MW01000408

Praise for *When Detroit Played the Numbers*

"The payoffs are many in Felicia B. George's deeply researched social history, which manages to be both engrossing and illuminating—placing Detroit's often maligned numbers community within the rich context it so rightly deserves. Even as the child of a numbers runner, I learned more than I ever knew and gained a better understanding of what I thought I knew. Honestly, I couldn't put this fascinating book down."

—Bridgett M. Davis, author of *The World According to Fannie Davis: My Mother's Life in the Detroit Numbers*

"Filled with fascinating detail—champion boxer Joe Louis's career was initially funded by numbers gambling profits—George's narrative is accessible and entertaining. Readers will be engrossed."

—*Publishers Weekly*

"Professor George tells the lively story of those archetypal minority entrepreneurs who used the gambling industry to build their role as community influentials and make a place for themselves in an economy structured by racial inequality. Charting the rise and fall of the black numbers business in Detroit, from its early roots into the late twentieth century, her book sheds light on the interconnections between the city's underground economy, politics, community building, and race."

—John J. Bukowczyk, professor of history, Wayne State University

"*When Detroit Played the Numbers* is the best researched and most comprehensive case study of one city's numbers games. Full of fascinating details about gamblers and game operators, this book is a must-read for anyone interested in gambling, the history of Detroit, African American culture, or the story of the American Dream."

—Jonathan D. Cohen, author of *For a Dollar and a Dream: State Lotteries in Modern America*

"Although it is seemingly a book about a guessing game that people played with small change, this book is in fact a complex and fascinating history that will be of great value to scholars of race, migration, capitalism, American leisure, and crime. Most importantly, it is a book that allows readers to better understand the city of Detroit."

—Matthew Vaz, assistant professor of history, The City College of New York

WHEN DETROIT PLAYED THE NUMBERS

To Brother Dan,
With much
Detroit Love,
Felicia Gaze

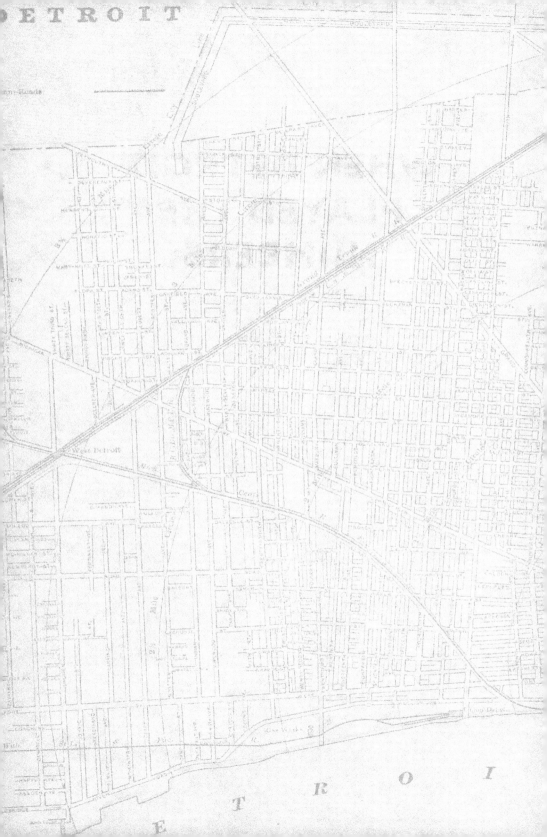

WHEN DETROIT PLAYED THE NUMBERS

Gambling's History and Cultural Impact on the Motor City

FELICIA B. GEORGE

WAYNE STATE UNIVERSITY PRESS
DETROIT

ISBN 9780814350768 (paperback)
ISBN 9780814350775 (hardcover)
ISBN 9780814350782 (e-book)

Library of Congress Control Number: 2023942235

Cover images © Elec/123RF.com and © Garyhider/123RF.com.
Cover design by Tracy Cox.

Wayne State University Press rests on Waawiyaataanong, also referred to as Detroit, the ancestral and contemporary homeland of the Three Fires Confederacy. These sovereign lands were granted by the Ojibwe, Odawa, Potawatomi, and Wyandot Nations, in 1807, through the Treaty of Detroit. Wayne State University Press affirms Indigenous sovereignty and honors all tribes with a connection to Detroit. With our Native neighbors, the press works to advance educational equity and promote a better future for the earth and all people.

Wayne State University Press
Leonard N. Simons Building
4809 Woodward Avenue
Detroit, Michigan 48201-1309

Visit us online at wsupress.wayne.edu.

For my Detroit players

Contents

Preface

In order to fully conduct this study, I took a holistic approach to my research. I used archival research methods and oral histories to achieve the historical goals of my project. These methods were necessary for the success of this project in order to show how the culture and community of numbers gambling in Detroit has changed over time. One of the strengths of using archival documents and sources in undertaking the research was the fact that archival information reflects the views and values of the person interviewed, the author, the newspaper, or mainstream society at that time. This subject matter spans more than eighty years, and as such, living sources for some phases of study were limited or nonexistent. To properly document and understand the history, culture, community, and political economy throughout this period, historical documents provided rich and much-needed evidence and data.

I obtained court records from Detroit Recorder's Court, Wayne County's 3rd Circuit Court, Michigan Court of Appeals, Michigan State Supreme Court, and the U.S. District Court. I used the Freedom of Information Act (FOIA) to obtain several records from the Federal Bureau of Investigation (FBI). Several newspapers were used, including the *Detroit Free Press, Detroit News,* and *Detroit Times.* These publications reflected the attitudes of the majority populace of Detroit at the time. I also used a number of black newspapers, such as the *Detroit Tribune* and the *Michigan Chronicle.* These papers captured the black perspective, which at times was not reflected in the mainstream papers. The Archives of Labor and Urban Affairs located at the Walter Reuther Library, Detroit Public Library's Burton Historical Collection, and the Bentley Historical Library were used throughout the study as well.

Three key informants with direct experience with numbers gambling were interviewed through a life history approach. This allowed informants to discuss past conditions and change over time, which in turn provided insights into the values and beliefs that helped tie numbers gambling to communities and vice versa. All of the informants were black and had ties to numbers gambling in Detroit. Semi-structured and open-ended interviews took place on a weekly basis over a one-year period. Two informants were related to or friends with numbers operators, and one informant was a former numbers operator and runner who organized, owned, and operated numbers gambling establishments. The key informants ranged in age from fifty to ninety. The collective memory of this age group covered the period from 1930 to 2000.

In addition to the three key informants, five other adult informants were interviewed over a twelve-month period. These participants, three women and two men, were black Detroit residents who at one time lived and played the numbers in the targeted research area. The participants ranged in age from fifty-two to eighty. These informants were included in the hope that they would provide information on how and why they participated in numbers gambling. They recounted what numbers gambling meant to them, as well as to the communities in which they lived.

Finally, when writing and organizing this project, I chose to deviate from the traditional format. I use a number of quotes because I want the reader to see the actual words used when discussing certain topics throughout this study. Actual word choices at times reveal values and emotions and demonstrate biases and acceptable attitudes better than summations can. Instead of having longer chapters with subsections, I instead used shorter thematic chapters with the goal of presenting a variety of diverse topics over time that are interlinked with Detroit's history of playing the numbers. This method provides a linear picture of how numbers gambling over time influenced, and was influenced by, major events in Detroit history. The story of *When Detroit Played the Numbers* actually unfolds in three phases. Chapters 1–12 cover, in great depth, the first phase of numbers gambling when it was controlled mostly by blacks. It explains the history and development of playing the numbers. Chapters 13–16, or the second phase, introduce the new leaders of Detroit's numbers gambling and follow how blacks slowly lost control of the game. Phase three is covered in chapters 17 and 18, when the state became the source of the ultimate takeover, and shows where illegal gambling still thrived after its legalization.

Acknowledgments

This book has been over a decade in the making. For more than ten years, I researched and wrote about this Detroit story. Throughout this process, my husband and soulmate, Anthony, has been in my corner. He cheered me on, comforted me when I needed it, and gave me tough love when I was ready to throw in the towel. I can never thank him enough for all of his love and encouragement. Without his faith in me, I am not sure this project would have become a reality. Another person who has been in my corner throughout this process has been my mother, Barbara Dale. Not only did she support me and this project, but she was the best free assistant ever. Thank you for working with me in the archives for countless hours. I owe gratitude to my father, Rayburn, for instilling in me his love of history and to my daughter, Jasmine, who has been a pillar of strength.

I am grateful for Sandra Korn, acquisitions editor of Wayne State University Press, who believed in me and this work. I am also indebted to Andrew Brandsasse, who was my "unofficial" editor. Many thanks go to Bridgett Davis for sharing her mother's story with me and for being my advocate. I owe much gratitude to all of my informants, who trusted me enough to tell their story.

Special acknowledgment goes to my original dissertation committee, Todd Meyers, Stephen Chrisomalis, and Andrew Newman, whose input planted the seed for this book.

Thank you to my brother A. P. and the rest of my family and friends who encouraged and supported me in ways both small and large. You all knew when I needed a hug, a word of encouragement, a story, or a simple laugh. I am so thankful you all listened to me go on and on about Detroit and playing the numbers.

Finally, Detroit is a multifaceted city that I love. It is not devoid of problems, but its good far outweighs the bad. It is a gritty city, yet it is filled with "Detroit Love." Detroit is a proud city where its inhabitants are not afraid to grind. For too long it has been cast in an unfavorable and unfair light. To everyone who takes the time to read this Detroit story, to those who want to learn about this city and truly see it, I hope you enjoy this book.

Introduction

One of the areas that is not talked about, and why our dollars turned over in the community, was the black numbers business. Our local people here developed it, and we controlled it. Of course, it was considered illegal, but that money was put to good use in the black community, with the dollar turning over in the community five or six times. The pickup man, the lady that wrote the number, pickup man, the other pickup man, to the owner. The owner had all blacks working for his area.

—William Hines, *Untold Tales, Unsung Heroes*

Playing the numbers . . . numbers gambling . . . street numbers . . . numbers—no matter what you call it, it all used to mean the same thing: illegal lottery. These games of chance have been around for years, and the Michigan Daily Three is a copy of the illegal version from years ago. Players chose three numbers from zero to nine, and to win, those numbers had to be selected. These illegal lotteries were operated by men and women called numbers bankers or numbers operators. At times, for as little as a few cents, a bettor could place a wager on a three-digit number, and if their number "fell," the payout could be as high as 600 to 1. These games of chance were more than just wagering on a three-digit number for entertainment. For some, it brought a sense of hope and a few dollars when they were desperately needed. Playing the numbers provided for much-needed community resources at times and was an activity that contributed to community building and solidarity. Yet for others, this illegal game of chance was their key to achieving wealth and the American Dream. Playing the numbers was many things to many different people. For some it symbolized hope and faith; for others it brought sorrow. The story of Willie Douglas Mosley tells the good, the bad, and the ugly of this game of chance in Detroit.

For black Detroit numbers banker Willie Douglas Mosley, extravagance defined how he and his family lived, and the numbers game helped him achieve this. Mosley was originally from Pratt City, Alabama, and worked in the coal mines before eventually settling in Detroit with his wife in search of a better life. When he first came to Detroit, he was penniless and worked in a factory before acquiring his first taxicab in 1921.[1] With hard work and determination, Mosley eventually purchased ten taxicabs and became the owner of the Midway Taxi Cab Company. According to Polk's City Directory, Mosley was listed until 1930 as proprietor of the Midway Taxi Cab Company, but by 1931, he was in the "real estate" business. This may have been when Mosley became a numbers operator/banker; being in "real estate" was the cover occupation of numbers operators. Exactly why this profession was adopted once someone became a numbers operator is not clear. As his numbers operation grew, so did his wealth, his social capital, and his legal businesses. Through both his legal and illegal businesses, Mosley was able to employ many people, and the money stayed within Detroit's Black Bottom, the community where he lived and worked. Black Bottom was located on the city's east side and was the forced residential area for most of Detroit's black citizens at that time. In March 1933, as the city and many of its residents struggled as a result of the Great Depression, the *Chicago Defender* reported that he threw a birthday party for his wife, and several wealthy and influential black guests attended the affair.[2]

In April 1933, he started the *Detroit Tribune*, a black weekly newspaper. This was a significant achievement and considered a much-needed resource in the black community. The major Detroit newspapers scarcely covered stories and events about black Detroiters, and when they did, they were usually negative, one-sided in coverage, and at times racist. An editorial in his first paper proclaimed, "With this initial issue, the *Detroit Tribune* makes its bow to the waiting public. It comes at a time of local and national crisis, when our people in this city and men and women everywhere are grappling with serious economic conditions, and are struggling to find their way back to better times."[3] In the open letter to readers, they were promised a weekly newspaper that unlike mainstream papers would serve everyone, would be factual, and would be free of prejudice. In the first edition of the newspaper, an ad was taken out by twenty individuals welcoming the *Detroit Tribune*, "the paper for which we have long been waiting," to the city. Of the twenty individuals who signed the "welcome," twelve were involved in the numbers business.[4] Three months later Mosley, described as "a new man of destiny," a "money maker," "a prince of good fellows," and a "shrewd business man," purchased the Detroit Stars, a Negro league baseball team.[5] Some blacks looked at Mosley's success and shared in it. He showed that blacks too could be successful and achieve the American Dream by using the principles of capitalism and the notion of pulling yourself up by your bootstraps. At one point during the Great Depression, when many of the country's leaders of industry were penniless, Mosley's wealth exceeded $500,000.[6]

Although Mosley lived lavishly, he was also generous to the Black Bottom community. On December 25, 1933, he served free Christmas meals to 1,500 children and 400 adults.[7] The following Christmas, Mosley, described as one of Detroit's "Big Brothers who annually brings Christmas cheer to thousands of underprivileged children and adults in the community," gave gifts of candy, nuts, and fruit to 2,000 needy children and 500 dinners to indigent adults.[8] As Mosley's wealth grew, so did his power and political influence. As a member of the Wolverine Republican Club, he was considered one of the Republican leaders of the black community and attended Republican state conventions as a delegate. Mosley was also an active member of Shiloh Baptist Church.[9] In a nutshell, he was a member in good standing with Detroit's black elite in spite of his illegal numbers business.

William Mosley's life and contributions came to a tragic end on May 24, 1935, when William Penix shot him twice in the chest. A numbers writer, Penix was one of about 100 people who worked for Mosley for several years. For about four years, Penix faithfully played the number "756." On that fateful day, Penix had placed ten cents on his regular number and it fell. The winning number should have paid him $50. Drunk and loudly swearing, Penix went to retrieve his winnings from his employer at Mosley's poolroom and smoke shop located at 2452 St. Antoine. When Mosley refused to pay, Penix demanded his money, but Mosley again refused because the date on the numbers ticket was wrong. Penix vehemently disagreed and insisted he was an honest man. Penix stressed he had written the ticket and would never cheat his boss. Mosley refused to listen and ordered Penix out of his establishment with the parting remark, "Bill, I guess you're out of luck."[10] Mosley escorted the enraged Penix outside where Penix shot Mosley to death.[11]

Two days after his murder, the *Detroit Times* covered his homicide and declared, "The body of Bill Mosley—the Alabama Negro boy—who became king of the policy makers in Detroit—political chieftain and reputedly the richest member of his race in Michigan—lay in state Saturday at the McFall Funeral Home, Canfield avenue and Hastings street." At his funeral, Mosley's pastor, Solomon Ross, stated, "I don't know how Bill Mosley got his money, but I do know that for five years he was a faithful attendant at services. I know also that Bill Mosley was loved and respected by his race and that untold thousands owe much to his genuine charity. He was without doubt a true benefactor of his race."[12] In an editorial, Mosley was described as having championed causes on behalf of others even when they were unaware. He was praised as a self-made man and a business genius. It was noted that as his wealth increased, so did his efforts to serve the black community; specifically, he employed deserving men and women, built new businesses, and supported civic organizations that uplifted the black community. As for his being part of the numbers game, this was said: "All successful men and women have enemies and critics who envy them, and Mr. Mosley was no exception. Fair-minded people admit, however, that business men who operate honest lotteries for the masses who take chances on pennies and dimes, fill the same public demand and deserve as much consideration as the honest brokers on Wall Street, where wealthy citizens speculate in stocks and bonds."[13]

Two days before Mosley's funeral, a funeral was held for former Detroit Recorder's Court judge William Connolly. It was reported that more than 2,000 people attended;[14] however, more than 25,000 attended Mosley's viewing, and 7,000 attended the proclaimed policy king's funeral, causing massive traffic jams.[15] Like the Detroit Times, the Detroit Free Press covered Mosley's funeral, describing him as a "Notorious Negro." He was laid to rest in a $5,000 bronze casket, and at the time, Mosley's funeral was described as the largest for a black man in the city of Detroit.[16] The police provided an escort to the 200 cars in the funeral procession, and Mosley's pallbearers included a few other prominent numbers bankers.[17] When he died, it was reported that Mosley was worth over $200,000 and owned twenty-five residential and business lots in Black Bottom, the Midway Taxi Cab Company, the Detroit Tribune, a nightclub called the Midway Café, and a pool hall. His numbers business generated approximately $10,000 daily, and his home, located on Vinewood, was described as a well-appointed residence.[18]

On June 13, 1935, the Detroit Times ran the following headline to announce that Mosley's murderer had been charged and was awaiting trial: "Policy King's Pals Cheer Death Charge." The paper reported that the courtroom was packed with Mosley's friends and supporters when William Penix went on trial.[19] His trial was heavily attended, and on October 2, 1935, thirty-eight-year-old William Penix was found guilty of second-degree murder in Detroit Recorder's Court. He was tried by an all-white jury made up of seven women and five men, who took two hours to deliberate before finding him guilty. Charles W. Jones, a black assistant prosecutor, was assigned the case by prosecuting attorney Duncan C. McCrea. Years later, it would be revealed how McCrea benefited from and protected the illegal numbers game in Detroit. McCrea wrote a letter to Mosley's newspaper, the *Detroit Tribune*, at the conclusion of the trial. In the open letter, he acknowledged the strong public interest concerning the trial and stated he was pleased with the conviction. He also stated, "I am especially pleased and proud of the splendid manner in which one of my assistants, Charles W. Jones, who is a member of your race, conducted the trial. Mr. Jones has justified in every respect the confidence and belief that I have, not only in him, but in the Negro group generally."[20] On October 14, 1935, William Penix was sentenced to fifteen to thirty years in Jackson Prison. As expected, Mosley's death did not cause the numbers game to cease. Upon his death, Mosley's lucrative numbers operation was taken over by his brother Charles.[21]

Willie Mosley's tragic story is just one example of the role numbers gambling played in Detroit. It highlights the complexity of self-made black entrepreneurs who overcame poverty and successfully navigated the pitfalls of racism and capitalism by mixing both legal and illegal activities. His story shows how important these men and women were in terms of the welfare of other blacks in Detroit, and it also provides a glimpse into what hitting the numbers meant for those who were not the wealthy operators. In Detroit, playing the numbers served several functions within society, most obviously as entertainment and sport, and among the most important of those functions, it served as a vehicle for achieving power and wealth in the city for the men and women who ran the game. The history of numbers gambling in Detroit provides insight into the power of community solidarity within the urban landscape of the United States. This book offers a detailed account of how the informal economy of neighborhood-based gambling took shape and thus formed a place within local communities over time and space. It describes how numbers gambling served the community both economically and as an institution that bound members of the community together socially.

Anthropology offers tools for taking a broad look at numbers gambling that is not limited to legal, economic, and political contexts. It accounts not just for the etic but also for the emic. In other words, this study provides not just a researcher's perspective on numbers gambling but includes the perspectives of the people involved in this activity: players, numbers writers/ collectors, and operators. This work examines how numbers gambling evolved within mostly black communities from 1919 to 2000 in Detroit, using both historical and ethnographic methods. The communities and historical framework were chosen because they represent where and when many southern blacks migrated to Detroit. According to the U.S. Census, in 1920, the total population of Detroit was 993,678. Blacks accounted for 40,838 or approximately 4 percent of the total population. At that time, blacks owned about 360 businesses, and Detroit was a beacon to southern blacks who dreamed of settling in a place that offered better educational, employment, and living conditions.[22] By 1930, the black population had increased to 120,000, and Detroit's Paradise Valley, located on the east side of Detroit, was known throughout the country for being a center for black businesses and entertainment. Detroit became the Promised Land for blacks wanting some semblance of equality and prosperity.

When studying numbers gambling, the issue of race is a key component of its history. At the peak of numbers gambling, in the early 1940s, the city of Detroit was experiencing rapid change and turmoil. Issues of race and inequality caused tension in neighborhoods and the workplace as blacks were segregated from whites and denied equal opportunities. This segregation caused conflict that created an "us versus them" mentality. In addition, Detroit was dealing with tensions caused by labor disputes and war production. Less than a year after the United States entered World War II, *Life* magazine noted that Detroit was rife with race, religious, political, and economic problems, and its people were loyal to their own groups.[23] It was reported that "the peculiar forces in Detroit have made the racial situation much more acute there than in most other cities."[24] This created an environment conducive for numbers gambling to operate and flourish. It can be argued that racial solidarity formed in response. Racial solidarity has been described as having no philosophical or conceptual implications beyond the desire of blacks to organize based on shared oppressive conditions in an effort to lessen them.[25]

The conflict caused by racism, and numbers gambling's role in righting it, caused people in the affected neighborhoods to rally behind gambling as something of their own. Numbers gambling not only provided resources that were otherwise denied but also brought people within the community

together. As a result, the community rallied around the institution of numbers gambling for entertainment, as a source of pride, and for basic financial
needs. I argue that numbers gambling established relationships and bonds
within the community because it circulated and redistributed resources.
There was power in numbers gambling that compelled gambling operators to engage in reciprocal relationships with the communities and people
who supported their operations. In some way, each party was dependent
upon or tied to the other. Numbers gamblers and community members
depended on the resources generated by numbers gambling, and numbers operators depended on the players' business for their own wealth.
Numbers operators felt obligated to assist neighborhoods financially and
socially due to the community's support of their business, and this contributed to the solidarity and social binding of the neighborhoods. The
reciprocity displayed by the numbers operators solidified their place and
status as leaders and race men and women in their respective communities
while at the same time ensuring the masses continued to place bets with
them. Race men and women were dedicated to improving the plight of
black people, and for the most part neighborhoods and neighbors trusted
the men and women who ran numbers operations and respected them.

Numbers gambling provided professional and non-professional employment opportunities for blacks when they were denied other ways to earn a
living because of their race and when jobs were in short supply.[26] The money
generated from playing the numbers allowed numbers bankers to serve as
a legitimate financial institution for blacks and black businesses that were
denied access to banks' financial resources.[27] This allowed Detroit's black
community to have access to neighborhood businesses and services that are
essential to any self-sufficient, thriving community. These neighborhood
businesses included hotels, bars, insurance companies, loan offices, real estate
firms, newspaper stands, barbershops, and shoeshine parlors.[28] Numbers
operators also ensured they contributed to charities and churches and provided funding for entertainment, including the arts. These flourishing businesses, which were supported by numbers gambling, gave the community a
sense of pride in the numbers men and women, as well as the businesses in
their community. People viewed the businesses and the people responsible
for them as positive examples of what the black race could produce.[29] This
conflicts with the assumption that numbers gambling pulled wealth out of
the community; in Detroit, it provided resources that could be measured

financially and socially. These men and women were a symbol of black success, and they leveraged some political power that benefited the community as well. Oftentimes, they were the informal leaders of the community and were looked upon to advance the race. In a nutshell, numbers gambling became a means to remedy economic and social injustices and offered a chance at the American Dream for blacks who were otherwise denied it.

In addition to the numerous economic advantages playing the numbers provided, in this study, I argue that it brought social benefits as well. Similar to anthropologist Jayne Curnow's work studying the Ngadha people on the island of Flores in eastern Indonesia, I argue the illegal lottery was not considered risky business by the players. Curnow found that "for the Ngadha people, gambling is primarily a social activity that provides a forum for the public circulation of cash."[30] Numbers gambling did the same for its black community seventy-five years earlier in Detroit, and this study will expand on the prominent role that numbers gambling has had as both a social and economic activity.

This is not to say that playing the numbers was without problems: it was illegal, and some viewed it as immoral. Others pointed out its exploitive nature and bemoaned the fact that the poor had the audacity to "waste" money on it while the numbers operators profited from what they deemed irrational foolishness. Previous studies have looked at the economic, criminal, and moral aspects of playing the numbers. I do not romanticize playing the numbers, nor do I vilify it. Rather, I lay out its history, illustrate its influence on culture in Detroit, challenge assumptions, and at times offer different perspectives from those involved.

In order to understand the foundation of playing the numbers, it is necessary to explain how it had its roots in the lottery. Chapter 1 looks at the history and purpose of the first lotteries in the United States. It also briefly examines the criticism reflected in newspaper accounts concerning the lottery and lottery players. Chapter 2 takes a closer look at how policy, an offspring of the lottery and a precursor to the numbers, developed in Detroit and how it was used to unjustly define, portray, and blame blacks for what was characterized as a public evil when most players were not black. In chapters 3 and 4, John Roxborough is introduced; he brought the game to Detroit and developed it. These chapters explore why and how first policy playing was brought to the community by Roxborough and how it later changed over to the game of numbers. For Roxborough, who was considered a race man, numbers gambling, an illegal activity, would become the vehicle for his enrichment and to help other blacks. Chapter 5 explores how white Detroiters, when they discovered the profits to be made in playing the numbers, unsuccessfully attempted to take control of the numbers game in Detroit from the black numbers operators through police protection and later with the help of an elected mayor. This chapter describes the racial climate in Detroit, further revealing why racial solidarity and an alternative to the formal economy were needed in Detroit.

Chapters 6 and 7 focus on the role playing the numbers had not just for the numbers operators but for the community during the Great Depression. When the legal formal economy failed black Detroiters, it was the numbers operators who came to the rescue by giving people jobs, a helping hand at times, and hope. Although the numbers operators profited off of the pennies of some poor players, it is important to understand that the people who participated did so willingly. Some played for entertainment, or for the chance to be able to pay a few bills and put food on the table, while others played for the feeling of "hope," to make it through another day. Whatever the reasons, these players did not see themselves as victims; rather, they were active participants taking control of their lot in life by the choices they had the freedom and right to make.

Chapters 8, 9, and 10 describe how playing the numbers and its operators evolved through the 1940s. It examines another round of corruption within the government and how this first phase of numbers gambling ended in the city. Throughout these chapters, the reader will see the role numbers gambling played in community building. Chapter 8 describes how Everett Watson, who was called Detroit's numbers czar because of the size of his operation, and who like Roxborough was a race man, poured money into the community by saving businesses, funding the arts, and providing employment to those in need. Chapter 9 reveals how payoffs and the funding of political campaigns kept blacks in control of the numbers game and gave the black community leverage in hiring black policemen to serve their communities. Chapter 10 builds upon chapter 7 and pays special attention to how John Roxborough developed Joe Louis's image with the income from his numbers business and turned the boxer into an American hero and a source of pride for blacks. The huge takeaway is that without the profits from numbers gambling, Roxborough would not have been able to support and "create" the image of Joe Louis. When blacks were hungry for a hero and for positive representation, and when some white Americans needed to see that blacks were not inferior caricatures but equal Americans, in stepped Joe Louis. Not only did Joe Louis, with the guidance and financial support of John Roxborough, provide this, but because of his status, he was able to break a number of racial barriers in the military, sports, and society. This chapter also highlights what Everett Watson did to address the black housing crisis in Detroit. Again, this shows how these men put money and resources into the community. This occurred as all the key players in the numbers racket had their day in court, which led to their downfall and the first step in the loss of control.

Chapter 11 is told from the perspective of someone who grew up during the first phase of playing the numbers in Detroit. His story illustrates what the numbers game meant to the community and the role numbers operators played in Detroit. Chapter 12 summarizes what happened to the powerful men who controlled numbers in Detroit during the 1940s, closing out the first phase of numbers gambling in the city. The chapter also discusses and reiterates how the profits generated from the game benefited not just the operators but the black community as well.

Chapters 13, 14, and 15 focus on the next generation of numbers operators in Detroit from the end of the 1940s until the 1970s. These chapters explore the continuing social aspect of numbers gambling in neighborhoods and the Italian mafia's eventual takeover; the next generation of black numbers operators who ran the game; the contribution that the latest and largest numbers operator at that time, John White, made to the community; and the role that urban renewal played in fracturing the numbers community and game. Chapter 16 introduces a woman who ran a small numbers business in the city and concludes the second phase of numbers gambling in Detroit. This chapter shows what it meant to be not just a woman but a mother and breadwinner in the male-dominated numbers game. Chapter 17 covers the legalization of the lottery and its effect on the illegal numbers game.

Illegal numbers can still be found in several automotive plants where there is a captive audience. Chapter 18 explores illegal numbers gambling's history and popularity in Detroit-area automotive plants and reveals how these locations have kept numbers gambling alive. In addition, this chapter includes the personal experiences of a major numbers operator in a large Detroit-area plant. His experience further explains why the illegal numbers exist and how they helped him achieve his American Dream. The last chapter provides final thoughts on playing the numbers in Detroit's history.

1
First There Was the Lottery

A lottery is at best but systematized gambling, a splendid lure for the unwary, in which the chance of remuneration to the adventurer is in no proportion to that of any other mode of gaming. Yet, like the Mirage of the desert, it lures and deceives, not only the unconscious, but the most practised beholder. The old and young, the economist and the spendthrift, the knowing one and the innocent, the poor man and the rich, with equal eagerness crowd around this gorgeous temple of fortune and though to-day the dupes of its-deceitful promises, return to-morrow with eyes as anxious and inquiring, to gaze upon and seek the glittering favors it affects to offer.

—*Democratic Free Press & Michigan Intelligencer*, March 8, 1832

In order to understand what numbers gambling or playing the numbers is, it is necessary to define the term and to explore the lottery from which it originated. The term "numbers gambling" refers to the practice of wagering on the outcome of certain numbers in a variety of games, which differ principally in the way the winning number is determined. Two types of numbers gambling are "policy," in which the winning number is obtained by a drawing, and "numbers," in which the winning number is derived from various published figures, outcomes, and numbers.[1] Policy has been called the lottery's "illegitimate offspring" because it originally derived from legal lotteries in London.[2] In the first half of the eighteenth century, it was developed by a lottery dealer as a side business. Its purpose was to bring the lottery to people who could not afford to buy a ticket. For a sum smaller than the full cost of a lottery ticket, a player could "insure a number." In other words, they could bet that any number of their own choosing would be drawn.[3]

To fully grasp how policy, and later numbers, evolved from the lottery, it is imperative to briefly describe the lottery's history in America. At its most basic, a lottery is a prize contest based entirely on chance. It requires no true skill but players must pay a fee to participate.[4] Lotteries have been around since antiquity and played a major role in the development of America. In England, lottery tickets were sold to fund the first American colonies.[5] Early American colonists took direction from the British and used lotteries as a source of revenue as early as 1719. Lotteries were used by the colonies to build schools, colleges, churches, bridges, and roads, and lotteries funded the American Revolution.[6] They were a popular way to raise revenue because they were an alternative to taxes, did not require large amounts of capital to run, and were a way to raise large sums of cash quickly. Lotteries were generally accepted and popular and, by 1790, were deeply entrenched in the economy and beloved by the American people. Due to this, state legislatures did not dare consider abolishing them.[7] By 1790, there were approximately 2,000 legal lotteries in the United States, and legislators throughout the country were authorizing the use of a lottery for one reason or another.[8] In 1833, it was estimated that $67 million in lottery tickets were sold in at least eight states. This figure was five times the federal government's budget at the time. Although all levels of government used the lottery to help finance a number of public projects, there were also many privately run lotteries whose purpose was personal gain and in some cases charity.[9]

As the lottery business grew, the need for people to run these lotteries grew as well. Several enterprising individuals became ticket brokers, lottery contractors, lottery managers, and promoters. Ticket brokers bought lottery tickets at a discount rate and then resold them at a profit at their own lottery shops or through the mail. Lottery contactors set up branches throughout the country to represent various lottery companies. Lottery managers oversaw the overall operation, and to increase lottery sales, promoters sent out handbills and placed advertisements in newspapers throughout the country. Lottery tickets were not affordable for everyone, and this opened the door for some brokers to sell a ticket to a number of people in fractions. This practice of selling tickets in shares enabled poor people to play.[10]

The participants who won lotteries used their winnings for several ventures. For some, lottery winnings meant instant wealth, but for others it meant life and freedom. In 1800, Denmark Vesey, a slave, won a lottery prize in the amount of $1,500.[11] With his winnings, he purchased his freedom from his master and opened a carpentry shop. Vesey crusaded against slavery and later enlisted over 9,000 slaves and free blacks in a failed insurrection. Vesey's story demonstrates how the lottery leveled the playing field between the "haves" and "have-nots." It illustrates how, with luck, the poor and those without power gained a fortune.[12] This flew in the face of the conventional Protestant work ethic, which stressed the importance of hard work to achieve success; however, this did not matter to the "have-nots," who played policy and gambled on what some considered an irrational and unjust game.[13]

While many lotteries were legitimate, fraudulent activity became increasingly widespread in the 1820s. It was not uncommon for agents and lottery managers to elicit large fees, rendering the profits for winners small to nonexistent. Some unscrupulous agents and managers would advertise nonexistent lotteries then flee the area with all money garnered from ticket sales.[14] As a result of the frauds plaguing the masses, a number of newspapers warned against the evils of the lottery. On March 8, 1832, the *Detroit Free Press* reported that the lottery was like a "mirage of the desert," which deceived the poor and the wealthy with promises of riches. The article warned readers of the "evils" of this form of gambling and the perils of trying to get something for nothing. The article also cautioned citizens to avoid avarice, advised against using the lottery as a "miserable plan of finance," and foretold of the need to "eradicate this cancer from the bosom of the state."[15] On September 5, 1855, the *Detroit Daily Free Press* told readers about a hardworking man, "a poor but industrious mechanic" out of New Orleans, who labored for years to purchase a home for his family. Every Saturday night the man gave his wife his weekly salary to put away for the purchase of a family home. After a couple of months, the man believed he had accumulated at least a few thousand dollars with which he wanted to purchase a piece of property at a bargain rate. When he attempted to retrieve his hard-earned savings from his wife, he learned she had "wasted all his hard earnings in the purchase of Havana Lottery tickets!" Upon hearing this, the hardworking husband broke out in a maniacal laugh, left his wife and children, and committed suicide.[16] A few years later, the paper reported how a man who had won $15,000 from the lottery lost all of it in a spending spree and then died. In the same article, the paper also told of another young man who won $1,500 and then went "crazy in consequence."[17] Northern newspapers during the 1840s and 1850s reported on black men and women fervently playing policy. They also wrote about how dreams and various superstitions were tied to the play. For them, policy playing revealed dangerous thinking by players who could never be good citizens who possessed the common sense needed to be a part of a rational, profit-seeking society. They claimed that policy play only benefited criminals and supported organized crime.[18]

Many states began to tire of lotteries and started banning them. When a state declared a lottery illegal, a policy shop would open in place of the closed lottery shop. These policy shops no longer sold policy insurance, but they allowed clients to bet on individual lottery numbers in other states. In the 1830s, the winning lottery numbers were based on the drawings of the New Jersey Lottery; when this lottery was banned in the 1840s, the winning numbers were based on the drawings from the Kentucky Literature Lottery.[19] Policy, like lottery, had the reputation of being a bane on society. In 1858 the *Detroit Free Press* reported that policy was dependent on the lottery business and generated about $10,000 daily: "The policy tickets vary in price from one cent to one hundred dollars, and find customers mostly among the poor, ignorant, and superstitious part, of our population. With the downfall of lotteries, the policy business must cease to exist."[20] Although both the rich and poor gambled, it was the poor who suffered harsh criticism for "wasting" money. When the poor played it was a dangerous vice, but when the wealthy played, it was for the greater good of society.[21] By 1858, all state-sanctioned lotteries in the United States were located in the South; northern states had outlawed them.[22] However, roughly three-quarters of lottery profits came from the sale of tickets in the North. It was estimated that one lottery spent more than $200,000 annually on advertisement and sold more than $200,000,000 in tickets. At this time, the lotteries sold about $800,000,000 in tickets yearly but only paid out $10,000,000 in prizes.[23] This was a clear indicator that lotteries were very profitable.

By 1860, many Americans viewed the lottery in a less favorable light. John Ezell, in his work *Fortune's Merry Wheel: The Lottery in America*, attributed this change in attitude to the shifting culture and values of Americans.[24] Some Americans at this time were several generations removed from their native countries and had established their own belief systems. These "new" individual-centered Americans believed in the principles of hard work, and the lottery, with its something-for-nothing logic, did not fit into this belief system. In 1868, the federal government made the sale of lottery tickets by mail illegal, and by 1878, with the exception of Louisiana, all states outlawed lotteries.[25] The Louisiana lottery continued to operate until 1893, when its charter expired, but policy continued to flourish throughout various locations as an illegal activity, including in Detroit.

2
Policy Playing
Comes to Detroit

Yes, sir, policy is played in fifteen or twenty places in this city. Of course you don't understand that game—nobody does.

—*Detroit Free Press*, December 3, 1880

By 1880, the lottery was dead in Detroit, but policy was alive and well. Detroit's population at that time was 116,340; it was the eighteenth largest city in the United States. Detroit's natural resources and location as a port within the Great Lakes made it a significant trading center. During this time, Detroit was not yet an industrial giant, but it was beginning its ascent to becoming a major industrial city. In 1880, the city was made up mostly of whites, comprised of native-born Americans and established immigrants from Canada, England, Ireland, and Germany; there were only 2,821 blacks at that time.[1] Most blacks lived on the near east side, in an area later referred to as Black Bottom, with whites of all nationalities. Although blacks lived among whites, social interactions were limited. This area of the city housed mainly poor people and was considered crowded with several dilapidated buildings and "alley houses." These dwellings were former sheds and stables that were erected in the alleys, which were created to remove ashes, trash, and sewage and to provide access to stables.[2]

It was during these times and conditions that the *Detroit Free Press* published one of the first accounts of policy playing in Detroit on December 3, 1880. In this article, a reporter who overheard a conversation between "a fresh young gentleman" and a "wisely gentleman" described what he learned while walking home at midnight in Detroit. According to the author, policy was being played openly in the city. There were fifteen to twenty policy shops frequented by hundreds of passionate policy players. It was known that the winning numbers were drawn out of Covington, Kentucky, and

Detroit policy writers who sold the tickets received a percentage of their sales before sending the rest to Covington. At Covington, numbers from 1 to 78 were put in a wheel, and each day twelve were drawn at noon. The twelve drawn numbers were telegraphed to the main office in every city and the process repeated again at 6 p.m. To play policy, a person visited one of the numerous shops and paid up to $2 for a "gig." A "gig" was any combination of three numbers from 1 to 78. For example, a person could play the combination 4-11-44, and if those three numbers were drawn, they would win $400 for their $2 wager. A $1 wager for a "gig" paid $200, and a fifty-cent bet paid $100.[3]

Policy playing was not viewed as a favorable pastime; many newspaper stories, in fact, were cautionary tales against it. For example, policy playing was described as the reason a married bookkeeper in Detroit embezzled money from his employer. The policy-playing bookkeeper admitted he had stolen the money from his employer and was later found guilty of his crime.[4] Five years later, it was reported that a Detroit detective arrested a sixty-five-year-old man for running a policy shop in the heart of the city. According to the detective, he paid ten cents for three numbers to be drawn that evening. When the man was arrested, he questioned why other establishments were being allowed to operate unmolested in the city.[5] Americans had acquired a mania for the lottery and particularly for policy playing, and these forms of gaming were not confined to age, sex, occupation, or social rank. Everyone played: "the leaders of society and the outcasts of the slums . . . the reckless young blood, who takes a flyer by day and leads the german at night . . . the decrepted old negro, who risks his last dime upon 4-11-44 . . . the veteran and the school-boy, . . . the philosopher and the proletaire."[6]

At this point, policy playing was not linked to a specific race, although most players were white, and was played by people of all socioeconomic classes. Charles Bertrand Lewis and others, however, would change the reality of who played policy in Detroit. Lewis was a famed humorist who wrote for the *Detroit Free Press* under the pseudonym "M. Quad" and once was credited with making the paper wildly popular in America.[7] At this time, the *Detroit Free Press* catered to Democrats. It frequently featured negative stories about blacks to appeal to the anti-black, white working class.[8] Lewis wrote a series of weekly stories from the point of view of "Brother Gardner," which appeared throughout the United States. The fictional character was a member of a social club called the Lime-Kiln Club. Brother Gardner was portrayed as an elderly philosophical "negro" who offered sage advice to readers in what was considered a "negro dialect."[9] The character of Brother Gardner was described by Lewis as "a shrewd and quaint gentleman of color, who has all the idioms and characteristics of his race, but is not a burlesque of our colored fellow citizen; he handles his own people gently, but satirizes the foibles, frailties and weakness of the whites inimitably. His sayings might be termed explosive wisdom—the reader is sure to imbibe a wise thought, but it is certain to explode within him."[10]

Lewis admitted in a *New York Times* article in 1912 that "Brother Gardner" and his Lime-Kiln Club associates were characters loosely based on an "old negro who used to frequent the market in Detroit with a dog and whitewash pail, looking for a job. That nigger, two other niggers, and the dog were the only real basis of the Lime-Kiln Club."[11] The fictitious Lime-Kiln Club was made up of "negroes" from across the country. Among its honorary members were sixteen former judges, twelve captains, twenty-four colonels, ten majors, seven generals, twenty-two elders, eight deacons, thirteen reverends, and a few other professional men. Although the club members were portrayed as professional, Lewis had the men speak in rough "negro" dialect and gave them names such as "Judge Holdback Johnson," "Giveadam Jones," and "Professor Tranquility Hanover." The discussions about politics and philosophy could only be described as ridiculous and nonsensical. This served to portray blacks as inferior and primitive, poked fun at them, and strengthened stereotypes under the guise of white humor. The derogatory images took away humanity, justified the mistreatment of blacks, and reinforced the need for segregation. It sent the message that even when blacks were educated, they were still not capable of knowing right from wrong and needed guidance. The pictures of the men further reinforced this notion. They were drawn as stereotypical black caricatures who, in a monolithic misrepresentation, all had dark skin tones that ranged from dark to very dark, and with oversized lips that varied from bright pink to deep red. This travesty ensured that whites viewed all blacks, whether educated or not, negatively.

In addition, Lewis portrayed these so-called professional men engaging in stereotypical activities. For example, it was not unusual to find the members of the club eating watermelon, physically fighting among themselves, and drinking to excess.[12] Numerous letters and people arrived at the *Detroit*

Free Press wanting to know the location of the Lime-Kiln Club. When confronted, Lewis never confessed that the club and characters were fictitious but rather made excuses as to why people could not visit the club or meet the members. Lewis's Brother Gardner and the Lime-Kiln Club were so prevalent that Brother Gardner was a household name. The popularity was largely due to the fact that Lewis's column appeared in ten thousand newspapers across the country.[13] Lewis first penned a play about Brother Gardner and the Lime-Kiln Club in 1882, a book about the club's meetings in 1892, and later, Brother Gardner and the Lime-Kiln Club's image were used to sell tobacco, cigars, and stove polish.

With a strong following in October 1880, Lewis wrote a column whereby Brother Gardner admonished a member of the Lime-Kiln Club for frequenting a policy shop in the city. Brother Gardner admitted to the members of the club that he, like any other black man in the country, knew the workings of policy playing because he had heavily played: "Now, gem'len, I've bin right dar. In da y'ars gone by I knew as much about 'gigs,' 'saddles,' 'blinds' and 'straddles' as any black man in this kentry will eber get frew his wcol. I played high an' low. I played till I couldn't rest. I played out all de money I could airn or borry, an' I neber cum widin fo' hundred miles of makin' a strike. It's a mighty enticin' bizness. Put a black man in one eand of Michigan an' de policy shop in de odder an' de two would find each odder by de shortest route. Yet, as I said befo', it's a losin' game an' it's mean bizness."[14] Although most policy players were white, Lewis ensured that the minority black population of Detroit was singled out for playing policy and said that it was a compulsion that black men could not resist. Since many people thought Brother Gardner and the Lime-Kiln Club were real and that the portrayal was not burlesque in nature, Lewis's column reinforced the notion that policy playing was a widespread "negro" activity and as such vilified it further.

Ten policy shops in Detroit were closed on February 17, 1881, when managers out of Chicago came to the city and took away the policy writers' books. The *Detroit Free Press* reported that policy shops were closed due to "local pressure against gambling dens and immoral places."[15] A year later, the Common Council of Detroit passed an ordinance to put an end to policy playing. The ordinance made both lottery and policy illegal within the city.[16] Upon the passing of the city ordinance, five policy shops immediately ceased operations, and the remaining ones were set to close the following day.[17] By May 21, 1882, seventeen other policy shops were served orders to close in the city of Detroit.[18] By the end of the year, as reported by the *Detroit Free Press*, policy was still being played by the "lowly, the vicious and the heathen."[19] One reporter described going to a dark, smelly, filthy saloon, occupied by a "short burly Negro" who served as a bartender, a cripple who played the fiddle, and a young man who was selling policy numbers. Unable to stomach the filth and smell of the saloon, the reporter ran from the establishment before he could place a bet.

On April 18, 1883, the Michigan Supreme Court rendered an opinion concerning the city's lottery ordinance. As part of its opinion, the court noted that lotteries involved large sums of money and operated all over the country: "All classes and persons of all ages are tempted to invest in the chances of sudden riches, and it is [a] matter of history that the passion for such investments has led to serious and widespread mischief. No other form of gambling operates so extensively in its dealings, or demoralizes so many people. It is this extensive reach and not merely its speculative purposes which makes lottery gambling so dangerous."[20]

In a continued effort to prevent people from playing policy, Detroit newspapers carried dozens of articles reporting on the irrationality of and disaster that resulted from playing policy. One article described the ignorance of a policy player who could not grasp the concept that it took him $1,500 to win $300.[21] In 1884, an unknown man named "Mr. Merryweather" allegedly gave a *Detroit Free Press* reporter an interview. According to the reporter, Mr. Merryweather, an expert on policy, played daily and had recently won $50 when he played the numbers 56-52-44 for a mere twenty-five cents. Mr. Merryweather advised the reporter that "there's very few coons in Detroit that don't play policy, I'm tellin' you, and then again there's as many white folks into it as coons." Mr. Merryweather then went on to tell of two people who hit the numbers for large sums of money, and of a woman who missed out on her riches when she neglected to play the numbers from her dream. Mr. Merryweather at that time endorsed policy playing;[22] however, a few weeks later, he changed his tune and warned readers to be leery of policy shops: "The fellers that runs dem gits twenty percent of all they git out of the suckers. They have ropers-in all 'round town and you can't hardly strike a saloon in some parts of the city that don't write up policy books." Mr. Merryweather further warned readers that players ultimately lose and pay more than they win: "No, sir, don't you tackle policy, if you know when you're well off; 'n' if you've got any boys a growin' up tell 'em to learn the burglar's trade b'fore goin' into policy. The feller in State's prison's better off than the feller that's once gone on policy."[23]

Although newspaper articles had indicated that both blacks and whites played policy, three years later, in 1887, the *Detroit Free Press* reported that policy playing at the 160 policy shops in the city was "one of the greatest hindrances to the prosperity of the colored people. When once infatuated with policy, as many of the colored people are, it readily relieves them of all their spare change."[24] This article appeared a few years prior to the 1890 census, which disclosed that blacks accounted for only 3,431 of the city's 205,876 residents. On April 19, 1892, the *Detroit Free Press* reported that at least 15 policy shops existed in the city, and at least 25 subagents made their living from the sale of policy numbers. If one were to believe the newspaper, in just five short years, 147 policy shops closed. Policy players at this time were able to buy their numbers directly from subagents or from saloons, pawnshops, barbershops, and small stores. Nine-tenths of policy players in Detroit and all other cities were "colored people":

> Barbers, waiters, roustabouts, servant girls, washerwomen and whitewashes—who, earning from $4 to $15 a week, devote at least one-fourth of their wages to "policy." Their purchases of numbers are chiefly in fifteen or twenty cent investments and when they fail to win, their first thought is as to what combinations they shall play next. They waste no time in regrets and one failure or fifty failures do not rob the game of its fascination. When they win they do not lose their heads and spend the winnings in idleness and dissipation but renew their dream-book and omen studies buying numbers more frequently and for larger amounts of cash, until their prize returns from whence it came—to the lottery company.[25]

A city official who was credited with investigating policy playing indicated that over $200 worth of policy tickets were bought daily in Detroit by about 500 regular policy-playing "fiends."[26] The numbers given by the newspaper and the city official are questionable; at no point does either tell how they arrived at these figures. The depictions of blacks by the *Detroit Free Press* and the police came at a time when the reported incidents of discrimination against black citizens increased considerably in the city.[27]

By 1902, Albert Adams, a white millionaire gambler out of New York, was credited with controlling the Frankfort and Kentucky Policy Company, which was a $3,000,000 a year operation. His company had been in existence for approximately forty years and was operated in every major city in the United States, including Detroit, where forty to fifty policy shops were in operation in 1902. Adams was able to run his policy shops because various high-ranking politicians and the police allowed him to operate while preventing rival companies from setting up shop in Detroit.[28] The Detroit police, however, indicated that the police did not protect policy shops: "About that policy game in Detroit? It is nothing but a negro's game, and I considered it not important enough to pay much attention to it. They are a sly lot, you know, and it is hard work to catch them with the 'goods.' They carry their policy plays and policy sheets in their hats, up their sleeves and make their play in a secret manner."[29] In May 1902 the *Detroit Free Press* reported that roughly 4,000 poor, ignorant, and superstitious people played policy. Twenty-two years after reports of policy playing appeared in the *Detroit Free Press* (when blacks only made up 2.4 percent of Detroit's population), blacks (who now numbered 4,111 residents in the 1900 census or 1.4 percent of the total population) were attributed with making up the majority of the 4,000 policy players in Detroit. If one were to believe the *Detroit Free Press* and the superintendent of Detroit's police department, virtually every black man, woman, and child played the "vilest" gambling game in the city: policy.[30] This was not unlike what historian Ann Fabian noted: "The northern press had long singled out African Americans of both sexes as the particular patrons of the lottery, although patrons were certainly numerous in many poor and immigrant communities."[31] While the Detroit Police Department blamed blacks for being the majority of policy players in the city, the press accused the police department of protecting the policy houses in the city.[32]

Throughout the beginning of the twentieth century, more and more blacks migrated to Detroit from the South for better wages, jobs, housing, education, and anticipated improved social conditions, among other things. What they found, however, amounted to more of the same. Housing was hard to come by, and when it was found, the cost was astronomical. Due to the lack of housing, it was not uncommon to find blacks being forced to live in unconventional locations, including saloons, gambling places, or "buffet flats," defined as "a sort of high-class combination of a gambling parlor, a blind tiger and an apartment of prostitution." These establishments were run in what were considered respectable private homes that catered especially to unsuspecting youths.[33]

By 1903, the *Detroit Free Press* reported that "there has never been more than a very brief time in the modern history of Detroit that the game of policy has not been open to those within her gates who wanted to squander their substance in this one-sided form of gambling. . . . It is largely the gambling field of the ignorant, superstitious, and the poor."[34] The poor played because they needed the money "at home for the necessaries of life." On April 2, 1903, the *Detroit Free Press* raised fears by reporting that the taste for policy playing was now corrupting young people, especially girls.[35] The article's tone struck fear in religious, hardworking Detroiters. From about 1904 to 1907, it was believed policy was eradicated from the city; however, in August 1908, the *Detroit Free Press* accused the "colored" population of Detroit of attempting to bring back policy. Allegedly a "well dressed colored man" with an abundance of money arrived in the area of Gratiot and St. Antoine, or Black Bottom, and tried to revitalize the game. The man was only partially successful in inducing policy playing because "the colored population" was suspicious.[36] This denunciation of blacks came at a time when it was reported the "colored" population in Detroit had reached approximately 17,400.[37] Policy's reputation as an evil, whether fair or not, was already being linked to blacks in spite of the fact that it was reported that a white counterfeiter was accused of running a policy operation in Detroit on Hastings Street.[38] Nevertheless, it would take another decade before blacks would successfully operate policy in Detroit.

3
John Roxborough

Hope Dealer and Numbers King

I made up my mind that when I got a chance to make money, no matter how, I'd take it. I would avoid embarrassing situations, like asking for a job when I was qualified. I also promised myself I'd help myself first then I'd help my black brothers.

—John Roxborough[1]

For those eleven short years, it appeared as if policy playing was gone from Detroit. That is, until John Roxborough successfully reintroduced the game to a population that wanted to try their luck. John Walter Roxborough was born February 21, 1892, in Plaquemine, Louisiana, to Charles and Virginia Roxborough. His parents were of Scottish, Jamaican, Spanish, and Creole descent.[2] Charles Roxborough was born a free man in Cleveland, Ohio, in 1860 before relocating to New Orleans with his family. While attending high school in New Orleans, Charles found he was the only black person in attendance. Never accepted or treated fairly, he was routinely assaulted and once stabbed by whites who did not want him at the school.[3] In 1877, Charles, considered a good student, was set to graduate but was refused a diploma because he was black. Undeterred, he later studied at Straight University and received his law degree in 1885. Shortly after, he opened a law office in Plaquemine and married Virginia Simms on December 23, 1886. The couple had four sons: Charles Jr., born in 1887; Thomas, born in 1889; John, born in 1892; and Claude, born in 1894. As time passed, because of his race, Charles Sr. dealt with a number of social and economic pressures and, seeking a better life for his family, eventually moved his family to Detroit in 1895. The Roxboroughs moved into a mostly Polish neighborhood, where the Polish people treated the family well despite the fact they were black.[4]

Charles Sr., once settled, set up a law practice in 1899 and became involved in Republican politics, published and edited a four-page newspaper called the *Republican Colored Independent*, and at age fifty was a candidate for Michigan's state legislature.[5] The Roxboroughs eventually became part of Detroit's black bourgeois establishment. Both Charles and Virginia expected their sons to follow in their highly educated parents' footsteps; however, Charles would not live to see his sons reach their full potential. He died on August 18, 1908.[6]

Charles Jr., like his father, became an attorney. John also began to follow in his father's footsteps to become an attorney, but after one semester at the Detroit College of Law and one and a half years at the University of Detroit he dropped out.[7] For one year while at Detroit College of Law, at just under 5'9", John played basketball for the college. During that time, several incidents made a lasting impression on him concerning race inequality. John Roxborough's college team played and practiced at the Young Men's Christian Association (YMCA) in Detroit. Each player was required to pay gym and locker fees; however, John was banned by the executive secretary of the YMCA from using the gym and the locker room facilities because he was black. On another occasion, John posed as a Native American to play in Anderson, Indiana.[8] He found these experiences humiliating and unfair, and they colored his views and opinions. As such, John felt that college was not worth the effort because of established social inequalities, which prevented educated blacks from obtaining employment in their fields of study. "You'd ask for a job, tell them you were a college graduate, and they'd say, 'Oh yes, we have a porter's job for you.' To hell with education. What good would it do me?"[9] John Roxborough's attitude reflected the realities of the time. With this mindset, John, at the age of twenty, was first employed as a clerk with the United States Post Office. He stayed there for approximately six years before becoming a clerk in the Wayne County Clerk's Office in 1918. A short time later, he became a bail bondsman.[10]

While John was attempting to find his niche in life, he was no stranger to the black newspapers that followed the antics of the city's black elite. In 1917, John was good-naturedly described by the *Chicago Defender* as being a member of the gentry who had mastered the "art of elbow crooking."[11] In other words, John was an accomplished drinker of alcoholic beverages. During Prohibition in 1920, a reporter with the *Chicago Defender* noted that John Roxborough, "the best hustler in Detroit, introduced us to a barrel of homeless brew that was a knockout; Johnny can always be relied upon to look after the strangers."[12] Roxborough's behavior was never classified as indecent or lowbrow, although the same behavior was looked down upon if committed by southern black men or women who were not considered part of Detroit's leading black citizens.

As Detroit grew into an industrial powerhouse in the 1920s, blacks and whites from the South continued to migrate into the city. For many southern blacks, Detroit promised an opportunity to leave behind all memories of slavery. Some were for the first time leaving the plantations where their families had been enslaved. Others were leaving these same plantations where they had tirelessly labored as sharecroppers. This past life was one of misery, where harsh treatment by whites and by the land they tended could be abandoned for a better future. After these southern blacks arrived in Detroit, they found they had to contend with discrimination not only from white immigrants but also from southern whites who migrated with them and with whom they competed for employment.[13] As blacks made their way into the city from the South, they were expected to adopt the mainstream middle-class values of the time, including being efficient, thrifty, sober, clean, industrious, and orderly.[14]

Detroit's preexisting black community, like whites, worried about the influx of "uncivilized" migrants. Detroit's black leaders felt that whites viewed all blacks the same, and the influx of migrant blacks' negative behaviors would be seen as representative of all blacks. The fear was whites would assume all blacks were dirty, loud, and discourteous. Black leaders tried to remind whites that "the Black population of Detroit had been mainly families of a high grade, both in intelligence and well-being . . . self-respecting and respected for their intelligence and well-being. Some of them held responsible places in the commercial professions and community life of the city."[15] In 1917, the Detroit Urban League formed the Dress Well Club. The purpose of the club was to improve race relations in Detroit between whites and blacks by educating southern blacks on the proper way to behave in public and to stem the tide of increasing segregation in the city caused by "uncouth" blacks. The Dress Well Club distributed a brochure outlining the "dos" and "don'ts" of proper public behavior for blacks. For example, the brochure advised black men not to crowd inside a streetcar while wearing dirty clothing, not to loiter, and to avoid speaking loudly in public. The club urged blacks to maintain employment by being industrious, efficient, prompt, and sober. Being clean and going to church and school were important, as well as saving money and avoiding buying on credit. The brochure went on to say that those who followed these rules would get better jobs and help decrease prejudice and discrimination.[16] In spite of all these efforts, most whites treated all blacks in Detroit as a "single entity."[17] Justine Rogers Wylie noted that all black Detroiters, the unemployed, working poor, and middle class, were forced to live in overcrowded accommodations in the oldest part of town. They were excluded from most establishments and struggled to survive daily.[18]

By the mid-1920s, southern blacks were coping with health issues brought on by filthy, substandard housing, cold winters, and lack of immunizations for diseases such as smallpox. This all made for a hard existence for the newcomers.[19] In spite of this, blacks felt their community was a city within a city. They were tied to each other not only by their race but also by religion, family, and the sense of community. To survive, people shared their homes with families and, at times, strangers, creating a "communal spirit." Family and communities provided support for their members against racism and inequality found everywhere in Detroit. For blacks, hope, dreams, and determination pushed them through difficult days and the many barriers that were put in place to deny them the American Dream.[20]

During the 1920s, Detroit would gain its reputation for putting the world on wheels with the automobiles it manufactured. The 1920 census reported Detroit's population at 993,675; 40,838 were black citizens. By 1930 there were 120,066 blacks in Detroit as the city's overall population ballooned to 1,586,662. People from all over the country were lured to Detroit shortly after World War I in an effort to address the shortage of workers needed to run various factories in the city. Companies recruited blacks from the South to Detroit via train and bus.[21] As the number of blacks increased in the city due to southern migration, criticism concerning their behavior continued to intensify as well. Blacks who were originally from Detroit continued to complain about the influx of the "southern negro," whom they still considered coarse and vulgar. According to a 1922 article in the *Chicago Defender*, some of the original "cultured" blacks of Detroit were upset that race relations were deteriorating between them and the white citizens in the city. The original black Detroiters complained that they were being denied access to theaters, restaurants, and other public places because of the actions of the newly arrived southern blacks, who, they felt, were unrefined and crude hoodlums. These "low-brows" were blamed for the indecency in the city, which included prostitution, gambling, bootlegging, stabbings, and shootings. They were accused of cursing and using coarse language and wearing indecent clothing. In the opinion of some of the refined black Christians, the "parasites should have been jailed and put in the workhouse."[22] However, these leading black Detroiters did not recognize that more southern whites had migrated to the city than blacks. These southern whites brought with them their prejudices, which included support for segregation. These attitudes likely impacted race relations more than the "uncouth" behavior of southern blacks.

As a bail bondsman, John Roxborough found that when someone was locked up and needed bail, they did not care who provided their freedom, black or white. As chance or luck would have it, being a bail bondsman introduced Roxborough to the game of "policy." One night, Roxborough provided bail for a Kansas City policy operator. The policy operator offered Roxborough some advice that would change his life and financial status. The policy operator noticed the large population of blacks in Detroit working for the Ford Motor Company. He surmised this population had the money and was ripe for the playing of policy, which would bring riches to whoever set up a policy operation.[23]

Policy, like other games of chance, had its own rules. The winning numbers in policy were determined by a drawing. The range of numbers was 1 to 78 with 12, 24, or 36 numbers drawn. In Detroit, the numbers were written on 78 pieces of rubber-like cloth. Each piece was put into a two-inch metal tube. The tubes were placed in a large container from which they were drawn.[24] A player could place a wager on either a single number or on multiple numbers.[25] Policy playing required a large investment in money and resources. It required a policy wheel, containers, printing presses, and large gathering spaces to accommodate the writers and other personnel needed in the actual operation of the game, as well as the public whenever possible.[26]

Roxborough listened and learned, and shortly after, in 1919, he established the D&M Big Four policy house located in Detroit's Black Bottom. Roxborough claimed he set up his policy house for two reasons: he had witnessed firsthand how the game helped the economic situation of those who operated the game and improved the finances of members of the black community.[27] With the establishment of the D&M Big Four, Roxborough became a policy operator, and like other policy operators of the time, he listed his occupation as being in "real estate" in Polk's Detroit City Directory of 1919/1920.

By 1920, Detroit's total population had doubled, and 100,000 people found themselves without employment as a depression hit the city. As a result, people found themselves living in deplorable conditions, including unheated and leaking barns, shacks, and tents. Food was scarce, and proper clothing for the harsh winters was nonexistent.[28] Despite this, Roxborough successfully began operating his policy establishment during the depression of 1920–21. Business was good, and by 1923 or 1924, Roxborough acquired a partner, Everett Watson.[29] It was during this tumultuous time that John Roxborough, who was from one of the original privileged black families of Detroit, made his mark and wealth in Detroit by selling numbers to many who dreamed and hoped for a better future. Roxborough's customers were found in Detroit's Black Bottom, which was not looked upon favorably by some. One paper reported, "The social and economical progress of the Negro in this city is badly hampered by such practices as are usually carried on in that section called Black Bottom. That Detroit has a black bottom section is appreciated only by the lowest type of underworld characters, who themselves are afraid to enter the section alone at night. The more intelligent Race folks are really ashamed to walk along the streets and establishments where such characters hang out."[30]

As Roxborough continued to amass his wealth from policy, he invested his money in legitimate businesses as well. For example, in 1927 he co-founded the Great Lakes Mutual Insurance Company with other prominent black Detroiters to ensure blacks had access to affordable insurance. These men were unable to secure loans from mainstream banks and, as a result, financed this venture with their own money. For Roxborough, this money came from the pennies, nickels, and dimes wagered on policy. At its inception, the Great Lakes Mutual Insurance Company had 250 policyholders and $10,000 in capital. The company was open for only twenty months when the stock market crashed. While banks and other financial institutions were unable to meet their financial obligations, the Great Lakes Mutual Insurance Company remained in operation. Thanks to the founding members' personal funds, the doors remained open, new policies were written, and all expenses and claims were paid.[31] Five years after it was founded, the insurance company reported it had issued more than 14,000 policies, which represented more than $5,500,000 worth of life insurance.

The all-black company located in the community had paid its employees more than $75,000 and had issued $25,000 in death claims to policyholders. The insurance company also established free visiting nurse services to sick and injured policyholders.[32] The Great Lakes Mutual Insurance Company continued to flourish for many years. By 1934, it had expanded and created two new companies. The first company, the Great Lakes Agency Company, founded the Great Lakes Country Club in Holly, Michigan. Its purpose was to provide recreational space for blacks who otherwise were denied access to such facilities. The second company, the Great Lakes Land and Investment Company, purchased investment properties for blacks. By the mid-1950s, the Great Lakes Mutual Insurance Company had become the largest black-owned business in Michigan, with 275 employees, 106,000 customers, and $5,000,000 in assets.

Just as John Roxborough was known as the founding father of numbers in Detroit, his one-time business partner Everett Watson was known as the black "numbers czar" of Detroit. He, like Roxborough, played a huge role in numbers gambling in Detroit. In addition, Watson had a hand in developing Detroit's black community. Whereas Roxborough came from a prominent black family, Watson did not; he was truly a self-made man. Everett Irving Watson was born in Woodstown, New Jersey, in 1884 and moved to Detroit in 1910. At that time, Watson worked as a waiter on the boats that traveled the Detroit River. Being a waiter was one of the few jobs that a black man could obtain that was considered prestigious and paid well.[33] Watson first appeared in the Detroit City Directory in 1916; his occupation was listed as a waiter. By 1919/1920, Watson's occupation had changed to janitor. The next year, Watson changed occupations again and was listed as the manager of the Eastside Social Club. He entered the policy gambling business as John Roxborough's partner in 1923 or 1924;[34] however, from 1922 to 1929, he is listed as either a waiter or manager for the Waiters and Bellman's Club located in Detroit's Black Bottom. The Waiters and Bellman's Club was a black gambling establishment that offered liquor during Prohibition as well as dice and card games. Sometime during this period (possibly in 1927, when the opening of the "new" club was announced in the *Pittsburgh Courier*), Watson bought the club. With his newly acquired wealth, Watson quickly became a prominent figure in Detroit's black community; it did not take long for him to be mentioned in black newspapers. For example, on December 31, 1927, the *Pittsburgh Courier* reported that he, John Roxborough, and some of Detroit's other "successful business men of the Race, gave funds to the Detroit Urban League to bring Santa Claus to over one hundred and fifty children."[35] The same article also noted that Watson was a guest at a banquet given for a newly elected city council member.

Watson was able to amass enough wealth to purchase $100,000 in contract certificates. Contract certificates were similar to annuities and entitled the holder to a lump-sum settlement after a set period of time.[36] At 162 pounds, standing at 5'6", with a strong face, Watson was described by some as a visionary who had expensive tastes. In 1928 he bought 200 acres of land in Grass Lake, Michigan, and a short time later added another 200 acres to his spread. On his 400 acres, Watson and his second wife, Ida, built what was described as a beautiful estate called Cherokee Farms.[37] Ida, with her fair coloring, was both proud and powerful. She was responsible for the building of the beautiful estate. It included a lagoon, a series of knolls, a ten-acre private lake, a large barn, a milk house, a large chateau with dog kennels, a two-bedroom house, an equipment building with living quarters, horse stables, a three-car garage, and an English-style main house comprised of nine rooms with three bathrooms.[38] Watson and Ida kept to themselves, which caused their neighbors to wonder about them and their home. Some speculated that Everett was an "Oklahoma Indian" who made his money from oil, while others argued he was a "Negro gambler from Detroit related to Joe Louis." Other neighbors thought Ida was an "Indian" based on the aggressive way she ran them off her premises when they tried to obtain information concerning the Watsons.[39] For years, Watson and Ida entertained the "who's who" of Detroit's black society, including Joe Louis, at their estate. In contrast to the wealth of Everett Watson and John Roxborough, for the average Detroiter, whether black or white, life was much harder. Watson's and Roxborough's wealth would continue to grow as a new numbers game was introduced to Detroiters and inaugurated a significant new chapter in the history of the illegal lottery.

4

312 Plays for Playing the Numbers in Detroit

Since the beginning of time the human race has placed much importance and significance in dreams. Those of us who are familiar with Biblical History will recall the many events that were rendered in deference to dreams. The fact cannot be overlooked that dreams have always been a deciding factor for good or evil in the World's History.

—Professor Zonite, *The Original Three Wise Men Dream Book*

As the numbers operators compiled their wealth from the policy racket, another game of chance was created and brought to Detroit. This new game would become more popular than policy, amass more wealth for the numbers operators, and eventually render policy nonexistent in Detroit. In 1928, John Roxborough learned a new game of chance simply called "numbers" from out-of-town numbers operators Gus Greenlee, Teddy Horne, and Casper Holstein.[1]

Holstein, originally from the Virgin Islands, moved to New York as a child with his mother in 1894. As an adult, Holstein worked as a store porter on Fifth Avenue; he was also a bookmaker and operated a gambling house.[2] While sitting in a janitor's closet in 1920, Holstein envisioned a new game of chance. While staring at the clearinghouse totals in the paper, he realized the figures differed every day. For six months he pondered that fact until the idea for a new numbers game was fully formed. In this new game, players would try to guess the correct three-digit number from 000 to 999 for the day. The three-digit number would come from the thousands column from the daily clearinghouse totals.[3] For example, if the closing figure on a certain exchange was $7,313,358, the winning number for that day would be 313.[4] From this, the "numbers" game was born. Unlike policy, numbers was a simpler game, which required fewer resources and people to operate. The winning numbers did not have to be drawn from a policy wheel or printed and distributed to players. The winning numbers for the Detroit numbers game from 1928 to 1931 included the ending numbers/totals of the financial clearinghouse and later were derived from the winnings of horse races.[5] This change occurred when the clearinghouses began publishing their figures in round digits rather than exact figures to prevent the published numbers from being used for gambling.

Roxborough learned this new numbers game from numbers operators Gus Greenlee and Teddy Horne. It is not clear how John Roxborough came to know both Greenlee and Horne, but the men were similar in several ways. William "Gus" Greenlee was from a family that valued education. Greenlee's brothers all obtained either a law or medical degree, while Greenlee only attended college for a year. He earned his money first from running bootleg liquor and then later from operating a numbers bank or organization. With his wealth, Greenlee purchased a Negro league baseball team, the Pittsburgh Crawfords, and built a baseball park for the team in a black Pittsburgh community. Greenlee also owned nightclubs, a pool hall, and a café and grill; managed numerous boxers; and was a generous philanthropist in Pittsburgh's black Hill District.[6] Edwin "Teddy" Horne Jr. was from Harlem. His father was a teacher and editor of two newspapers, and his mother was an active member of the Urban League, the National Association for the Advancement of Colored People (NAACP), the suffragette movement, and a few other social organizations. Like Roxborough and Greenlee, however, Horne was impatient with education and wanted to amass wealth quickly. For Horne, gambling was the way to do it.[7] Horne had one daughter, Lena, who later became world renowned for her beautiful voice. Horne moved to Pittsburgh and ran a hotel called the Belmont, which had both a restaurant and gambling room in the rear. In addition to the hotel, restaurant, and gambling club, Teddy Horne was involved in a lucrative numbers business. Lena Horne stated, "Numbers are a poor man's preoccupation. You can buy a number for a few cents and you may strike it rich. It's not likely, but it is a hope, and in the Negro ghetto it is about the only hope you can afford."[8]

Although many hoped to win, the odds of correctly choosing the three-digit number were 1,000 to 1. With these steep odds, some turned to religion and spiritual guidance to select numbers to play, and there was no shortage of self-proclaimed prophets, mediums, and spiritualists willing to help for a fee. Black published newspapers were filled with their advertisements offering a variety of services to numbers players. In 1928, one paper reported,

Almost every week there springs up in a different street a spiritualist who sells numbers to policy players that are sure to "come out" in one to five days. The purchasers dare not, under penalty of losing their luck, show them to anyone but the policy writer. The prospective buyer is asked to "cut" a deck of cards; if a red card is turned up, the luck is bad, and no numbers will be sold him that day. They go in droves sometimes waiting in line, two and three deep. The law is evaded under guise of giving spiritual advice free, as no charge is made for the numbers, but each customer must toss a quarter over his left shoulder as he passes out. This of course, adds to the customer's luck and to the spiritual adviser's wealth.[9]

Some players played "special numbers," which could be any number that had significance to the player. Those numbers were considered more powerful or had what anthropologists call mana.[10] Special numbers, commonly played for years, were often birth dates, anniversaries, and addresses. Others, called hunch players, derived inspiration from numbers found anywhere. They live by the credo "take a hunch and bet a bunch."[11] Hunches can be found anywhere: license plate numbers, traffic tickets, or change owed at a cash register. During the 1930s, it was not uncommon for black numbers players to play Joe Louis's weight. At one time the telephone numbers that were broadcasted on the popular *Amos 'n' Andy* radio show were heavily played as well. "Playing the numbers each day means thinking about numbers all the time. The number on a dry cleaning slip. A bill from a restaurant. The number of pages in a book. Things that people who don't play the numbers take for granted are very important to people who play."[12]

Finally, some numbers players hoped to be successful in hitting the numbers by examining their unconscious dreams. These players believed that their dreams had meaning that could be translated with the use of dream books. Dating from 1862 and first popular among whites from eastern Europe, dream books link dreams or other experiences to number combinations in a dictionary-like format.[13] Anthony Comstock, an early American reformer and post office agent who fought against obscenity in 1883, felt that policy houses were fodder for the superstitious. He noted, "The negro dreams a dream, the Irishman or woman has a 'presintiment,' and the German a vision, and each rushes to the 'dream-book,' kept in every policy-den, to see what number the dream or vision calls for."[14] Like numbers gambling, dream books were used to paint minorities as ignorant and superstitious. By the early 1900s, *Old Aunt Dinah's* and *Aunt Sally's Policy Players* began to appear on the market. The cover of these books featured caricatures of elderly black women advertising the washwoman's row or "4-11-44." As one white magazine writer wrote, "Dreams are very popular among Negro players as a means of determining the number to be bet on and books interpreting dreams in terms of figures are best sellers in darky districts."[15] The books were simple to use; a player merely looked up a key word that corresponded with their dream or other significant event in their life. For example, if a person dreamed of dogs, in policy playing, the number that corresponded to dog in *Old Aunt Dinah's* dream book was "73"; however, in *The Original Three Wise Men Dream Book* dog corresponded to "616." Every dream book was different, thus numbers assigned were commonly not the same. This inconsistency in dream books did not faze users, however; one user noted that some books worked for some people and not for others.[16] The numbers published in dream books were so popular that a few songs about playing the numbers used the assigned dream book numbers in their lyrics. In 1930 Arthur "Blind" Blake wrote and sang a blues song called "Playing Policy Blues." In the song, he talks of dreaming and playing the numbers that correspond to his dream.

> Numbers, numbers 'bout to drive me mad
> Numbers, numbers 'bout to drive me mad
> Thinking about the money that I should have had
> I dreamed last night the woman I loved was dead
> I dreamed last night the woman I loved was dead
> If I'd have played the Dead Row I'd have come out ahead
> I acted the fool and played on 3, 6, 9
> I acted the fool and played on 3, 6, 9
> Lost my money and that gal of mine
> I played on Clearing-House, couldn't make the grade
> I played on Clearing-House, couldn't make the grade
> Lord, thinking of the money that I should have made
> I begged my baby to let me in her door
> I begged my baby let me in her door
> Wanted to put my 25, 50, 75 in her 7, 17, 24
> I want 15, 50, and 51

I want 15, 50, and 51
I'm gonna keep playing policy 'til some good luck come

Blake cleverly inserts numbers in place of words. He uses a sexual double entendre when he says he wants to put his "25, 50, 75 in her 7, 17, 24." Depending on the dream book he could be saying he wants to put his phallic symbol into the woman's yonic symbol, or that he simply wants to wash his underwear in the river or washtub. When he says he wants "15, 50, and 51," in one dream book this could mean he wants to have sex with a "colored" woman in bed or that he wants to make noise, sing, and dance.[17]

It is not clear how the numbers in dream books were derived, although some authors claimed biblical inspiration. Dream books tended to be written by people with sage or scientific names. For instance, *The Original Three Wise Men Dream Book* was penned by "Professor Zonite"; Zonite was Detroiter Mallory F. Banks. Banks copyrighted his dream book in 1933, and in addition to selling his dream books, he sold "Iramir Hit Perfume with free numbers" and Jacob's Ladder incenses.[18] Like Mallory Banks, dream book authors tended to offer multiple services to their users. H. G. Parris of New

Figure 1. Three Wise Men Dream Books.

York, writing under the name of Professor Konje, in his *Lucky Star Dream Book* told users, "When Luck comes your way make a sound investment in A Home for you and your family. Before purchasing, see me at once. I have real bargains, in private houses and apartment buildings in and out of the city."[19]

In 1938, Mallory Banks sued eight people, including numbers bankers John Roxborough, Everett Watson, Pete Kelly, and Louis Weisberg, as well as Otis Sanders, H. L. Bolar, Delbert Lee, and a John Doe, in federal court for copyright infringement.[20] Banks had previously sent letters to each of the defendants warning them to cease plagiarizing the contents of his copyrighted book; however, they refused.[21] H. L. Bolar was the owner of the Bolar Publishing Company, Delbert Lee was a printer, and Otis Sanders was a jobber or small-time wholesaler.[22] Banks claimed that Sanders, who had previously worked as a columnist for a Detroit newspaper, had been employed by the numbers men to print Banks's book for free distribution to numbers players.[23] The defendants admitted they copied and distributed the dream book without permission but argued that because the dream book was used for illegal numbers gambling, they were exempt from paying Banks. This defense did not hold up in court, and two years later, the eight defendants settled the lawsuit with Banks.[24] When the *Detroit Times* ran a story on March 14, 1938, about Banks's plagiarism lawsuit against the numbers kings, they explained how dream books work. The example they used was of someone dreaming of snakes, which played for 263. Numbers players flooded numbers banks by playing 263 the next day, and it fell. It was reported that numbers banks lost as much as $25,000.[25]

Policy playing proved to be lucrative, but the new three-digit numbers game would generate even more wealth for numbers operators/bankers. For a while, Roxborough offered this new game to players in addition to policy before focusing exclusively on numbers. To generate interest in numbers, Roxborough stressed the payout for wins or hits was more lucrative than policy playing. For example, in policy, a five-cent wager paid ten dollars if the winning number fell; however, in numbers, a five-cent wager paid out twenty-five dollars. To generate trust in his numbers games, he made sure he was seen with his writers and paid off winning bets called "hits" with new money. He also enlisted fortune tellers to predict numbers and preachers to sell them to their congregations.[26] Roxborough's presence with numbers runners sent the message to the masses that numbers gambling was acceptable and could be trusted. It was said that "Honest John" lived by the motto,

"Play fair with me and I'll play fair with you, otherwise I don't want any deal-ings with you."[27] In addition, Roxborough ensured everyone could play by allowing penny bets.[28] By 1931, numbers became more popular than policy playing in Detroit because the players felt "that there is more fairness, despite the great odds, than is true in policy where the slips are likely to be juggled or the policy wheel fixed."[29]

In 1928, Everett Watson severed his partnership with Roxborough's Big Four numbers establishment and opened his own numbers house called the Yellow Dog in Detroit's Black Bottom neighborhood.[30] This eastside num-bers establishment was located just a block and a half from Detroit's police headquarters. Watson named his numbers operation after a busy southern railroad line called the Yazoo Delta.[31] The Yazoo Delta was nicknamed the Yellow Dog and ran north to south in Mississippi. For some, the Yellow Dog represented an escape from despair in Mississippi to a future filled with hope in the North. Like the railroad line, the Yellow Dog numbers house offered an escape as well. For the cost of a few pennies, it offered the dream of winning a windfall.

For a numbers organization to run effectively, several people were needed to fulfill specific roles. Every numbers organization required writ-ers, who were essentially salesmen whose main job was to solicit business. Some writers worked solely for a particular numbers organization and gen-erated door-to-door sales, while other writers wrote numbers as a part-time job. The neighborhood milkman, for instance, took bets for the custom-ers on his daily route. Both men and women served as numbers writers and were paid 25 percent of the total numbers they wrote or sold. If a writer wrote or sold $100 worth of bets, his pay or commission would be $25. Writers were found in neighborhoods going door to door, in office buildings, stores, and factories. Candy and cigar store owners, barbershop porters, and bartenders doubled as numbers writers as well.[32] A large num-bers organization hired thousands of writers, and an average-sized organi-zation employed 300 to 500 writers. When a writer took a number or a bet, he or she would write the number in a book that recorded the transaction in triplicate. The original copy, usually yellow, was turned in to headquar-ters, the white copy was given to the person placing the bet, and the final copy remained in the writer's book. Once writers completed taking bets on numbers, they turned the numbers or their "book" over to a pick-up man, who was assigned to a specific area.[33] The pick-up man then transported the books and money to the numbers house. The number of pick-up men varied and depended on the number of writers an organization employed. Pick-up men received 10 percent of the total amount of money collected from the writers in their territory. Cashiers, located at the numbers organization's headquarters, tabulated the money and checked the betting slips for accuracy. Cashiers then turned the money over to clerks, who entered the information into the house books. The betting slips went to checkers, who examined the betting slips for winning numbers.[34] Checkers were normally paid $10 per week, and numbers houses, depending on their size, employed 10 to 20 of them.[35]

After 1931, the winning numbers were derived from the newspapers via the total winnings of horse races.[36] For several years, John Roxborough chose which racetrack would be used to gauge the winning numbers. This information was communicated to players via cards, which were given to customers. By controlling which racetrack was used, Roxborough wielded great power over all other numbers operators. The winning number was obtained by totaling the figures in the win, place, and show columns of certain races. For example, if a player placed a wager on the three, five, and seven races on a given day, and the total paid for the three races was $129.20, the five races was $235.20, and the seven races was $301.00, the winning number for that day would be 951: the winning number was derived from the digit directly preceding each race's decimal point. The winning numbers could be found in several Detroit newspapers, and this made it easy for any player to ascertain the winning number. This method of determining the winning numbers also assured players that the winning numbers were not manipulated.[37] Newspapers published the winning numbers because of the popularity of the numbers game in both the black and white communities, and this in turn stimulated newspaper sales.[38] Sometime after 1935, however, Detroit newspapers stopped printing race mutuel totals in an attempt to end numbers gambling.[39]

Each policy or numbers house, also referred to as policy wheels or numbers banks, also employed a manager. The manager ran the organization for the owner, also called a numbers operator or numbers banker, and was paid $50 to $200 per week depending on the size of the organization.[40] Every organization had various other employees, including accountants, adding machine operators, typists, security officers, and telephone operators who answered the phone and gave out the winning number.[41] According to the *Detroit Free Press*, "Many skilled black comptometer operators, adding machine operators, secretaries, stenographers, accountants and lawyers served their apprenticeships in policy and number houses in the Valley. Before the policy operations, few black-owned businesses required highly trained help, but policy money came in so fast that adding machine operators soon became proficient, and well paid."[42] Security officers for policy

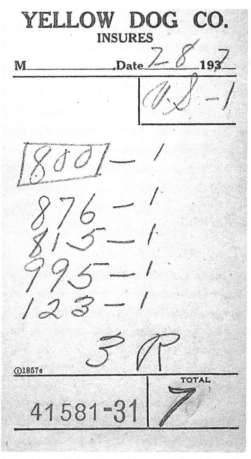

Figure 2. Losing numbers ticket from Everett Watson's Yellow Dog numbers organization. The winning number for the day was 874. The ticket is for the first three races. Five numbers were played. One number, "800," was boxed, the other four numbers, "876," "815," "995," and "123," were played straight. The wager could have been for a penny or a dollar.

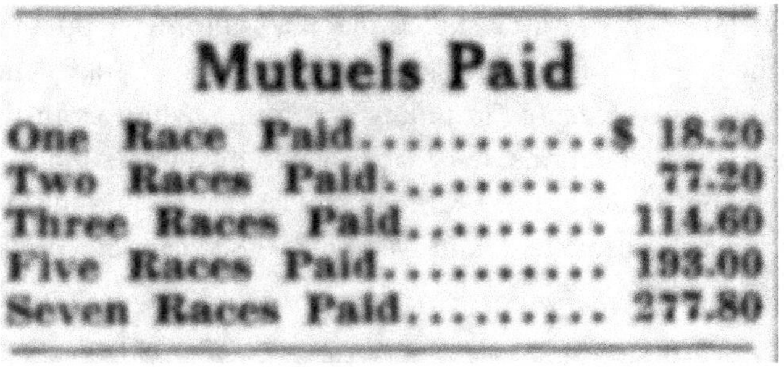

Mutuels Paid

One Race Paid.	$ 18.20
Two Races Paid.	77.20
Three Races Paid.	114.60
Five Races Paid.	193.00
Seven Races Paid.	277.80

Figure 3. Racetrack results for July 8, 1937, printed in the *Detroit Free Press*. The winning number was 874. It was derived from the digit directly preceding each race's decimal point.

organizations applied to the city to be private policemen. The Detroit City Charter provided security officers with special police badges and allowed them to carry guns. These special policemen were paid by the numbers organizations but had the same authority as police officers.[43] Finally, bail bondsmen and attorneys were retained to bail out and defend employees when they were arrested and charged. Black attorneys were usually not hired by white clients and appreciated the work generated by the policy and numbers houses.

By 1928, black numbers organizations were growing and had a corner on the numbers game in Detroit. In New York, it was a different story. By the end of 1928, Casper Holstein, the father of the numbers game, had abandoned his numbers empire in New York. On September 20, 1928, Holstein was kidnapped by white gangsters who beat, bound, gagged, and blindfolded him. The gangsters allegedly demanded $50,000 and that Holstein give up his numbers empire. On September 24, he was released by the thugs, who gave him three dollars for cab fare.[44] Holstein refused to identify his assailants, and after the kidnapping, he retired from the numbers business. It was revealed during an investigation by Samuel Seabury that several unsolved murders took place from 1928 to 1931 as a result of what was called "factional strife in the policy slip racket."[45] Seabury was the legal counsel for the Hofstadter Committee, also known as the Seabury Investigations. The committee not only exposed the murders connected with the takeover of the numbers racket by gangsters but also found widespread corruption in the court system and the police department. One of the last black numbers

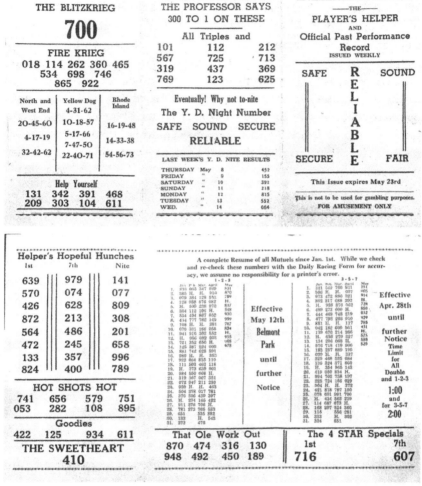

Figures 4 and 5. The front and back of a numbers tip card from the 1940s. It indicated which racetrack (in this case Belmont Park) was used for choosing the winning numbers. It also provided the winning numbers for the year and even suggested numbers for both policy and the numbers to play. The tip cards allowed some organizations, like the Yellow Dog, to advertise directly to their customers.

operators who was able to hold on to the numbers game in Harlem after 1928 was Stephanie St. Clair. She fought for four years, but by 1932, she too was forced out of her $100,000-per-day numbers business by white gangster Dutch Schultz. In September 1932, she called upon the mayor to complain that Schultz had "muscled" into the Harlem numbers game with other white gangsters and effectively closed down her operation and those of other black numbers operators.[46] It was estimated that at least fifty murders were committed by the Schultz gang as a result of their takeover of the numbers racket.[47] When an attempt to take control of the numbers racket in Detroit occurred, the methods and the outcome were different than what occurred in New York.

5
The White Invasion

A short time later, another mob made an invasion, setting up an elaborate office and began doing business in the white neighborhoods. Colored writers working for the colored numbers barons, in many instances, were beaten and barred from the neighborhoods where they had been working for a number of years.

—Russ Cowans, *Afro-American*, September 17, 1938

For a while, black numbers organizations in Detroit were able to operate without outside interference and controlled the business. This did not last long; they soon found themselves having to deal with three groups that threatened their control: white gangsters who entered into the numbers game; the clergy, other businesses, and homeowners; and Detroit politicians who controlled the police department.

In 1928, white numbers operators became involved in numbers gambling. Prohibition was still in effect in 1928 and would not be repealed for another five years; however, white gangsters, who had earned much of their money from bootlegging, decided to diversify their enterprises by branching out in both legal and illegal businesses. For example, some became involved in the cleaning and dyeing industry or owned taxi companies, while others dabbled in bookmaking and numbers gambling operations.[1] White number operators were attracted to numbers gambling for the same reason the black numbers operators were: huge profits. In addition to opening policy/numbers houses in Detroit's black communities, they also opened blind pigs or illegal establishments where they peddled prohibited whisky. Despite the misconception that only blacks played the numbers, the reality was that all races did and many wanted a piece of the action. Sunnie Wilson in his memoir, *Toast of the Town*, recalled hearing the story of a numbers operator who, while taking a sack of money from his numbers operation to the bank, was stopped by a Chinese man. The Chinese man asked the black numbers operator what was in the bag, to which the numbers operator responded,

"I've got black folks' dreams." Sometime later, the numbers operator saw the same man holding his own bag of money. As they passed, the Chinese man told the numbers operator, "Chinese people got black dreams too."[2]

These new numbers entrepreneurs were criticized by the black press for taking resources from Detroit's black community. The *Chicago Defender* wrote, "Many white gamblers, attracted by huge policy profits, have opened up policy houses. Other syndicates taking advantage of lax conditions, have scattered blind pigs over the black belt, where various brands of whisky are displayed with a recklessness indicative of high police protection. These bootlegging syndicates drain resources without giving anything in return."[3] In response to whites' attempted takeover of numbers gambling, black numbers operators formed the Associated Numbers Bankers. The organization's purpose was to ensure blacks stayed in control, established payoff rates, retained attorneys, and paid for police protection.[4] As a result of this, eventually, the united black numbers operators were able to successfully drive out a white takeover.

The white operators had several advantages over black operators, their race in particular. While black numbers operators were restricted to working in mostly black communities, the white operators set up shop all over the city in both black and white communities. One such white numbers operator who was able to capitalize on this was Louis "Lou" Weisberg. Unlike Roxborough and Watson, Weisberg had a reputation for dishonesty. He gained this reputation after he closed his business and failed to pay winners on a heavily played number.[5] When another white numbers house refused to pay on a $3,000 hit, black operators accused them of being crooked and blamed them for bringing unwanted attention to the numbers game. When the winner did not receive his money, he hired an attorney who brought the story to the attention of the press. At one point, black operators were ordered to cease operations by police and other authorities, while white operators continued to operate without police interference.[6] In an effort to eliminate competition and to stay in business, Walter Norwood, a black numbers operator, partnered with Weisberg. The two operated without police interference while other black operators were forced to relocate or close.[7]

Walter Norwood was described as a "grand little man." He owned the Norwood Hotel and Club Plantation located in Paradise Valley. Club Plantation was a swanky black and tan club that catered to Detroit's well-established. It was known for its revolving floor, where guests listened to Ella

Fitzgerald, Billy Eckstine, Sugar Brown, and McKinney's Cotton Pickers on a regular basis. Norwood operated his numbers house, called the Manhattan, in his hotel at 550 East Adams. Approximately sixty employees worked for the Manhattan, and Norwood, in addition to Weisberg, had a few partners who for $7,500 bought into his business.[8]

The main operations for the Manhattan took place on the second floor. Pick-up men collected the numbers from writers and brought them to the first floor. The numbers were then put in a pail attached to a conveyor rope, which was pulled through a hole to the second floor. Pick-up men were not allowed on the second floor, and the second-floor location added a layer of security against would-be robbers and raiding police.[9] Once the number tickets reached the second floor, they were distributed to six to eight employees to be sorted.[10] Adding machines were used to get the total dollar amount of tickets played for the day. Once this was done and the first horse race completed, the tickets were examined for winners or hits.[11] After checkers identified the winning tickets, they wrote up envelopes showing what the winning number was, how much it was played for, who wrote the ticket, the writer's route number, and the date.[12] The organization's manager would fill the envelope with the payout cash, seal it, and place it back in the pail. The pail was lowered back to the pick-up man on the first floor for distribution to the writer, who in turn delivered the payout to the winner.[13]

Numbers and policy houses became so successful that small business merchants, ministers, landlords, insurance agents, and other professionals united to rid Detroit of its "arch enemy" in 1928. These groups claimed numbers gambling drained more money out of the community than all other forms of gambling and left little money for people to patronize their businesses and contribute to the church.[14] If those allegations were not bad enough, they also purported that even schoolchildren were playing numbers with their lunch money. These groups estimated that 3,000 people were employed as numbers writers and about $10,000 was played daily in Detroit in September 1928. By December of that year, one source reported that there were 51 policy houses in Detroit, and 5,000 numbers writers, who took $30,000 daily in bets from players. These writers were accused of going door-to-door and enticing women to play; as a result, these women neglected their homes and children and failed to buy insurance. Police blamed the players, whom they estimated to be in the thousands, for wanting to "get something for nothing."[15]

The community was outraged at the gambling taking place and went into action. Westside Detroit merchants decided to take on numbers gambling by raising money to hire private investigators to obtain evidence for grand jury proceedings, and a number of ministers decided to attack the problem from the pulpit. They described numbers gambling as the "greatest evil" to assault the black race; it also threatened the development of Detroit businesses.[16] At a time when black Detroiters were facing high unemployment, inadequate housing, meager education, lack of health care, rampant tuberculosis, and prejudice, none of those was thought to be the greatest evil to assault blacks. One black minister stated, "There is nothing in Detroit that so affects the Negro as this policy wheel."[17] These views were indicative of what some blacks who had embodied middle-class values felt. These black Detroiters were not in tune with the problems that assailed poor blacks, and for them, the embarrassment of numbers gambling was truly an evil. On the other hand, blacks who faced numerous ailments caused by poverty found numbers gambling to be the least of their worries. In fact, many poor people played the numbers because it was a chance for them to live a little easier if just for a moment.

As time went on, the number of people playing the numbers continued to surge. The *Detroit News* estimated that daily policy playing in Detroit ranged from $50,000 to $80,000 and was mostly played by "Negros." Once again, poor blacks from the South were being blamed by Detroit's black and white middle-class leaders for the evils of numbers gambling and policy playing. The *Detroit News* reported that according to one prominent black resident, "The Negro workman comes here from the South, where he never had any experience in handling money, and at once begins to make what seems to him to be large wages. He is superstitious, and easily led. He falls an easy prey to the policy runners. Unfortunately, we haven't been able to obtain much cooperation from the Police Department in our efforts to protect him."[18]

White property owners who lived in the east-central district of Detroit formed an organization called the East Central Detroit Improvement Association to fight crime and vice in their neighborhoods. The association wanted to maintain property values by improving and promoting the beautification of the area. According to the association, property values had declined because of gambling, bootlegging, and disorderly houses. The chairman of the organization declared that "policy gambling among the Negro population in the district must be abolished." He stated that the association would ensure that other property owners were informed of the activity in the neighborhood and that the laws were enforced.[19]

Although some ministers and community leaders spoke out against the numbers game, they did not speak for all ministers and leaders in the community. For example, John Roxborough enlisted some "store front ministers" in 1928 to sell numbers to their congregations. These ministers worked out of churches housed in former stores. It was not uncommon for ministers to ask Roxborough, who at this time was wealthy, for cash donations. In return, he requested they encourage members to play.[20] Community leader John Dancy, who served as the executive secretary of the Detroit Urban League, had no problem associating and vacationing with Roxborough. In the fall of 1928, Dancy traveled to Idlewild, a black resort in the western part of Michigan, as Roxborough's guest. While there, Roxborough honored Dancy at an elaborate dinner party for his work in the community.[21]

Due to the mounting press coverage and pressure from various citizen groups, the Detroit Police Department cracked down on numbers gambling by conducting raids and arresting black violators. As a result, black numbers operators were forced to shut down their businesses while white numbers operators were not. Meanwhile, the black community leaders of Detroit indicated they were not specifically fighting black numbers operators but rather were fighting numbers gambling because it was detrimental to the city's youth. While delivering this message to the masses, they also relayed a contradictory statement. On one hand, they were trying to eradicate numbers gambling, but if numbers gambling were to remain, they wanted to ensure that black numbers operators were treated fairly and did not lose control of their businesses.[22] In spite of this, however, that is what occurred to some extent. A black weekly newspaper reported, "The police got busy and closed up all the policy houses, for a time, with a bluff at scaring the Negroes out of the business. In the interim whites tried unsuccessfully to gain control. When the houses opened up again several new places backed by 'white money,' opened, but as before soon went to the wall. As far as the ministers were concerned they were sincere in their efforts but the undercurrent opinion of the whole thing was that it was a crusade against the Negroes who control the activities."[23]

Throughout 1929, both John Roxborough and Everett Watson were expanding their legal and illegal businesses. Roxborough acquired the black Detroit newspaper *The Owl* and saved it from bankruptcy by investing $20,000 in it.[24] This was important because black newspapers provided not only information that was relevant in the black community but also professional jobs to blacks in the newspaper industry. Like other publications, Roxborough's *The Owl* employed college students as staff members.[25] During the same period, Roxborough was elected as a director to the National Benefit Life Insurance Company, where his biography described him as being engaged in the real estate, newspaper, and insurance business.[26] In July, the *Pittsburgh Courier* reported that he, along with other prominent Detroit men, had been elected to the Crudential Bond and Mortgage Company.[27]

In 1929, at the age of forty-four, Everett Watson continued to build his wealth; however, in June of that year the police raided his realty office, Watson Realty Company. Detroit police officers confiscated $20,000 worth of jewelry from the office and $1,200 from Watson's pocket. Although he did not have a license to run a pawn shop, Watson had accepted the jewelry in an interest-free loan transaction. During the raid, the police also found small rubber tubes, which were used in policy play, and upon their discovery, he admitted to running a policy game.[28] On July 22, Watson was charged with violating the gaming law when he took a $50 bet from someone who filed a complaint against him.[29]

A few months after Watson's office was raided, in October 1929, the stock market crashed. A month prior to this, 56,800 people were out of work in Michigan; approximately thirty days after the crash, that number ballooned to 212,500.[30] In the midst of this financial catastrophe, the citizens of Detroit elected a new mayor, Charles Bowles, who had been endorsed by the Ku Klux Klan.[31] The Klan at this time had a strong base in Detroit. Members could be found in all levels of government and exerted great political influence. Bowles's election, at first, opened the door for white numbers operators to try to take over the numbers racket from black operators. It would eventually prove unsuccessful.

Charles Bowles was born in Yale, Michigan, in 1884. He obtained his law degree from the University of Michigan in 1908, eventually settling in Detroit to practice law, before serving as a judge in Detroit Recorder's Court. As a political unknown, he first attempted to become Detroit's mayor in 1924, when he ran against Catholic candidate John Smith. At that time, 25 percent of Detroit newcomers were foreign born, and most were Catholic.[32] Detroit's population swelled and the make-up of neighborhoods began to change. Some lower- and middle-class whites could not tolerate the new-comers challenging their perceived social status, and this intolerance led to Detroit being a KKK stronghold.[33] A Klan official estimated that 70,000 Klansmen lived in Detroit in the early 1920s.[34] In 1923, the Detroit Klan tried to prevent a city council member, Dr. Frank Broderick, from being reelected. Broderick was narrowly reelected, but on Election Day, as votes were being counted, a five-foot cross was burned on city hall's lawn. By 1923, the burning of crosses in Detroit near public buildings was not unusual.[35]

In September 1924, a primary election was held in Detroit to deter-mine who would run for a final one-year term as mayor. The former mayor, Frank Doremus, had become ill and was unable to complete his full term. Attorney Charles Bowles threw his hat into the ring. Bowles lost the primary but decided to stay in the race as a write-in candidate or a "sticker candidate." A crowd of 6,000 Klan members showed their support of Bowles at an anti-Klan rally in October of that year by blocking the entrance to the rally and proceeding to march on Woodward Avenue. As they marched, they shouted Bowles's name, and some put Bowles stickers on windows of passing vehicles. The Ku Klux Klan of Detroit posted the symbols of the Klan and the logo of the Bowles campaign side by side up and down Wood-ward Avenue.[36] Police were called to disburse the Klan in an effort to allow the rally to continue.[37] Joseph Martin, who was running against Bowles, felt the Klan's actions revealed to citizens that Charles Bowles was their can-didate for mayor.

The other candidate, John Smith, who had strong support among Catholics, blacks, and immigrants, garnered support by criticizing the Klan's transgressions against minority groups. Smith called southern whites "ignorant hillbillies" and referred to the Klan as an "ugly monster from the South."[38] Although supported by the Klan, Bowles never acknowledged their backing. A few days before the election, the largest Klan meeting in Detroit's history was held in a field in Dearborn Township. Anywhere from 25,000 to 50,000 Klan members attended the rally, where vehicles were plastered with Bowles stickers and instructions on how to vote for him.[39] On the day of the election, several fights broke out between supporters of Smith and Bowles. Voters turned out in heavy numbers, and at the end of the day, Smith was declared the winner. Bowles came in second place, and it was noted that more than 15,000 votes for him were not counted because of various mis-takes people made in casting their vote for him. The voters either misspelled or shortened his name, rendering the votes invalid. Bowles demanded a recount, and the recount showed Smith had won by approximately 14,000 votes. Bowles, a Klan write-in candidate, was nearly elected to Detroit's top political position that year.

A year later, during what was described as a "hot campaign," members of the Klan distributed campaign literature for Bowles before burning a cross on the east side of the city.[40] Although his campaign was one of the smoothest Detroit had ever seen at the time, with Klan members driving voters to the polls, the support of the Klan and Klan sympathizers was not enough to pull off the victory.[41] Bowles then ran for a position as a judge in Detroit Recorder's Court and won. He was reelected for an additional three-year term before he once again ran for mayor in 1929.

The 1929 campaign was no different than the previous campaigns; it was hotly contested and controversial. Three candidates were fighting to be elected: incumbent John C. Lodge, former mayor John Smith, and Charles Bowles. Lodge, elected for one term from 1928 to 1930, was fighting to be reelected, and Smith, who had been elected for one year in 1924 and then again in 1925, wanted to reclaim the job from Lodge. Lodge, a quiet man with years of public service under his belt, was referred to as the man who did not talk. He made no campaign promises or speeches, which caused voters to be unsure of where he stood on issues. His opponents felt he was not dynamic enough and new leadership was needed. It did not go unnoticed by black voters that Mayor Lodge had never welcomed them or their causes; however, a small group of black citizens threw their support behind him based on an incident that occurred shortly after he first entered office. When a black family moved into a home in a white neighborhood outside of Black Bottom and the white neighbors began to intimidate the homeowners to make them move, Lodge ordered the police department to provide protection to the family.

Many black voters did not support John Smith because they felt he had not done enough in 1925 when several race disturbances broke out in the city. Specifically, many were upset that then Mayor Smith did nothing when black doctor Alex L. Turner was forced to abandon his home on Spokane in a white neighborhood in the summer of 1925 when a mob backed by the Klan broke into Turner's home and removed his furniture and property. As Dr. Turner and his wife left their home, they were attacked by a mob and received no help from the police. Other black voters, including Dr. Ossian

Sweet, were staunch supporters of Smith. Sweet was a black physician, like Turner, who in 1925 bought a home in a white working-class Detroit neighborhood. When he and his family moved into their home, a mob gathered to force him and his family out. Armed, Sweet and several family members and friends attempted to defend his home and family. In the process, a man was shot and killed. Sweet was tried with his brother Henry and several others for murder. None were found guilty, and Mayor Smith was credited with ensuring the Sweets were protected by police during this ordeal. Nonetheless, several blacks took exception to comments Smith made concerning blacks and housing—that they should not move into neighborhoods where they were not wanted.

Meanwhile, Charles Bowles openly denied ever being a member of the Klan and had earned a reputation on the bench as being a fair judge. With three candidates, black Detroiters were torn about whom they would vote for, and because they could not unite, their divided vote carried little weight in the primary.[42] Eventually, the election came down to two candidates, John Smith and Charles Bowles. Smith, a Catholic liberal, was known as a wet candidate, meaning he was against Prohibition, and Bowles was the dry candidate. Anti-Catholic voters, many of whom were Protestants, expected Bowles to soundly defeat Smith, whom they felt was pro-immigrant, pro-black, and pro-Jewish. Bowles ran on a platform of municipal reform and promised to be tough on crime and vice in the city. In a bitter campaign, Bowles beat Smith by just 6,000 votes. It was noted Smith did well with blue-collar districts, while Bowles was strongly supported in the "silk stocking" areas.[43]

Bowles took the oath of office in January 1930 to serve a city with a deficit of $12 million, a high unemployment rate, uncontrolled crime caused by illegal rum running and gambling, and a corrupt police department.[44] Just one month later, on February 13, 1930, John Roxborough was cited by the Detroit Police Department for violating the gaming laws when a numbers player placed a four- to five-dollar bet on fifty to sixty numbers from one of Roxborough's numbers writers. The bettor had winning numbers that should have paid him $1,820, but he was not paid his winnings. The case was eventually quashed.[45]

It took the citizens of Detroit approximately six months to decide that Mayor Bowles was not the man they wanted or needed to lead the city. He was accused of not keeping his campaign promises and charged with being "in bed" with criminals after he fired a popular police commissioner who was aggressively enforcing anti-vice laws in the city, including numbers gambling.[46] Immediately after Bowles was sworn into office, a number of gambling establishments and speakeasies opened. Citizens took notice and newspapers published pictures of various gambling activities. At first, the police department denied the gambling activity existed but eventually consented to accompanying some newspaper reporters to the gambling locations. When the police arrived at the locations, they raided them, and 300 people were arrested. Bowles, who was out of town attending the Kentucky Derby, promptly fired Police Commissioner Harold Emmons, who had authorized the raids and arrests.[47] Upon hearing this, angry citizens drew up a recall petition, and approximately 90,000 voters signed it in an effort to recall Bowles. According to the petition, Bowles had committed a number of transgressions including instituting "a policy of secrecy in public office" and "tolerating lawlessness and countenancing license."[48] Emmons alleged that Bowles had warned him that enforcement of vice and gambling laws would destroy his political career. Bowles ordered the formation of a centralized vice squad against Emmons's recommendations. The purpose of centralizing the vice operations was to make political and police payoffs easier and to ensure selective enforcement activities occurred. Emmons felt that vice crimes should be handled by each police precinct, which had more resources, and not centralized into one small squad. Emmons further charged that once the vice squad was centralized, organized criminals became more aggressive in their illegal activities. Some even openly declared they were untouchable because of the payoffs made to members of Bowles's administration.[49]

During the Bowles administration, Eddie Levinson, a Jewish gangster, formed a partnership with black numbers operator Walter Norwood. Once again Norwood crossed the numbers game color line and, with Levinson, planned to form a monopoly in Detroit. Levinson had strong ties to members of the police department, as well as the mayor's office. Levinson ordered a Detroit police lieutenant to call a meeting of all the numbers operators in the city. In a show of force at this meeting, the lieutenant advised the operators that Levinson would now control the numbers racket in Detroit. Upon hearing this, John Roxborough told Levinson in no uncertain terms that he would not and could not get away with taking over the numbers racket from him and the other black numbers operators.[50]

After firing police commissioner Emmons, Bowles hired Thomas Wilcox as his replacement. Thomas "Tom-Tom" Wilcox was a former special agent in charge at the Bureau of Investigation. During World War I and into the 1920s, he worked in the Detroit area investigating dynamite plots, German spies, and draft dodgers.[51] In an effort to show Mayor Bowles was not soft on crime, in May 1930 Wilcox met with the leadership of the Detroit Police Department and informed them to "go the limit" against vice.[52] Wilcox ensured raids and arrests were carried out throughout the city against numbers gamblers, bookies, and other gambling establishments. The results of these raids were captured by the newspapers and helped reinforce Wilcox's image as an upstanding lawman who was committed to cleaning up vice in Detroit. This action ended Levinson's attempt to take control of numbers gambling in Detroit and temporarily ensured blacks maintained control over their lucrative numbers businesses. These raids, however, did not stop Bowles's recall.

Two hours after the results of Bowles's recall were announced, at 1:45 a.m. on July 23, 1929, Gerald "Jerry" Buckley was murdered. Buckley

Figure 6. Thomas Wilcox (*center*) is sworn in as Detroit's police commissioner by City Clerk Richard Reading. Detroit mayor Charles Bowles stands by. Photo courtesy of *Detroit News*.

was a popular radio personality who had vehemently opposed Bowles during his short tenure as mayor. He had thousands of followers that tuned in to his show on WMBC out of the La Salle Hotel. Buckley used his radio airtime to crusade against gambling and other vice and had been warned his radio addresses were putting him in harm's way after he called out specific gambling locations and alleged collusion between city hall and Detroit's mob. Buckley had campaigned for pensions for seniors and employment opportunities for the unemployed and was credited with obtaining jobs for hundreds of Detroit residents.[53] Buckley was the first to suggest the recall of Mayor Bowles, and on the day of the recall urged voters to vote "yes." As he sat in the lobby of the La Salle Hotel, three men approached him. One shot Buckley eleven times, five in the head and six in the body, before running away. The day after Buckley was murdered, the Central Vice Squad was abolished, and raids on blind pigs and gambling establishments commenced.[54] Eventually, seven people, who were connected to the Italian mob, including mob boss Peter Licavoli, were indicted by a grand jury for Buckley's murder. At the time of his death, Buckley was the eleventh murder by the mob in the metro Detroit area in nineteen days.[55] Three stood trial for his murder, and during opening statements, it was revealed that the mob organization to which the three accused belonged had contributed $11,000 to Mayor Bowles's campaign. It was also alleged that on the night of the recall, one defendant was overheard saying, "If this recall goes through, you know what we will have to do tonight."[56] Despite the prosecutor's best efforts, after thirty-three hours of deliberation, all were acquitted in 1931.

In January 1931, the *Afro-American* reported that black Detroiters were wagering $50,000 daily on numbers gambling and the new mayor's campaign against lotteries appeared to be nonexistent.[57] A black newspaper heaped praise on some of the numbers operators and noted, "Underworld control seems to be lodged in three principal racial groups, Negroes, Jews and Polacks with the Negro syndicates seemingly far outdistancing their rivals in the amount of daily business." The paper also noted that John Roxborough was the "most outstanding of the Negro operators." He was viewed as a "demi-god" among his customers and with his keen business sense he made "an institution founded on and governed on the spirit of fair play—for there is such a thing as fairness, even in numbers he insists."[58] That same year, the Italian mafia got into the numbers businesses in Detroit. Peter Corrado, and others who were accused of being a part of the Italian mafia, opened a numbers operation called the Murphy House. They entered into the racket when "white" business began to greatly increase. Corrado and Roxborough formed a gentlemen's agreement. They agreed not to intrude on each other's business, to pay the same odds, and not to solicit the other's employees: "These Italians were described as honorable and cooperative men who stated they were now legitimate businessmen and were through with violence and killings."[59]

With notoriety came problems for the black numbers operators. They not only had to worry about the police and crooked politicians but were constantly looking over their shoulder for criminals. It was common knowledge that numbers operators made large sums of money. On October 25, 1931, numbers operator Irving Roane was robbed at gunpoint by three white criminals and had his Buick coupe stolen in front of his residence. Before they took his vehicle, they made him drive to his barbershop located at 2441 Hastings Street, in the heart of Black Bottom. Once there, they forced him to open his safe and took two guns and reportedly just $76.[60] It would take two months before the men were arrested, and it was later revealed that the trio of bandits had in fact stolen $632.[61] The armed robbers were connected with six robberies of handbooks and blind pigs. Their modus operandi was to trail the owners of the establishments to their homes, then force them to return to their establishments at gunpoint. From there they would rob the safes and flee with whatever money they could procure.[62] On January 30, 1936, three men tried to rob Everett Watson while he was at his home on Seminole in Detroit. Watson was convalescing at home with an injury when the three armed men confronted him in his living room. What the men did not expect was that Watson's wife, Ida, was in a second-floor bedroom and heard the break-in. Quickly, she ran downstairs to protect her husband with a gun of her own. She fired three shots at the men as they fled.[63]

As Charles Bowles's career as the city's mayor imploded, numbers operators John Roxborough and Thomas Hammonds worked with other prominent black Detroiters to get Roxborough's brother, attorney Charles Roxborough, elected to the Michigan state senate.[64] With their financial backing and support, Charles Roxborough became Michigan's first black state senator from 1932 to 1934. Although a state senator, Charles Roxborough still found time to represent his brother in legal matters in July 1932. Charles was John's attorney of record when John, described as a wealthy clearinghouse operator, was charged in a reckless driving case. He was accused of driving his new luxury sedan in a reckless manner and was fined $40.[65]

While the numbers continued to greatly enrich the numbers operators, they ensured they gave back to the community during the Great Depression. For numbers players and other members of the community, the numbers operators were their saviors.

6
Detroit Numbers to the Rescue!

Eventually, even the worst jobs dried up. You had to live, so you scammed or stole or played the numbers in the policy houses that thrived in Paradise Valley, the black entertainment district that hummed in the middle of Black Bottom.

—Cathy Trost, *Detroit Free Press*, October 25, 1979

Detroit's numbers operators had to deal not only with fighting for control of the numbers racket they created, and corruption in government, but also with the ramifications of the Great Depression. Even before the stock market crashed, however, economic problems were evident in Detroit because of Henry Ford's vehicle model changeover. In 1927, Ford decided to cease making the Model T and began production of the new Model A. As a result, Ford laid off 60,000 employees in Detroit and an additional 40,000 in other parts of the country. Because of Ford's change in production, 45 percent of welfare or relief recipients were former employees of Ford Motor Company.[1]

Even as the Depression overwhelmed the city and the people within it, numbers gambling continued. As banks failed and automotive jobs and other forms of employment declined, numbers gambling gradually increased. At that time, hope was needed, and numbers gambling was a comforting constant for the masses. For a few nickels, the poor, hungry, and downtrodden could wager on the hope that their number would fall and temporarily uplift them from the misery of the Depression. Ulysses Boykin, a former editor for the black newspapers the *Detroit Tribune* and *Michigan Chronicle*, recalled, "One day my mother told my father that she'd had a dream, Ulysses Boykin says. He said, 'Well, Miss Curtis'—that's what he called her—'will you loan me a dime?' That evening he came back and handed her an envelope with 50 new dollar bills inside. She said, 'You know I'm against the numbers because that's gambling but I'm not going to say anything more against it.' And they both went out and bought groceries and stocked up the house."[2]

Jobless and hungry people frequented the numbers houses in a desperate effort to survive.[3] Out-of-work numbers players claimed that playing the numbers was the only way they could make money and not go hungry.[4] One numbers operator alleged that numbers gambling helped keep the welfare rolls down because many people were able to make just enough money on small bets to carry them through the week.[5] John Roxborough and the other black numbers operators encouraged the residents of Black Bottom to play certain numbers. People could play those suggested numbers for a penny and up to twenty-five cents, which meant the hits would not be very large, but the payouts were large enough to buy needed food and fuel. The suggested numbers would often turn out to be the winning numbers. The numbers operators did this because the small hits or winnings allowed players to hit regularly and created goodwill in the community.[6] Numbers operators also assisted the community by creating soup kitchens, distributing baskets of food, and providing fuel to community residents in need.[7] Everett Watson was known to pass out five-dollar bills twice a week to the poor during this time.[8] For others playing the numbers gave them hope when it was in short supply during the Depression. One player stated, "When I goes home and finds no coal and nothing to eat, and the kids bawling it's pretty hard times believe me. But you know if I got as much as a penny or nickel on that old number it gives me a good feeling, cause it might be my lucky day."[9]

Not everyone saw the numbers bankers or operators as positive for the community. After the police raided and arrested two workers at a numbers/policy house owned by black numbers bankers Thomas "Rooster" Hammonds and Irving Roane, they received scathing criticism from a black newspaper. The paper noted that the two arrested workers pled guilty to operating and maintaining a gambling establishment while Hammonds and Roane, who actually owned the business, were not arrested or prosecuted. They further noted, "This is enormous and strikingly sad when we think of the hundreds yet thousands of our Negroes who are living on welfare and saving their pennies and nickels which they sadly need for food and clothing to maintain 'Rooster' Hammond and James Roan [sic] in magnificent luxury and furnish high powered cars to transport them about the city." The paper also hinted that police corruption protected Hammonds and Roane's numbers business. "It is very strange that the police have never raided their magnificent main office maintained at 420 Ferry street east, where they transact their main business with the aid of about twenty-five clerks. This place is situated just next door to Fairview hospital and in a decent neighborhood. A number of leading citizens have come to the office of this paper and a committee has been formed to call on the mayor and council to ascertain just who protects nefarious enterprises and sets such [a] bad example for our young people. This octopus is strangling the Negro."[10]

During the Depression, not only did blacks play the numbers in hopes of "hitting the number" for temporary riches, but whites did as well. Marie Norveth, a wife and mother during the Great Depression, smoked to drive away her hunger; however, this strategy never fully worked because she would run out of cigarettes, causing her to trade what little food she did have for cigarettes. She, like other poor Detroiters, held out hope that one day she would make a big hit playing policy. Her savings and escape plan was playing policy with the Yellow Dog.[11] Playing the numbers not only gave people the chance to win temporary riches but also provided employment to many who could not find it elsewhere.[12] For example, in 1930, Leonard Reid testified during a criminal hearing that he worked as a clearinghouse writer for John Roxborough's numbers bank. He was paid to take people's numbers and received a 25 percent commission for every numbers ticket he sold. Roxborough hired him on January 1, 1930, after he was laid off from the Ford plant in the summer of 1928 and could not find employment elsewhere.[13] Another numbers writer described as being "a clean cut chap" noted, "I never dreamed that I would fall into this racket; but hard times causing me to lose my job, forced me to find something to do to keep the wolf away from the door. This was the only thing I could find. I make a fair living, but I'm telling you, as soon as I can get a legitimate job again I'm going to drop the whole business. There are many others in the same predicament in which I find myself, but what is a fellow to do if he's hungry and has no place to stay I ask you?"[14]

As the unemployment numbers increased and overall conditions deteriorated, about 2,000 unemployed people gathered and demonstrated in front of city hall in October 1930. They demanded that the city give $20 per week to unemployed families plus $5 for each child, as well as a termination on eviction proceedings, and free meals and housing for the homeless.[15] By July 1931, conditions had not improved for the poor and unemployed. The city of Detroit's welfare department was running out of funding, and countless men, women, and children were going hungry.[16] By 1932, blacks were hit the hardest because they were the last hired and the first fired. The practice of firing blacks from jobs and filling them with whites was commonplace. The Detroit Better Business Bureau contacted stores, hotels, and other businesses throughout the city and informed them "that idle white workers should be employed instead of colored workers."[17] The Urban League reported that government programs gave blacks little to no consideration despite the fact that black unemployment was four to six times higher than that of other racial groups. During an informal canvas of black neighborhoods in Detroit, the *Chicago Defender* found that every other black person was out of work. This in turn meant blacks commonly were malnourished, increasingly sick, and had higher death rates, juvenile delinquency rates, and crime rates.[18] One crime that was noted to have increased was petty gambling, which included policy and numbers gambling. Due to segregation and limited housing, blacks had much higher living costs than whites. By March 1932, Detroit's welfare department announced that blacks made up only 8 percent of Detroit's population but accounted for 30 percent of welfare recipients.[19]

While ordinary Detroit citizens were feeling the intense pressure caused by the Depression, larger corporations, municipalities, and banks were collapsing. Banks were victims of their own greed, and a Senate investigation in January 1933 exposed just how much. These men of finance were tax dodgers, manipulators of stocks, and frauds. The investigation brought into question the integrity of Detroit's justice system when it was revealed that more than forty judges had a total of $600,000 in outstanding loans at just one Detroit bank, and the state treasurer had an outstanding loan of $100,000. When these special customers failed to make payments, the banks looked the other way.[20] By February 14, 1933, banks had simply run out of money because their on-hand cash could not support depositors' demands. In response to this problem, Michigan's governor, William Comstock, signed a proclamation declaring a bank holiday. This meant 436 banks and trusts were closed, and more than $1.5 billion in deposits were frozen.[21] The closing of the banks caused Detroit to default on its bonds, and panic spread throughout the city. People with money feared going hungry and bought all available food, which caused prices to skyrocket.[22] The lack of available money caused the city of Detroit to issue scrip in its place. Scrip was accepted as a form of legal tender, and as such, was used to pay city employees. Over a short period of time, approximately $42 million worth of scrip was placed in circulation, which helped the flow of commerce in the city.[23] However, not every business accepted scrip, and those who held it at times found themselves being limited in terms of where they could shop and what they could buy. In response, John Roxborough and other numbers men exchanged scrip for cash. This allowed city employees paid in scrip to shop wherever they wanted.[24]

It was in 1933 that John Roxborough first met a young Detroit boxer named Joe Louis, and because of this meeting, another one of Roxborough's dreams was realized. For years he had "the idea of one day finding a Negro boy with a particular gift—preferably an athletic gift—that would make him outstanding, and of molding this boy into a veritable ambassador of good will from the Negro race to the white race."[25] Roxborough first saw Louis fighting out of the Naval Armory in Detroit. At that time, Louis knew that Roxborough's real estate office was a front and that he was a "big-time numbers man." Louis recalled Roxborough as a true gentleman who had great wealth and style and was impressed with Roxborough's reputation for helping so many people.[26]

Initially, Roxborough provided Joe Louis with boxing equipment, money, and clothes. He managed and guided Louis through his amateur career before he turned professional. Over time, their relationship evolved into that of a father and son. Roxborough invited Louis into his home first for dinners and then later allowed him to move in with him as his "adopted" son.[27] By December 1934, Roxborough was officially Louis's manager. One newspaper proclaimed that the Detroit businessman and philanthropist had been offered $50,000 for Louis but refused because Louis meant more to him and "the glory of the race" than money.[28]

Roxborough ensured Louis received academic tutoring and was educated in the finer points of being a gentleman. He knew that Louis had to live down the negative racial connotations created by former black heavyweight champion Jack Johnson. In 1908 Johnson had won the heavyweight championship and held onto the title until 1915. During his reign as champion, Johnson refused to conform to racial mores of the times. He would frequently gloat over beating white men in the ring, had numerous public affairs with white women, and married two. Johnson at one point owned a cabaret in Chicago where whites and blacks socialized together, and he frequently infuriated local police by driving his fancy automobiles too fast. His behavior so bothered the white public that the Mann Act was deliberately drafted with him in mind. The act made it illegal for individuals to take women across state lines for immoral purposes.[29] It did not take long for Johnson to be charged with violating the Mann Act, and as a result he fled the United States to avoid prosecution.[30] No black person from the time Johnson was champion had been allowed to fight for the heavyweight title. Roxborough was aware of this and knew it would be difficult for Joe Louis even to aspire to fight in a heavyweight championship bout; however, he believed in Louis and thought, "But he is a good boy. He was born that way. If we can only make white people believe it—if we can only make them *want* him to fight for the title—provided, of course, he gets good enough to."[31]

Roxborough advised Louis, "Joe, a colored fighter has to be a gentleman at all times if he ever expects to win respect."[32] He further instructed him that his toughest fight would not be in the boxing ring but in the ring of public opinion. Louis was instructed never to say anything bad about an opponent before or after a fight and never to smile after beating a white opponent. Louis was not allowed to go into a nightclub alone and was told to avoid having his picture taken with white women.[33] If Louis ever forgot this and allowed success to go to his head, Roxborough would no longer manage him. Roxborough further stated, "If you make good and should get to the top, we'll be no party to your letting your race down, for then you'd do your people a lot more harm than your success would be worth."[34] To this Louis promised, "I won't let my people down."[35] Louis would comment in his autobiography that Roxborough talked about "Black Power" before it became popular in later years.[36] After eight wins, former heavyweight champion Jack Johnson approached Roxborough to train Louis after first being critical of him. Johnson told Roxborough he could make a champion out of Louis if the reins were turned over to him. Roxborough told Johnson Louis had a good trainer in Jack Blackburn, and his services were not needed because he wanted to develop Louis into a great, clean-living champion, which he felt was the exact opposite of what Johnson had been.[37] Numerous articles were written about Joe Louis's clean and devoted lifestyle, including one that described the love, respect, and devotion Louis had for his mother and his boxing handlers and ended with a promise that Louis would never do anything to forfeit the faith that the black race had in him.[38] Having an all-black management team who were professional and efficient was a source of pride in the black community.[39] A letter written to the *Pittsburgh Courier* in 1935 summed up this sentiment: "To my mind the finest thing about Joe

Louis is the fact that he has a colored manager, and his whole working staff is made up of colored men . . . the colored man has the same ability as the white man."[40]

Joe Louis received several letters from both black and white fans that reminded him of his responsibility to race relations. For example, in 1935, Governor Frank D. Fitzgerald of Michigan wrote,

> I'm talking to you as a man more than twice your age just to give a little advice to a young fellow who has a real chance to do something for his people. . . . Your race, at times in the past, has been misrepresented by others who thought they had reached the heights. Its people have been denied equal opportunity. Its obstacles and its handicaps have been such that it has been saved only by its own infinite patience and its ability to endure suffering without becoming poisoned by bitterness. The qualities which may soon make you a world champion should call to the attention of people the world over that the good in you can also be found in others of your race, and used for their own welfare, and the welfare of humanity at large. So Joe, you may soon have on your strong hands the job of representative-at-large of your people.[41]

Joe Louis brought a sense of pride and joy to black families throughout the country. It was not uncommon when he fought for entire black neighborhoods to gather around a radio to hear the commentary. These fights made black Americans proud to be alive at a time when to be black was viewed by the masses as anything but cause for celebration. His bouts, like playing the numbers, allowed black Americans to escape the harsh reality of the hard times brought on by the Great Depression.

Although Roxborough tried to ensure Louis's image was one of a clean-cut, wholesome black man, the white press initially was not buying it. At one point, southern papers would not cover stories about or print pictures of black fighters in their papers; however, by 1935, a number of papers in the South carried stories about Louis and even printed his picture in their papers.[42] In 1935 a church pastor in the South wrote a letter to Louis which unwittingly was insulting—or maybe not. The pastor stated, "Some day I feel you will be the champion, and should this come to pass, try always to be the champion of your people, so that when you are no longer the champion, the world will say of you—he was a black man outside, but a white man inside, most of all in his heart."[43] Many articles were written about Louis in his early career, and they ranged from being unflattering to racist in content. *Life* magazine wrote that Joe Louis "rarely smiled, hated workouts and getting up."[44] In the same article, Louis was described as being "a powerfully built Negro, 23 years old, 6ft 1¼ in. tall, 200 lb. in fighting trim. He has the most impassive face. . . . In the ring, Louis is lithe, shuffling and stolid. Outside he is lethargic, uncommunicative, unimaginative."[45]

While Roxborough was having success with Joe Louis, things in Detroit were still hard for many. In 1935, 120,000 blacks made up less than 8 percent of Detroit's total population but were still feeling the stress of the Depression more than most. Black Detroiters accounted for 23 percent of the people receiving welfare from the city, partly because unlike their white counterparts, they were not being rehired once they were laid off.[46] In spite of how bad things were, the numbers game continued to be played by both whites and blacks. In 1936, "99 per cent of all the lottery bets come from the people who can least afford to gamble. By the same token, they are the people who are most tempted to gamble, because their lives are the most drab and the thrill and hope of long-shot gambling is the one release from that drabness available to them. . . . The numbers is a Negro game. To build it into the big money class you have to get the white people to playing it."[47]

In the same year, *Easy Money*, a mainstream magazine whose sole purpose was to publish stories about how easy money was made and lost in an attempt to quench people's fascination with it, featured an in-depth story about the numbers racket. The article emphasized that numbers gambling was "within the reach of everyone from a school boy to a grandmother, a beggar to a millionaire, and they all play it. . . . Play on the policy and the numbers is not confined to any race or class."[48]

7
Numbers Provides the American Dream

Now, you have to think back some. In those days it was hard living if you were black, and it was harder still because the Depression was on. If you were smart enough to have your own numbers operation and you were kind and giving in the black neighborhoods, you got as much respect as a doctor or lawyer. It was a kind of charge to me to know a man like him was interested in me. His brother Charlie was a lawyer and politician and a big wheel in the Urban League and the Young Negro Progressive Association. So Mr. Roxborough was well encased in dignity and legitimacy.

—Joe Louis, *Joe Louis: My Life*

As the Great Depression raged on, numbers operators, unlike the city, showed no sign of being short on money or resources. In fact, they continued to enjoy lavish lifestyles. Everett Watson fared well during and after the Great Depression. In 1930, Watson's official title was president of Watson Realty, and he was known around town for being a big spender and flashy dresser who owned an expensive automobile.[1] The society pages followed him and his wife, Ida, as they traveled on vacation from Detroit to Los Angeles. When not traveling the country, Watson was known to cruise and fish around the Detroit River in his Chris-Craft yacht, which held ten passengers for the parties he threw.[2] By 1933, he was an investor and a board member of the Great Lakes Mutual Insurance Company. Watson cultivated political power in the community by donating money and services for fundraisers and political campaigns. For instance, in February 1935, Watson donated the use of his nightclub to prominent black attorney Harold Bledsoe when he unsuccessfully ran for circuit court judge.[3] By July 1935, the *Detroit Times* named Watson the policy racket czar. The paper said that policy was a game "which annually fleeces small-time gamblers, mostly Negroes, of thousands of dollars." On July 12, 1935, police raided two of Watson's numbers houses. The paper reported that a guard at one of the houses was armed with a gun (he had a permit for it) and had a badge stamped "National Police." Watson drove by one of the locations as it was being raided, but police were unable to catch him; however, four others were arrested. The operation took up eighteen rooms and was located on the second floor of a building that had double doors, barred windows, flashing lights, and an elaborate buzzer system to notify workers of a raid. Inside the operation, the police found four safes, ten telephones, desks, hundreds of chairs, adding machines, typewriters, several bags containing $6,000 in coins, an automatic shotgun, several revolvers, and 150 rounds of ammunition. In one safe, a bank slip showing a deposit for $33,800 was found. Information indicating other locations and the names of hundreds of numbers runners were discovered. Thousands of slips of paper showing the average runner took in about $100 a day while only paying out $10 a day were also found. The payoff number "743" was displayed on the office walls and on desks where the bookkeepers and other operators worked.[4]

Numbers was such a lucrative business that along with wealth came political influence. The major black numbers organizations from all over the country realized this and formed the National Brotherhood of Policy Kings in 1933 to pool power and offer protection to all members. John Roxborough was a prominent member, as were several other Detroit bankers. The organization met annually in Cleveland and in Hot Springs, Arkansas, to discuss various issues.[5] At one such meeting in 1936, members gathered to discuss what consequences a United States court ruling would have on their operations. A Detroit policy king, described as being powerful because of his connections, presided over the meeting.[6] At this time, it was estimated that numbers games in the United States generated $1 billion per year.[7] Meetings such as this helped ensure numbers gambling continued as a lucrative business and enabled the election of corrupt politicians who allowed numbers gambling to flourish. Wayne County Prosecutor Duncan McCrea was one corrupt politician who did just that.

In 1935 McCrea demanded Everett Watson and other numbers operators pay him protection money to operate. McCrea was elected Wayne County's prosecutor in 1934. He was born in Roscommon, Michigan, and for a while worked as a lumberjack and a railroad brakeman before settling into a clerical job in Detroit. At night, he worked on his law degree at the

Detroit College of Law and by 1924 became an assistant prosecutor in Wayne County's Prosecutor's Office, where he gained a reputation for prosecuting gangsters.[8] Later, he was known for being involved in violent altercations and gained the nickname "Wayne County's Fighting Prosecutor."[9] While campaigning for office in 1935, McCrea, along with approximately seventy Detroit police officers, became members of the Black Legion, an outgrowth of the Ku Klux Klan organized in 1925.[10] According to its founder, the Black Legion was based on the "principles of the Old South," including the need to "maintain southern chivalry and the ideals of the south before the Civil War."[11] The Black Legion was notoriously ruthless and prejudiced against blacks, Jews, and Roman Catholics. In 1936, when McCrea's membership as a Black Legion member was exposed, he claimed that he unwittingly completed the application for membership.[12]

When McCrea demanded graft payments, a number of black numbers operators met at Everett Watson's Waiters and Bellman's Club to discuss the prosecutor's demands and how to best handle a group of Italians who were attempting to muscle into the numbers racket.[13] At this meeting, Watson was chosen by the other numbers operators, which included John Roxborough, Thomas Hammonds, Irving Roane, Charles Mosley, and Walter Norwood, to meet with the chief investigator for Wayne County, Harry Colburn, and Wayne County Prosecutor McCrea.[14] It was agreed that monthly payments of $1,500 would be made to the prosecutor's office to ensure the numbers organizations were protected and operated without prosecutorial interference.[15] Watson served as the graft collector on behalf of Detroit numbers operators for Wayne County Prosecutor Duncan McCrea from April 1935 to August 1939.[16]

In addition to being the payoff representative to the prosecutor's office, Watson was busy establishing the Everett I. Watson Real Estate Company in 1935. The company provided real estate brokers and investment mortgages to the community and bought, sold, rented, managed, built, and remodeled various properties. His agency sold individual, residential, business, vehicle, and property insurance as well. In February 1937, he leased an office in a former bank located at 1727 St. Antoine in Black Bottom. Here he announced the opening of the Everett I. Watson Investment Loan Company. The company provided cash loans ranging from $50 to $300 to people who otherwise would have had trouble securing financing.[17] The location, 1727 St. Antoine, would hold several other businesses over the years as well.

It was the headquarters of both Watson's and Roxborough's numbers operations, was the official office for Roxborough's Joe Louis interests, and housed the *Michigan Chronicle*, lawyers, accountants, and several other legitimate businesses.

Two years later, the Watson enterprises went from having one full-time employee to nine part-time employees. He was credited with saving several properties owned by blacks in Black Bottom from foreclosure when they were unable to secure loans elsewhere. Within one year, Watson had provided over $100,000 in loans.[18] In December 1937, Watson and two other men, Reuben Ray and Grady Jackson, formed the Paradise Valley Distributing Company. The beer distributing company was meant to be a sound business investment and provided employment opportunities for blacks.[19] Watson also supported community ventures by buying ads in cultural programs for the arts in Detroit's black community. One such production he supported was the Detroit Negro Opera and its presentation of *Aida* at the Detroit Institute of Arts in May 1938. Finally, by 1938, Watson was managing heavyweight boxer Roscoe Toles. Sunnie Wilson, the former owner of the Mark Twain Hotel and Forest Club, located in Paradise Valley and at one time the largest black-owned club in America, knew Watson and described him as "a soft-spoken, respectful man."[20]

John Roxborough's wealth was evident in divorce proceedings filed by him against his first wife, Dora, in 1934. According to the 1934 divorce complaint, the Roxboroughs lived luxuriously. Dora Roxborough had diamonds worth $10,000, a $4,200 grand piano, a Packard automobile, and monthly phone bills of $100 and required $1,000 per month for household and living expenses. John Roxborough owned a 12-cylinder Lincoln automobile, wore socks that cost $7.50 per pair, owned 250 neckties, which cost $1,625, and strove to maintain the "finest home of any colored man in Detroit."[21] Court testimony also revealed that John purchased Dora a home in Pennsylvania, furniture valued at $15,000, and numerous expensive articles of clothing. Dora contended her husband had bought her $10 stockings and numerous dresses and gowns ranging from $100 to $200 apiece for her to be the best-dressed woman in Detroit. These extravagant purchases were all made from July 1926 to October 1931.[22] Court documents revealed Roxborough sought a divorce on the grounds of extreme cruelty and an injunction to keep Dora away from him at home and at his business and from inflicting harm on him. Roxborough alleged that Dora at one time shot a gun at him, was addicted to gambling, spent too much money, and generally caused him shame. Dora alleged that she armed herself after he physically beat her and further contended that Roxborough failed to support her and was cavorting with other women.[23] During the divorce, Roxborough was accused of hiding his finances and was charged with contempt of court for failure to pay alimony to his wife.[24] He eventually settled and paid his ex-wife $30,000.[25]

In March 1935 John Roxborough was one of 50,000 people who attended the richest race in automobile racing history in Los Angeles. Many who attended were considered celebrities, and Roxborough wagered and won $20,000.[26] At this time, Roxborough owned four numbers and policy houses: the Big Four, D&M, Royal Blue, and Last Train.[27] It appeared everything he touched turned to gold, including an amateur baseball team he sponsored. The Big Four, named after his numbers operation, eventually won a championship.[28] He was described as one of Detroit's best-loved citizens and as possessing keen business acumen. He was so popular that when he was in his office, located in Paradise Valley on St. Antoine, it was not uncommon for people to seek him out and ask for assistance. He helped high school and college students, as well as athletes like Eddie Tolan, Eugene Beatty, Holman Williams, Clinton Bridges, and Willis Ward.[29]

Roxborough remarried in November 1936, and by December it was reported, "Mrs. John Roxborough will be the Queen of Detroit Society. King Roxy, one swell guy, will build a magnificent palace for his queen. An invite to an affair of Roxy's is like a ticket to the Blue Book."[30] A few years later, Roxborough hosted a lavish party at this magnificent palace. The beauty of his home was said to strike awe in the guests. His home was equipped with a crystal bar, elaborate lighting, and a recreation room, which contained a large jitter box and dance hall. The home also had spiral staircases, natural fireplaces, parquetted flooring, Venetian metal blinds, and leather furnishings.[31]

A year later, Roxborough was still riding high when Joe Louis beat James Braddock on June 22, 1937, to become boxing's world heavyweight champion. After he won, Louis's media coverage improved greatly. *Life* magazine carried an article about Joe Louis winning ribbons in America's first all-black horse show, which occurred outside of Detroit. In this article, Louis was no longer seen as lazy and lethargic. According to the article, Louis was a hero to his whole race and was far removed "from elderly religious Negroes who sing spirituals and the reefer-smoking jitter bugs." It was noted he was part of a better class of blacks who played golf instead of craps and gutter ball. Joe Louis was officially "well-behaved."[32]

John Roxborough had successfully crafted Joe Louis's image by alleviating white fears, which broke the color line. Louis's management team, which included Roxborough, was deemed his "Brain Trust" because they were astute men whose created image of Louis became a representation of racial progress.[33] Roxborough's "piloting" of Joe Louis to the heavyweight championship was a source of pride for blacks as well. One newspaper writer noted that what Roxborough had done to make Louis a champion, not to mention earning nearly $1 million in three years, was an unusual American phenomenon. The writer encouraged black Americans to take note and be proud that black men who were forced to abide by the rules of prejudice were able to accomplish a great feat in spite of them. The writer implored Joe Louis and his management team to "hold on to the money, and make it serve not only their personal ends, but the race at large, if in no other way than by keeping it in their possession, which adds prestige to the whole group."[34]

Roxborough continued to look out for the community in several ways in 1938. He was known for always extending loans to those in need and helping young people. He employed many young college graduates in the fields of accounting and business who would not have normally found work in their field.[35] Roxborough also used his wealth in 1938 to support science. He entered into an agreement with a black inventor, Joseph Blair, to provide funds that would aid in the development, patenting, and promoting of numerous inventions, including a non-slip fan propeller and designs for submarines, telescopic lenses, and a dishwasher. Later, Blair would sue Roxborough, claiming he wrongfully took advantage of him through their contract. Blair claimed the agreement he had with Roxborough "was one-sided, unfair, inequitable, oppressive, lacking in mutuality, and inadequate."[36]

In 1938 when Detroit was cited as having living costs higher than any other city at $1,486.50 annually, Roxborough's home was robbed of $3,000 in jewelry by his chauffeur.[37] For more than what one person earned in a year Roxborough owned in two rings and a diamond-studded watch.[38] If this excess in wealth and capitalist consumption represented making it in America, Detroit's numbers kings had truly arrived. However, their success did not come without a cost.

8
You Have to Pay to Play

With champagne flowing like water, Everett Watson and "Rooster" Hammonds two Detroiters named by police in connection with the policy racket in Detroit entertained Mayor Reading and his son, Richard, of that city and some twenty other persons at Small's Paradise the night of the Louis-Schmeling fight last June 22, Mayor Reading and his party, which was composed of one other person in addition to his son, entered the cabaret immediately after the fight and left for his suite of rooms in the Waldorf-Astoria about 4 a.m. the next morning.

—New York Amsterdam News, September 17, 1938

It may have seemed as if the numbers operators were living a rich and carefree life, but that was hardly the case. In order to operate in the city, they had to pay massive amounts of bribe money to politicians and the police. Their bribes primarily went to the mayor of Detroit, Richard Reading.

Detroit politician Richard Reading Sr. was called "Little Dick" because he stood just 5'3" tall. He was considered a self-made man who rose quickly as a political force in Detroit in the 1930s. Born and educated in Detroit, one of eight children, he did not come from a wealthy family. Reading started his career as an apprentice printer for the *Detroit News* before managing several different departments with the *Detroit Times*. From the newspaper business, Reading began purchasing properties in the city and selling them before obtaining a job as a city assessor. From this position, he was promoted to city controller, and then decided to throw his hat into politics and was elected Detroit's city clerk.[1] By 1937, Reading, a Republican, decided to run for mayor of Detroit. He had big plans that included not only running the fourth largest city in America but also profiting from his position of power. In June 1937, he attended a Board of Commerce pleasure cruise with several police officials and the chairman of the Water Board, William Skrzycki. Reading and Skrzycki had been political associates and friends for more than twenty years. As the cruise ship passed by Marquette Prison, the friends began to discuss Reading's run for mayor. During the conversation, Reading asked Skrzycki if he knew about the graft that was being paid to Detroit Police Department's Fourth Precinct. Skrzycki, like others, had heard rumors that the Fourth Precinct was receiving $5,000 per month in bribe money to allow gambling to operate without police interference. Reading estimated that other parts of the city, specifically the central district, which included downtown Detroit, Black Bottom, and Paradise Valley, would pay three times as much for police protection.[2]

"Little Dick" was known as a likable "showman" who was impulsive, hated advice, and rarely took it from anyone.[3] With big plans, Reading was easily elected after running a contentious campaign in the fall of 1937. Reading boasted he had been "backed by some of the finest men in Detroit; the men who made Detroit."[4] Blacks overwhelmingly supported Reading's election; he was no stranger to the men and women of Black Bottom and Paradise Valley. While city clerk, Reading read the oath of office to Roy Lightfoot, the owner of the B and C Club, when he was elected mayor of Paradise Valley in 1936. The *Michigan Chronicle* for eight weeks had urged readers to vote for the mayor of Detroit's black business district, Paradise Valley. Although the title had no power, it was a source of pride for black Detroiters who listened to Lightfoot take the oath of office over radio station WJR.[5] The Paradise Valley mayor's job was to be a ceremonial leader of the community. Several numbers men, including Walter Norwood and Everett Watson, supported Reading. Watson donated $3,000 to Reading's campaign fund.[6] Norwood's donation of $500 resulted in him being told, "Thanks, I'll take care of you boys."[7] Later, Norwood was given a special phone number to city hall and was instructed to call it if he had any trouble as it pertained to the operation of his numbers organization.[8]

Shortly after being sworn in as Detroit's mayor, Reading demanded a new limousine that cost taxpayers $6,000. When a delegate from the Common Council tried to persuade him to use the funds for much-needed police vehicles instead, Reading angrily refused, stating, "Gentlemen, I intend to take this mayoring seriously and I need that car." Reading hired his son, Richard Reading Jr., as his personal secretary at taxpayer expense. Reading insisted that handsome, tall, well-built policemen be assigned as his bodyguards, which would allow him to make grand entrances at all functions.[9] One such event occurred in July 1938, following Joe Louis's fight with Max Schmeling. A wine party was given at Small's Paradise by numbers operators/bankers Everett Watson and Thomas "Rooster" Hammonds. In attendance were various numbers operators, celebrities, and politicians, including Mayor Richard Reading.[10]

After being elected mayor of the city of Detroit, Richard Reading was approached by former campaign worker Ulysses Boykin. Boykin was also a columnist for the *Detroit Tribune*, which was owned and managed by Charles Mosley, the owner of the Michigan Policy Wheel, a numbers house.[11] Twenty-three-year-old Boykin was referred to as the "black mayor" by a number of black Detroiters because he had helped Reading get elected. Because of this relationship, Boykin was able to approach Mayor Reading with a proposition on behalf of the black numbers operators. Boykin had been contacted by Everett Watson, who asked for help in securing protection through the mayor's office and fixing payouts to 500 to 1.[12] The request to lower the payouts was in response to the actions of white numbers operator Louis Weisberg, who had increased his payouts to 600 to 1. His payouts were more lucrative to numbers players and lured them away from other numbers organizations. This spelled doom for several black numbers organizations if the mayor did not intervene.[13] As a result, all numbers operators were forced by the police department to keep or limit payouts to 500 to 1. If an establishment refused, they were raided numerous times until they complied.[14]

In addition, Everett Watson wanted a centralized racket squad formed and more black police officers hired and promoted. He felt that a special racket squad would "help the numbers operators by keeping them in mind."[15] Boykin took the requests to Reading and advised him that many black Detroiters depended on numbers for a living. Reading responded that "the colored people had conducted themselves like gentlemen, and that the policy and mutuels were their games." Reading further stated he "hoped something could be done to prevent them from going out of business."[16] Three weeks after Watson's request, Reading formed the centralized racket squad. In return, Watson and the other numbers operators began to make graft payments to Reading.[17] In order to prove that they were protected by the mayor, numbers pick-up men carried a metal tag with a cloverleaf engraved on it. If they happened to be stopped or arrested by police, they simply flashed the tag.[18] Boykin delivered payments to Reading from number operators Everett Watson, John Roxborough, Thomas Hammonds, Irving Roane, and Walter Norwood from September to December 1938.

In December, Reading became dissatisfied with Boykin and how the payments were made. A change was ordered, and Everett Watson began making the $4,000 monthly payment to Detroit Police Inspector Raymond Boettcher. This payment was then divided among a few people. Boettcher delivered $2,000 to Mayor Reading at the Book-Cadillac Hotel. Handbook operator and racing news service manager Elmer "Buff" Ryan, who controlled the wire service which provided winning horse information, received $1,000. Police Superintendent Fred Frahm received $800, and Boettcher kept the remaining $200 for himself. Police Superintendent Frahm was described by the newspapers as being handsome, intelligent, friendly, and popular. He had a national reputation based on his work as a detective and was known as the nemesis of criminals. Prior to being appointed to superintendent, Frahm had at one point overseen virtually every division of Detroit's Police Department. From December 1938 to August 1939, Mayor Reading was paid $18,000, Ryan $9,000, Frahm $7,200, and Boettcher $1,800.[19]

John Roxborough and Everett Watson visited Mayor Reading on numerous occasions to ask for favors. One time, Roxborough and Watson advised the mayor that mobsters from Cleveland were attempting to "muscle in on the numbers and policy games in Detroit." Reading promised the men the situation would be addressed. On another occasion, Reading was told that police lieutenant Frank Dombecky was a "good friend of Negroes." After being advised of this, Dombecky was promoted and put in charge of a police station on the city's west side that had a large black population. Watson and Roxborough also used their political influence with the mayor to get two black officers promoted to the rank of detective, and on one visit to the mayor, they brought Joe Louis. On this visit, the emissaries successfully had Louis's former bodyguard promoted to detective sergeant.[20]

By the fall of 1938, the numbers game was openly played throughout the city because many played the numbers, including law enforcement personnel. It was an open secret that numbers writers took bets from everyday workers as well as high-ranking officials at the Wayne County building and law enforcement looked the other way. Overall, the numbers game was a gigantic business that employed hundreds of people, including high school and college students. They could be found working all over the city in offices in the swankiest hotels and clubs, in factories, stores, barbershops, poolrooms, and restaurants, as well as in private homes.[21]

In September 1938, State Senator Charles C. Diggs Sr. of Detroit reported to the *Detroit Free Press* the findings of a study he conducted in Detroit's black neighborhoods. According to his report, blacks made up one-third of tuberculosis cases in Detroit, infant and maternity death rates were higher among blacks than whites, housing rent for blacks in black districts was much higher than in white districts because of the limited housing available, and housing, safety, and health laws were not enforced. Finally, Diggs reported that numbers gambling plagued black neighborhoods and went untouched due to lack of police enforcement.[22] In his report, Diggs also complained that numbers gambling was largely responsible for the crime and poverty in his district. His report was not well received by some black Detroiters. The report, submitted just prior to Diggs's election, brought down an avalanche of disgruntled protests from numbers players, and an effort was launched to defeat him.[23]

In response to Diggs's allegations, the Detroit Police Department declared war on policy/numbers playing and conducted a series of raids on those establishments. More than 200 police officers raided eleven numbers houses, including Roxborough's Big Four House, Watson's Yellow Dog, and George Cordell's Murphy House. Cordell, a white numbers operator and Purple Gang member, was a former bootlegger and rum runner who expanded his underground businesses to numbers gambling. In 1933, when the Detroit Police Department was crusading against hoodlums, he was sought and named as a public enemy. As a result of these raids, eighty-one men and five women were arrested, and roughly $2,200 was seized. When police were questioned about why so little money was found, they attributed it to conducting the raids too early in the day.[24] Black numbers organizations believed that the police activity was specifically orchestrated to turn control of the numbers racket over to white mobsters.[25] The police activity once again revealed that people from all walks of life played the numbers. Numbers writers were observed taking numbers from people in the Wayne County building, at police headquarters, from a local high school, and from a number of wealthy homeowners.[26] During a raid on the Murphy House, important documents were found including a fair trade agreement that showed the numbers organizations were in collusion with each other. The document was titled, "Detroit Policy Racket's 'Fair Trade Code,'" which went into effect on August 27, 1938.[27] The first part of the document outlined the "rules of organization," which established the standard rate and basis for all numbers organizations. The three rules of organization included payoffs of 500 to 1, paying 25 percent, and paying pick-up men 10 percent. All Detroit numbers organizations agreed:

1. Not to proposition any other companies, writers, station or pick-up men.
2. If any of the pick-up men or station men want a change from one company to another, such a change cannot be made until former company is consulted.
3. If a writer, pick-up man, station man or other employee is discharged for dishonesty, such a person or persons are to be placed upon a permanent blacklist and not to be accepted by any other company.
4. If for a personal reason or misunderstanding an employee wishes to make a change, former employer and prospective employer shall get together and affect an adjustment of the difficulty.
5. No station rents or fees are to be paid (this matter left open to discussion).
6. No short slips to be paid in part or otherwise.
7. Deadline for acceptance of business to be established the same for all companies, ten minutes before the off-time of the first and third races.
8. Each company to see that the agents and pick-up men do not give writers in stations more than twenty-five percent (25%) for the business.[28]

The agreement was compiled to ensure that all numbers organizations operated under the same conditions and no one had an unfair advantage. The larger numbers organizations were concerned that smaller "fly-by-night" organizations were ruining the numbers racket's reputation by not paying winners. The larger organizations hoped the agreement would drive out unscrupulous organizations and ensure their survival. The numbers operators agreed to lower the payoffs to 500 to 1 to cover the substantial graft payments that were being made to the prosecutor's office and police officials.[29] In addition, some numbers organizations were losing writers to other organizations that were paying commissions of 32 percent versus the standard 25 percent. When the agreement was made to pay all writers 25 percent, the writers who had to reduce their commission staged a strike. These writers eventually went back to work when they learned their commission would be 25 percent or nothing.[30]

Another agreement was later found and showed that both black and white numbers organizations were a part of the pact. The black numbers organizations included the Big Four Company, owned by John Roxborough, the Yellow Dog Company, owned by Everett Watson, the Michigan Company, owned by Charles Mosley, and the Daily News Company, which was owned by Brumal Penick. The white numbers organizations included the Murphy Company, owned by Joe Massie, Pete Corrado, and George Cordell; the Western Union Company, owned by Peter Kosiba; the Mexico Villa Company, owned by Louis Weisberg; and the Great Lakes Company, managed by William McBride.

As part of the war on numbers gambling, Detroit Police Commissioner Heinrich Pickert warned Detroit's good citizens to avoid playing the numbers.[31] He advised that by playing the numbers, decent citizens unwittingly contributed to crime, juvenile delinquency, rackets, gang feuds, and bloodshed. To illustrate this point, Pickert released the criminal records of the Murphy Company numbers operators Massie, Corrado, and Cordell, which showed the men had previously been arrested for armed robbery, carrying concealed weapons, rum running, bribery, and multiple murder charges.[32] These numbers operators' characters were very different from those of Roxborough and Watson, who were viewed as community businessmen and lacked violent and extensive criminal records. The so-called war on numbers gambling did have a short-term effect on numbers operations. The police raids caused the Great Lakes Mutuels Company to cease operations temporarily. When the police raided the numbers headquarters on September 20, 1938, they confiscated 300,000 betting slips, which represented bets placed over a two-day period. The Great Lakes Mutuels Company also posted a notice informing pick-up men that due to police enforcement, they were closing.[33]

During this raid, led by Lieutenant John McCarthy, twenty-two people were arrested. Of those arrested were manager William McBride and bookkeeper Janet MacDonald. Although numerous arrests were made during these raids, no one was convicted. The raids in August and September 1938 were shams and served two purposes: they made the public believe there was in fact a war on gambling, and they forced an increase in protection rates that gambling operators paid police and other officials.[34] The graft payments

Figure 7. Great Lakes Mutuels sign confiscated during raid on Great Lakes Mutuels Company on September 20, 1938. Pictured to the right is Lieutenant John McCarthy of the racket squad. Reproduced by permission from the *Detroit Free Press.*

increased fourfold, from $150 to $600 per month.[35] In addition to the monthly payoffs, numbers operators like Everett Watson found themselves contributing to the reelection of Mayor Reading. Watson donated $1,000 to Reading's campaign in June 1939. The money was used to supplement the operation of Reading's campaign headquarters. During this same campaign, Watson, Roxborough, and Norwood together donated an additional $3,600 to Reading's campaign.[36] A month later, in July 1939, Roxborough was acknowledged for all his good work in a black newspaper:

> John Roxborough is one of the most unselfish men I have ever known. No one knows how many people he has helped. No one will probably ever know how many Negro businesses he has saved from sinking. He has been good literally to everybody. Innumerable boys and girls struggling to make their way through school have been given financial assistance by him. He has given money to the Detroit Urban

League to establish a scholarship fund for deserving boys and girls. He makes a gift of five hundred dollars annually to the Detroit Community Chest for human welfare. He gives liberally to the YMCA and YWCA, the NAACP and many churches and schools. I have no means to estimate the exact amount he gives away, but I am in a position to know that it runs into sizeable figures. . . . He has never been known to forget a friend. He is never too busy to turn aside and recognize, with an enthusiastic and hearty handclasp, the most insignificant former acquaintance. He has gone out of his way to help set up his own employees in business when he saw some who were ambitious and promising and even when they have become competitors instead of trying to crush them he has shown them how it was possible to get further ahead through cooperation.[37]

Nothing lasts forever; some Detroit numbers operators were forced to deal with the illegal aspects of their financial empires.

9
Hell Hath No Fury like a Woman Scorned

Dear Sirs:

On this night, a girl has ended her life because of the mental cruelty caused by racketeer William McBride, ex–Great Lakes Numbers House operator. McBride is the go-between man for Lieut. John McCarthy. He arranges the fix between our dutiful Lieut. and the Racketeers.

—Janet MacDonald, August 1939

As Reading was preparing for reelection, little did he know thirty-six-year-old Janet MacDonald would play a major role in his future and impact several Detroit numbers operators. An English woman born and educated in Belfast, Ireland, MacDonald had recently become a U.S. citizen and lived alone in a rooming house on Detroit's east side, while her eleven-year old daughter, Pearl, lived with her sister, Sophia. MacDonald was an idealist, an avid reader who loved poetry. A bit of a romantic, she was unlucky in love. Just three years previously, she had been granted an uncontested divorce from her first husband because he was cruel, had cheated on her with other women, and had failed to take care of her and their daughter before finally deserting them. While working as a cashier at an eastside Detroit market in 1937, MacDonald met William McBride, manager of the Great Lakes Mutuels Company. Shortly after meeting him, McBride secured her a job there, and the two became romantically involved. McBride was born in Corktown, located on Detroit's southwest side, and previously made his living as a bootlegger before being hired to manage the Great Lakes Mutuels Company. Divorced, McBride at thirty-seven had a ten-year-old son. He was described as an "average sort of fellow." At five feet nine inches, 170 pounds, with brown hair and blue-gray eyes, there was nothing about him that really stood out. He was a former bootlegger, current numbers operator, and all-time gambler. He tried to paint the picture of success by the way he dressed, with the fancy coupe he drove, and by being a big tipper. Those who were truly successful made fun of him by calling him "Flashy" and "The Looking Glass Boxer" because of the way he pranced in front of mirrors whenever he wore a new tie. McBride was arrested nine times for various crimes, including possession of gambling equipment, and was known as the man who could get a Detroit police officer promoted to a sergeant for $300. McBride had a close relationship with Richard Reading Jr., who was not only the son of the mayor but also served as his father's secretary.[1]

In July 1939, McBride ended his on-again, off-again romantic relationship with MacDonald. McBride urged her for her own good to find some nice fellow.[2] McBride, in breaking up with MacDonald, had called her a "rat," accusing her of informing on another woman involved in a fraud scheme. In response to the ugly breakup, MacDonald became distraught and dramatically vowed McBride would have another woman over her dead body. Early in the day on August 5, 1939, MacDonald picked Pearl up from her sister's house to go on a picnic and horseback riding on Belle Isle. During the outing, MacDonald was irritable. She found fault with little Pearl and with the horses. By the time she and Pearl returned to her room, MacDonald's mood had improved. That night, MacDonald called McBride, saying she had to see him. At midnight, they met at Woodward Avenue and West Grand Boulevard in the city. MacDonald and McBride talked about their breakup. She wanted him to take her to get something to eat, but he refused.[3] Instead, McBride left MacDonald and met another woman at a cheap hotel in downtown Detroit for a tryst. Upon his refusal, MacDonald retrieved Pearl. MacDonald, distraught and distracted, with Pearl dressed in a pink taffeta dress, drove around that clear, warm night until Pearl fell asleep. With Pearl seated next to her in her automobile, she decided to take their lives. Janet parked her idling automobile in a rented garage, located in Detroit's North End, and ran a hose from the exhaust through the car's window. Carbon monoxide, the silent killer, did its job.[4]

Janet's and Pearl's bodies were discovered the next evening. Shortly before they were found, McBride was playing golf with Detroit Police Lieutenant John "Mac" McCarthy. Found near MacDonald's body were several letters and photographs. The letters were addressed to various officials, including Police Commissioner Heinrich Pickert, the newspaper editors of Detroit's largest papers, Michigan's governor, and the head of the FBI for

Detroit. In the letters, MacDonald accused several police officials of being guilty of taking bribes from McBride and other numbers organizations.[5] In the letter written to the FBI, she said there was a great deal of vice in the city of Detroit that included corruption within the Detroit Police Department. MacDonald recounted how McBride paid monthly bribes to a number of sergeants and to Lieutenant John McCarthy; in return, his numbers operation ran free of police interference. If a numbers operation was to be raided by police, it was alleged that McCarthy would tip off the organization, allowing evidence to be removed ahead of time.[6] In this same letter to the FBI, MacDonald said that McBride had failed to pay taxes for years, had a record for smuggling illegal liquor from Canada to Detroit during Prohibition, and possibly had a warrant out for his arrest.[7]

News of MacDonald's suicide hit the Detroit newspapers on Monday, August 7, and what was reported scared William McBride and Detroit's numbers bankers. The numbers bankers announced that their places would close for at least two days because they were under scrutiny. Players were notified that numbers writers would not be taking wagers and if any did, to be aware of the irresponsible organization that did.[8]

Upon reading the papers and seeing MacDonald's picture, McBride became physically ill. He jumped in his car and drove around waiting for the beer gardens to open. His plan was to drink away his nerves. He went to a lot of beer gardens, and then drank even more, before having a cab take him to the Michigan border near Toledo. While trying to hitchhike back to Detroit, he was arrested and eventually taken to the Monroe County Sheriff's Department, where he was questioned by a chief assistant prosecutor, two homicide detectives, and two federal agents for six hours. McBride alternated between drinking a massive amount of ice water and holding his head and pacing while answering questions in the hot room. His answers to questions about MacDonald's accusations were at times evasive and at other times contradictory. He denied being involved in any kinds of payoffs and at times rambled. At one point he said, "I haven't got nothing and I never gave a policeman as much as a cigar, never." When pressed about MacDonald's letters he responded, "I saw them in the papers but I didn't read all of them. They are lies." In an effort to get McBride to confess, the police told him to look at a picture of MacDonald and Pearl. The officer wanted McBride to look at what he had done to them. McBride pushed the picture away: "I won't look at them no more. I can't."[9]

Figure 8. Janet MacDonald with her daughter, Pearl, in 1937 at St. Joseph, Michigan. Reproduced by permission from the *Detroit Free Press*.

The deaths of Janet MacDonald and her daughter sparked outrage in the city. Her letters illuminated the need to investigate not just numbers gambling organizations but the police department as well. The *Detroit Free Press* reported that a previous attempt to investigate the connection between police officials and gambling had been made in 1936 when anthropologist

Gustav Carlson, from the University of Michigan, wrote his dissertation on it. Carlson stated that numbers operators told him they could not successfully run their business without protection from the police department. When faced with this allegation, Police Commissioner Heinrich Pickert said, "Carlson's charges that gambling rackets are operating under police protection is downright silly."[10] This time, however, Janet MacDonald's pleas for an investigation did not fall on deaf ears. Initially, Mayor Richard Reading indicated the police department would conduct a full investigation. When the higher-ups in the police department were questioned about what steps they would take, their responses were evasive. Within one day of MacDonald's allegations against Lieutenant John McCarthy, he was cleared of all wrongdoing by the department. Later, McBride met with McCarthy and in a face-to-face meeting denied knowing him. McBride maintained

Figure 9. William McBride, Lieutenant John McCarthy, and Assistant Prosecutor William Dowling at meeting where McBride denies knowing McCarthy on August 7, 1939, and is questioned concerning the deaths of Janet and Pearl MacDonald. Reproduced by permission from the *Detroit Free Press*.

his affair with MacDonald was of minor importance to him. He further contended that MacDonald's allegations were untrue and swore he was only a small-time racket guy who managed the Great Lakes Policy House for a mere $48 per week.[11]

The police department's official findings were that Janet MacDonald had fabricated the story about McBride because he had ended their relationship and lied about McCarthy because she had a grudge against him for arresting her previously. MacDonald was characterized as "very vindictive."[12] The investigating officer concluded, "There was not a semblance of truth in anything she wrote."[13] He also summed up MacDonald's claims as "just the outburst of an emotionally unbalanced woman."[14] Shortly thereafter, Wayne County Prosecutor Duncan McCrea called off any investigation being conducted by his office due to lack of manpower.[15] On August 19, 1939, Pickert professed, "There is not a more honest policeman in Detroit than Lieut. McCarthy, and it is unfortunate he has suffered because of this fellow McBride, a tin horn gambler and alley rat."[16] Superintendent Fred Frahm concluded McCarthy was "a fine officer with a fine record."[17]

In reality, McCarthy's employment record was anything but stellar. He joined the police department in 1923 and a year later resigned under charges. He was then rehired the next year. He was eventually promoted to the position of lieutenant in June 1938, and then in September 1938 he was made the head of the newly formed racket squad. The *Detroit News* reported that McCarthy had been handpicked and promoted by Mayor Reading on the advice of the mayor's son. The racket squad's focus was on eradicating vice in the entire city, and it operated independently of any direct supervision by reporting to top-ranking officials. McCarthy was placed in this unique position although he lacked an exceptional work record. He had three demerits for being absent from duty, sleeping on the job, and spending several hours in a hotel with a woman of "questionable character."[18] It was later established that McCarthy and the five police officers assigned to him all took graft payments from twelve numbers houses.[19]

These findings did not sit well with some citizens as Detroit's daily newspapers carried numerous stories about what was perceived as a whitewash of the graft allegations by the mayor, the police department, and the county prosecutor. A pastor of a downtown Presbyterian Church devoted a sermon to the evils of gambling and police graft and demanded a probe be conducted.[20] In response to the outrage, the Detroit Common Council passed a resolution calling for an independent grand jury to investigate. Altogether, four petitions were presented to the Circuit Court demanding a grand jury investigate MacDonald's allegations. As a result, the Wayne County Circuit Court appointed Judge Homer Ferguson to conduct a one-man grand jury into the allegations.[21] This caused the major numbers organizations, the Big Four, the Murphy Company, the Yellow Dog, the Manhattan, and the Daily News, to close for two weeks.[22]

On August 19, 1939, in a show of force and in an effort to show they were not soft on gambling, the Detroit Police Department, under the watchful eye of Detroit Police Commissioner Heinrich Pickert, and led by Lieutenant John McCarthy, raided ten gambling establishments and arrested 147 people. Numbers organizations then declared a thirty-day holiday as a result of this activity.[23] One source estimated that, as a result of the closing of the

Figure 10. Judge Homer Ferguson (*right*) was chosen to convene a one-man grand jury of the Detroit Police Department and gambling activities. He selected Chester O'Hara (*left*) as special prosecutor on August 25, 1939. Photo courtesy of *Detroit News*.

numbers organizations, more than 20,000 people were unemployed.[24] Many were eligible for unemployment benefits because their numbers organizations paid state unemployment taxes for them.[25] In addition, some numbers organizations also ensured their employees were eligible for Social Security benefits by taking the appropriate deductions from their paychecks.[26] At this time, Everett Watson owned four numbers houses, which brought in approximately $4,900 daily.[27] John Roxborough's Big Four numbers organization generated $800,000 annually.[28]

These events did not impact Roxborough's managing of Joe Louis. Louis's managers, including alleged Chicago numbers king Julian Black, issued the *Official Souvenir Scrap Book* about Joe Louis at this time. It cost thirty-five cents and was filled with pictures, sayings, and information about Joe Louis. For example, one page told the reader "Things You Ought to Know about Joe Louis," including the fact he had earned $1,250,000 and his hobbies included golf, horseback riding, table tennis, motor boating, and baseball. He was devoted to his mother and never drank intoxicating liquors nor smoked. Louis never forgot a friend, had lots of pet charities, was easy for his manager to handle, had a keen wit and great sense of humor, and never gambled. In one article, Joe Louis was described as a shy "mamma's boy" who was reared to fear God and to be loyal and honest.[29]

Less than two months after Janet MacDonald committed suicide and exposed the corruption in Detroit, on a cool Wednesday night, September 20, Joe Louis fought Bob Pastor at Briggs Stadium in Detroit. Famous people from Detroit and all over the country came to see the twenty-round scheduled fight. Fans who attended included the governor of Michigan, Luren Dickinson; Mayor Richard Reading; Prosecutor Duncan McCrea; Edsel Ford, son of Henry Ford; General Motors president William Knudsen; President Roosevelt's son Elliott; Detroit Tigers owner Walter Briggs; former heavyweight champion Gene Tunney; and FBI director J. Edgar Hoover.

In addition to the nationally known politicians, businessmen, and celebrities, several of Detroit's numbers kings and numbers operators from out of town made their presence known. Sam "Bolita" McCollum and his wife, Ruby, were among the out-of-towners who attended the fight. McCollum was known as the "king" of Suwannee County's numbers racket and was considered the wealthiest black man in Live Oak, Florida. When he and his wife attended the Louis/Pastor fight, Ruby remembered, "I called Pastor 'Bicycle Bob' because Louis had to chase him for 11 rounds before he could catch up with him."[30]

Black Detroiters were proud that their native son, Joe Louis, was back home. One black newspaper reported that the sun was shining brightly as hundreds of people walked and shopped in Paradise Valley. Allegedly, more blacks attended this fight than any other at that time. When introducing Louis to the crowd of 33,868, the announcer declared, "Weighing 200 pounds wearing the purple trunks, native son of Detroit, who proved himself to be a credit to his chosen profession and the race he represents, the current heavyweight king, Joe Louis." Louis knocked Pastor down six times before finally knocking him out in the eleventh round. After the fight, Louis was elated. He took his gloves off and gave one to numbers king Thomas Hammonds, because he attended every Louis fight and Louis considered him one of his best fans.[31] Louis left Briggs Stadium and went to Roxborough's home for a luncheon. He then attended parties at the Club Forest and Club Plantation in Paradise Valley.

The *Detroit Free Press*, with racial undertones, described how anywhere from 10,000 to 25,000 of Detroit's black citizens celebrated in Paradise Valley:

> There was swingin' and singin' and jivin' no end in Paradise Valley Wednesday night, for the dark town's hero had come through again. . . . Down from upper floor apartments and drinking places the listeners poured, to fall into one another's arms and to spin into the whirling dervish of the jit. . . . All of the garish colors so dear to the heart of the dusky brethren brightened under the street lamps, lending a hysterical background to flashing teeth and gleaming eyes. In red and green and yellow and blue the clothing of the celebrators flashed, while overhead drifted the faint odor of sizzling pork chops, fried chickens and spareribs, turning on barbecue spits against the moment when appetite would not be denied.[32]

After the fight, Joe Louis was commended for his clean living and for what he did for the fighting industry by the *Detroit News*: "Fighting is a dirty business as a whole, but the colored boy from 'Bama has done a lot to lift it from the gutter. He is the cleanest fighter in the ring today. He never has thrown a low punch, and he has never squawked about the dozens that have landed on him. His ring manners are impeccable, and try to name a heavyweight champion before him of which that could be said."[33]

While Roxborough prepared Joe Louis for the fight, Judge Ferguson and Special Prosecutor Chester O'Hara began their investigation. They first subpoenaed Lieutenant John McCarthy to appear before them and answer questions. McCarthy refused to answer any of their questions and was jailed for contempt of court.[34] William McBride, however, never made it to testify because he died of pneumonia in Fort Lauderdale, Florida, on November 11, 1939. McBride's former wife, Irene McBride, later claimed she was suspicious of his death due to the suddenness of it.[35] During this same time period, the voters of the city of Detroit overwhelmingly chose a new mayor, Edward Jeffries. The *Detroit Free Press* speculated that Reading lost to Jeffries because of Janet MacDonald's allegations of citywide corruption.[36] Jeffries wasted no time in naming a new police commissioner, Frank Eaman. Eaman immediately began making changes to reestablish the integrity of the police department. He fired the superintendent of police, Fred Frahm, for failing to properly investigate a case involving Dr. Martin B. Robinson.[37]

Dr. Robinson, a Detroit Army Reserve Corps lieutenant colonel, physician, drugstore owner, and real estate firm owner, was considered a minor political figure. Prior to Janet MacDonald's suicide, in July 1939, four men allegedly robbed Robinson at gunpoint at his real estate office. His firm, Great Lakes Development Company, had been legally inactive for five years, and Robinson never possessed a real estate license; his firm was a front for a numbers organization.[38] Initially Robinson reported the robbery, but he later decided he did not want to pursue the case when the men were arrested in possession of the stolen money. Against department policy, Robinson was given back $1,000 of the money recovered from the so-called robbers. In truth, Robinson owed a gambling debt to Detroit's Purple Gang after betting on a losing horse. The four arrested robbers were members of the Purple Gang and had attempted to collect the debt. Robinson did not have the total amount owed and gave the men a partial payment. He then reported to police the four men had robbed him to secure the remaining money with a fraudulent insurance claim. It later came to light that the upstanding Dr. Robinson had not only reported a fake robbery to cover a gambling debt but also provided financing to a number of numbers organizations, including the Great Lakes Mutuels Company.[39] When questioned by police concerning his ties to the Great Lakes Mutuels Company, Robinson stated, "I like to help people out. They need money and I lend it to them. That's the way I am. Always willing to help. I don't have any other interest in the places."[40] Robinson also owned a second policy house in Detroit and had used his influence as a lieutenant colonel to obtain the parole of a state prisoner who later worked for him at his policy house.[41]

The investigation into the fake robbery revealed that, after police officers learned of the fake robbery, they attempted to cover up Robinson's false allegations. In addition to Frahm, police inspector Raymond Boettcher and several others were fired for their part in the fake robbery cover-up.[42] When Judge Ferguson learned of this incident, he ordered a number of the officers involved to testify, including Boettcher, who received $1,800 for assisting Robinson in the staged robbery.[43] After numerous people testified before Judge Ferguson, several high-ranking officials were indicted for taking graft from baseball pool operators, handbook operators, houses of prostitutions, and numbers organizations.[44] Those indicted included Wayne County Prosecutor Duncan McCrea, who refused to investigate the allegations made by Janet MacDonald in her suicide letters; McCrea's chief investigator, Harry Colburn; and former Detroit police superintendent Fred Frahm.[45] Prior to being indicted, McCrea unsuccessfully attempted to undermine Ferguson's grand jury by appointing his own grand juror, a seventy-one-year-old justice of the peace from New Boston, Michigan, who was a full-time grave digger.[46]

After McCrea was indicted, he refused to leave office and, in a truly brazen move, had his aides and members of the Wayne County Sheriff's Department attempt to raid the office of Judge Ferguson on March 4, 1940. According to Judge Ferguson's aides, McCrea's staff tried to seize evidence against the prosecutor. Conversely, McCrea claimed his staff was attempting to identify a room that was used by Ferguson's staff to assault grand jury witnesses. One man claimed he was apprehended by two men, later identified as men working for Ferguson, when he left his home. He said the men took him to a small room and questioned him. At some point, the men began to beat him while demanding he tell the truth. The beating allegedly went on for hours. Based on this and two other allegations, McCrea's men went to the grand jury location and were confronted by Ferguson's staff. A battle ensued between members of Judge Ferguson's staff and McCrea's before Detroit police officers were summoned and ended the ruckus.[47]

Shortly after this incident, a warrant was issued for the sheriff of Wayne County, Thomas Wilcox, for conspiracy to accept bribes and allowing gambling and houses of prostitution to operate.[48] Wilcox had been hired by Mayor Charles Bowles in 1930 to clean up vice in the city as Detroit's police commissioner, but after Bowles's recall, Wilcox was fired by incoming mayor Frank Murphy. In 1932, he was elected for a two-year term as sheriff of Wayne County, and it was rumored that under his command, wild parties ensued at the jail. When "Tweedle-dee," as he was called, ran for reelection in 1934, he lost. He refused to accept defeat and demanded a recount. The recount's results were in his favor, but in spite of that, he was eventually ousted by a court order.[49] Wilcox successfully ran again in 1935 and was reelected with the help of various gambling operators who contributed to his campaign.[50] As sheriff, he appointed his friends as deputies and required them to contribute to the purchase of his diamond-studded badge; the newly appointed staff contributed $5,000 for Wilcox's $1,500 badge. Wilcox had been the butt of jokes for a few missteps he took while in office. For example, he requested the county budget two dollars to cover the cost of catnip for the Sheriff's Office cat before proposing to tattoo chickens to reduce chicken thefts.[51]

McCrea and Wilcox required organizations throughout Wayne County to pay for protection on an annual or monthly basis. Baseball pools had to pay $22,500 per year to operate and had to make campaign gifts of $500. Slot machine operators paid $800 annually. Numbers gambling organizations and houses of prostitution had to pay $1,200 per month, and handbook operations paid a monthly fee of $1,225. It was estimated that a total of $52,900 was paid annually to McCrea and Wilcox.[52] In return, the establishments would be forewarned of any planned raids, which allowed them time to remove money and other incriminating evidence. Once the raid was conducted, the establishments were able to reopen for business as usual.[53] Both Wilcox and McCrea were able to live extravagantly from the graft payments they received. Both had homes in the city and expensive second homes in Florida and Wisconsin. Like the numbers operators, they would have to pay the price for their corruption and illegal activities.

10
Detroit's Hope Dealers Go on Trial

The city's attempt to break up the numbers hurt the economic condition of the black community. Black Detroiters saw the trial as a direct attack on their community.

—Sunnie Wilson, *Toast of the Town: The Life and Times of Sunnie Wilson*

The number of people indicted by Judge Ferguson continued to grow, and by April 24, 1940, former mayor Richard Reading Sr. and 134 others were indicted, accused of accepting graft in return for allowing the $10,000,000 per year Detroit numbers racket to flourish. When indicted, Reading declared, "It's a lot of nonsense. It is ridiculous. I don't even know what policy is. I don't know what it is all about." Those indicted included Wayne County Prosecutor Duncan McCrea; his chief investigator, Harry Colburn; the former superintendent of police, Fred Frahm; Lieutenant John McCarthy and eighty-eight other police officers; John Roxborough; Everett Watson; Ida Watson; and forty additional numbers operators and employees.[1] Roxborough, smiling and smoking a cigar after being bonded out, stated, "I have been out of town and do not know what it is about, but maybe I ought to check up and see if I stubbed my toe."[2] The day after Roxborough was indicted, one of Detroit's major newspapers ran an article boasting of Roxborough's accomplishments. Roxborough was credited with being the unseen brains behind the management of Joe Louis and for ensuring Louis acted like a gentleman in and out of the boxing ring. The paper noted that Roxborough admitted to being in the numbers business at one point but had removed himself from it so he could manage Louis's boxing career. The article indicated Roxborough had made a great deal of money, which he invested in Detroit real estate, charitable activities, and the development of black youth.[3]

Figure 11. John Roxborough arriving at grand jury proceedings on April 24, 1940. Reproduced by permission from the *Detroit Free Press*.

The black papers across the country also came to Roxborough's defense after he was indicted and voiced their opinion on the role of numbers gambling in society. One paper, after noting Roxborough was an astute businessman who was a credit to his race, said that without the income from the numbers racket he would never have been able to accomplish all he did for Joe Louis, the boxing industry, and the black race:

Roxborough could not have done this because American democracy is so imperfect that there is little chance for a man of color to accumulate a real stake before he passes the age of usefulness without resorting to such shady enterprises as numbers or some other racket. . . . Few of our race have made a killing on the stock market, few have built factories and trading houses where they can exploit both the public and their employees in the quick accumulation of wealth because the inner circles are closed to them. They have turned to the outlawed enterprises more from necessity than by choice. . . . The whole thing narrows down to a class problem and the gambling instinct in the human race. If it is all right for the rich to play the stock market, it should be all right for the poor to play the numbers. But that unfortunately, isn't the case. The poor do not make the laws—they only go to jail for breaking them. After all somebody has to go to jail. That's what jails are for.[4]

Another black newspaper wrote about Roxborough:

He has keen insight into human nature but has never used it to undue advantage. He has his own code of right and wrong and has practiced it in its broadest sense always with the good name of the race in view. There is a touch of the gambler in all of us and Roxborough is no different from the man in Wall Street or the man who stages his raffle in a church. The count against him is just another step in the age-old battle between tradition and changing social trends. Numbers banking may yet become an accepted practice. I have seen it happen with pari mutual betting and prohibition.[5]

The indictment of eighty-nine Detroit police officers caused major problems for the police department and its operation. Officers were arrested

Figure 12. Everett Watson surrenders to Special Prosecutor Chester O'Hara on March 17, 1940. Photo courtesy of *Detroit News*.

Figure 13. Indicted police officers outside courtrooms in July 1940 smiling and laughing for the cameras. Reproduced by permission from the *Detroit Free Press*.

while they walked beats, sat behind desks, and were in patrol cars. Once arrested, the officers were relieved of duty and suspended. The grand jury investigation into numbers gambling once again proved that whites were involved in numbers gambling as much as blacks. Of the 135 people indicted, only twenty-eight were black, including eight black police officers.[6] However, the media reported numbers gambling as a black activity: "It was a blow to the entire numbers racket, which for more than 10 years has flourished in Detroit, particularly among the Negro population, and whose leaders have grown wealthy on the proceeds of the illegal enterprise."[7]

The court proceedings for the 135 defendants became a spectacle for the public, and at times, court watchers had to be turned away due to lack of space. There were so many defendants in the courtroom at times that it was hard to keep the proceedings orderly. It was not uncommon for defendants to jeer at the prosecutor and to talk openly to witnesses while they were testifying. Eventually, Judge Homer Ferguson, in response to the circus-like atmosphere, ordered all defendants to sit in permanent seats, banned them from placing their feet on tables, and prohibited the reading of newspapers in court.[8]

In an ironic twist, numbers operators who were granted immunity from prosecution in exchange for their testimony were still in business. Indicted Wayne County Prosecutor Duncan McCrea arrested them and in doing so attempted to silence and discredit them before they could testify.[9] For example, Walter Norwood testified concerning the payoffs he made to both the prosecutor's office and the mayor's office on May 9, 1940. He also testified against a few police officers and other numbers operators, including John Roxborough and Everett Watson. In retaliation for his testimony, the following day, someone put a stench bomb in the lobby of the Norwood Hotel.[10] By May 23, McCrea authorized Norwood's policy and numbers house to be raided and issued arrest warrants for Norwood and ten of his employees. On the day of the raid, crowds gathered outside Norwood's numbers house and cheered as police officers raided his establishment. A number of those cheering were Norwood's customers who were upset with him for failing to pay off on winning hits.[11]

The community had long felt that Norwood ran a crooked game. Sometime before Christmas in 1939, the number "437" fell. This number was heavily played by people because the number "437" corresponded with "Christmas" in some dream books. Because it was heavily played, this meant that numbers operators were set to take a huge loss. Norwood allegedly went to other numbers operators trying to convince them to delay paying winners. He also proposed that when the winners were paid, they should be paid only half of what they had won.[12] Between his failure to pay off on winning hits and his perceived betrayal of the other numbers operators, factions of the Black Bottom community turned against Norwood.

On April 29, 1940, Wayne County Prosecutor Duncan McCrea and Sheriff Thomas Wilcox were found guilty for their part in taking graft to protect illegal gambling in Wayne County and sentenced to four and a half to five years in prison.[13] Even though those around them were being convicted and sentenced for their part in numbers gambling, both John Roxborough and Everett Watson continued their various businesses and work in the community. Roxborough did not want his legal troubles to reflect on Joe Louis and the image that he had crafted for him. He made it clear that Louis had nothing to do with numbers gambling and continued to protect his image. In June 1940, Earl Brown, a black writer, wrote an eight-page, largely unflattering feature on Joe Louis in *Life* magazine. As a result, pressure was applied by John Roxborough, and Earl Brown was fired from his editorial job at the *Amsterdam News*.[14] Roxborough wrote a letter to the editor of *Life* stating that Brown's article was filled with lies and derogatory statements about Joe Louis and his management team. He took exception to comments that Louis walked around in his bare feet, snored, overate, and overslept. He reiterated that Louis was a golfer, rode horses, played baseball, hunted, was in good physical shape, and did everything to win and retain the goodwill and respect of the American public.[15]

At this time, Louis was so popular that presidential candidate Wendell Willkie solicited Louis's help while campaigning in 1940. Louis made over 123 speeches for Willkie, the last taking place in Detroit on November 3, 1940. Louis urged black voters to vote for Willkie because "he has put things down in black and white that we're going to get jobs and not have to take welfare checks. I'm going to cast my vote Tuesday for Willkie for our next president."[16] Louis also appeared in ads for Willkie, which appeared in the *Detroit Free Press*. Willkie won the state of Michigan but ultimately lost the presidency to Franklin D. Roosevelt.

Everett Watson's legitimate businesses were being lauded for their rapid growth and Watson himself was being praised for his support of black citizens. Black Detroiters were proud that Watson's was the only black-owned realty company in the country and entirely operated by blacks. Despite his legal troubles, Watson was praised for extending loans to blacks when no other lending institution would. The *Detroit Tribune* reported that because of Watson, thousands of black Detroiters were able to purchase homes and businesses.[17]

On September 17, 1941, the numbers graft conspiracy trial began. At the time, it was one of the largest gambling criminal trials in the country and the largest in Michigan. In less than a month, an all-white jury of ten women and four men were selected to preside over the 65 defendants. During jury selection, 619 people were rejected as jurors.[18] The prosecutor, Chester O'Hara, rejected every black person and prevented any from serving on the jury. John R. Williams, a black editor for the Detroit edition of the *Pittsburgh Courier*, asked O'Hara, "Mr. O'Hara, how does it happen that you have continually for days excused only the Negro jurors who have been called for service in this case when many of them are without question as qualified as any of the others who have been called?" O'Hara answered, "The Roxborough-Watson interest[s] are so wide that I prefer not to have any Negroes on the jury, and further practically every Negro in Detroit is a number or policy player anyhow, and as such is unfit to serve on a case involving such matters."[19] The prosecutor's prejudiced view was not uncommon, and it did not help that an academic, Gustav Carlson, had written a widely read dissertation about the pervasiveness of numbers playing in Detroit's black community.

For example, a Detroit police officer, after witnessing a black man who was an employed property owner with no criminal record enter and exit a grocery store, concluded the man was a numbers writer because he was black and arrested him. When the case was brought before a judge, the judge asked the police officer how he could tell the man was a numbers writer. The police officer stated the man was in a black neighborhood and therefore must have been a numbers writer. The judge threw the case out on the grounds the police officer had made an illegal arrest.[20]

One month before the trial began, Kern's, a major department store in Detroit, ran a full-page advertisement for a sale. The advertisement also perpetuated the stereotype and belief that blacks were gamblers and superstitious. The ad screamed, "Don't Gamble! THIS is a 'Natural!'" under a picture of two young black males, eyes bucked, rolling dice. The dice were landing on seven, and a rabbit's foot and horseshoe were present.[21] In response to the advertisement, the *Detroit Tribune* admonished Kern's along with those responsible for depicting blacks in a derogatory manner to increase their sales with white customers. "The picture speaks for itself. It links the modern schoolboy with 'craps.' There is the seven. There is the rabbit's foot, also the horseshoe, all carrying through the theme of gambling, superstition, and

Figure 14. Irving Roane and Thomas "Rooster" Hammonds in court after pleading guilty on September 30, 1941. Photo courtesy of *Detroit News*.

luck. Such pictures represent the Negro as being still the ignorant, super-stitious, handicapped, grinning individual that prejudiced men and women would have him remain. This is not so. It is embarrassing and unfair."[22]

The selected jurors were forced to live at the Tuller Hotel under guard and away from family and friends for the duration of the trial. The jury's mail and phone calls were monitored to ensure they were not influenced in their deliberations. While under guarded supervision, jurors were only allowed to visit their family for fifteen minutes twice per week.[23] When the trial began, numbers operators Thomas "Rooster" Hammonds, Irving Roane, and Harvey Cox pled guilty and later were sentenced to probation. As a result of their pleas, Roane and Hammonds were fined $1,500 and sentenced to two years of probation. Two months later, charges against Everett Watson's wife, Ida, were dismissed.

Many witnesses were called to testify during the trial. One such witness, Claude Semus, formerly worked for Everett Watson's Yellow Dog policy house before being fired in 1939 for cheating by manipulating the numbers drawn. Semus admitted he had in fact cheated but insisted he was only following Watson's instructions. Semus further claimed that Watson's wife, Ida, was the "boss" of the Yellow Dog in her husband's absence.[24] Another witness also testified that Ida was a major part of the numbers organization.[25] The claim that cheating occurred contradicted Watson's reputation within the community for running a fair game, and after the testimony, Watson denied Semus's assertion. Watson told reporters, "You will never make people on St. Antoine Street believe I did that."[26] A number of witnesses were loyal to Watson and refused to testify against him. One such loyal employee was seventy-seven-year-old Andrew Young, who had been friends with Watson for thirty years. They had been waiters together in 1916, and Young had hired Watson as a waiter on the Great Lakes Steamer in 1926. Watson later returned the favor and hired Young in 1934 for $20 per week. When Young was called to testify against Watson, he refused to answer questions and displayed a selective memory. At one point, the judge in the case threatened to jail Young for contempt of court. When this occurred, Watson asked to speak with Young. Watson smiled at Young, and then urged his friend of thirty years to "go ahead and answer all the questions Mr. O'Hara asks you. You tell him the truth—all of the truth." Young nodded his head and slowly walked away, "an old man who hated to talk about his friend."[27] Another Watson employee also refused to testify. When Watson advised him at a

Figure 15. Ida Watson. Artwork by Avery Sky.

recess to "get back on that stand and tell the truth," he refused and was sentenced to fifteen days in jail for contempt of court.[28]

As the trial dragged on, witnesses from all walks of life testified. One police officer testified that the rumors that police officials were taking bribes were so rampant that he and other officers decided they might as well take bribes. The trial also revealed that the numbers game was not a "black-only" industry. A number of whites played the numbers, while white numbers operators profited largely from running their own policy/numbers houses in the city.[29] Finally, after a three-month trial, on December 13, 1941, the final jury of eight women (which included seven housewives and one clerk) and four men (which included a retiree, an assembler, a salesman, and a brick-layer) was given the case to decide the fate of the accused. The jury, while sequestered, deliberated for more than eighteen hours. When they emerged from deliberations late in the evening on December 15, 1941, they found twenty-three people guilty of conspiracy to protect the numbers racket, while eighteen others were found not guilty. Those found guilty included former mayor Richard Reading, former lieutenant John McCarthy, and numbers operators John Roxborough and Everett Watson, who were both described as fight managers and prominent in politics.[30] Just like the trial, the rendering of the verdict was filled with drama, arrogance, and laughter on December 16.

When former mayor Reading heard the guilty verdict, his smile faded. Flushed and no longer smiling, with a grim face, in response he shouted, "The most inhuman thing since the Lord was crucified!" Richard Reading's son Clarence, upon hearing his father's guilty verdict, angrily approached the prosecutor, Chester O'Hara, and said, "If you were 20 years younger I would tear you to pieces." O'Hara's guards stepped in between the two men as O'Hara tried to reach Clarence Reading. George Cordell, convicted operator of the Murphy House who was standing nearby, playfully punched O'Hara on the shoulder and laughingly advised him to "take it easy" because Clarence Reading was "only a punk." Simultaneously, Richard Reading Sr. stepped in front of his son and told him, "You keep quiet." Clarence in response yelled, "I can't take it, I just can't take it!" Reading called his sons to his side, and as they exited the courtroom, Reading Sr. declared, "This is the greatest injustice since the crucifixion of Christ. I will appeal the case."[31]

The black community also felt the trial was unfair and blamed O'Hara. Blacks were offended by his exclusion of black jurors and concluded he was racist. O'Hara in response issued the following statement: "I am perfectly satisfied with the verdict rendered by the jury in the case relating to the policy and numbers conspiracy. I feel that the jury used good judgment in deciding who should or who should not be convicted. Some colored defen-dants were found guilty, but there were some, including all the colored

Figure 16. Ralph Reading, Richard Reading, and Clarence Reading leaving court, December 2, 1941. Reproduced by permission from the *Detroit Free Press.*

policemen, acquitted by the jury or upon my recommendation. I feel that all the defendants who were acquitted or dismissed will make splendid citizens from now on, and I trust that my conduct of the case throughout will once and for all tamp out the claim of prejudice against me. I brand as false the accusation of prejudice."[32]

Like many others, Everett Watson expected the verdict but was disappointed. He vowed to "fight it as long as I have any money left."[33] The guilty were sentenced on January 7, 1942; Reading was the first. No longer did he appear carefree as he had throughout the trial. When asked by the court if he had anything to say, Reading with tears in his eyes responded, "A jury said I am guilty, but I am not guilty. I never in any way conspired to accept any money or to protect any racket. In the future this will be shown." Judge Pugsley, before casting a sentence on Reading, said, "I have heard your testimony and your story, and I wish I could accept your story. But the proofs are conclusive. As Mayor you were responsible for good government. You violated a public trust and became part and parcel of a scheme of corruption."[34] Reading was given four to five years in the state penitentiary. Upon hearing his sentence, Reading's face flushed and, no longer cocky, he quickly went to the courtroom's water cooler to get a drink before having to be escorted back to his seat by his son Clarence.

Former lieutenant John McCarthy received eighteen months.[35] Roxborough and Watson were sentenced to two and a half to five years for being vital in the conspiracy. Also sentenced on that day was John Roxborough's brother, Claude. Claude, with William H. Robinson, former manager of the Big Four numbers bank, was fined $2,500 and had to pledge never to engage in the operation of any illegal enterprise.[36] A few days after they were sentenced, a black newspaper ran a picture of both John Roxborough and Everett Watson on the front page with the caption, "They still have friends." Under Roxborough's picture, the following was printed: "John Roxborough, co-manager of champion Joe Louis, and prominent business man, who has filed for an appeal from the sentence imposed Wednesday in the local alleged policy graft case. Through his generous gifts to charity and investments in business enterprises, Mr. Roxborough has been a public benefactor." The statement under Watson's picture read: "Everett I. Watson, one of the principal defendants in the local grand jury trial conducted by Circuit Judge Homer Ferguson in connection with charges of graft in the policy numbers field. Watson has filed for an appeal to the higher courts. He is financially interested in many local business concerns, provided employment for many men and women of the race."[37] Another black newspaper concerning John Roxborough stated, "He was known as a man of varied interests in a business way, but he had only one interest in a personal way. That was the elevation of his race to a position of pride. He wanted it clean, admired, respected.

He wanted it given its fair and honest chance in the American way."[38] Just a few days after Roxborough was sentenced, a columnist in the *Washington Post* mentioned his guilty verdict and noted that although he had been found guilty, Roxborough, described as a "suavely college bred lawyer," had managed Joe Louis better than any other fighter had ever been managed.[39] Although both men were found guilty, the message to them and to the public at large was simple: they were supported.

True to their word, both Roxborough and Watson appealed their sentences because they felt they had been denied the opportunity to be judged by a jury of their peers when Chester O'Hara excluded all blacks from serving on the jury. In their appeal, lawyers for the two argued that when O'Hara said "every Negro in Detroit is a number or policy player," he had essentially tarnished a whole race.[40] Watson and Roxborough's legal team found that O'Hara's statement went beyond censuring an individual; it censured all 149,119 blacks who resided in Detroit. O'Hara had condemned blacks based on his assertion of a "supposed racial characteristic."[41] As the appeals were being fought in court, both men remained free on bond. For Everett Watson, he had to deal with the possibility of going to jail while grieving. On May 3, 1942, his twenty-five-year-old son, William "Stompey" Watson, died of a heart attack in Los Angeles. His son had appeared in vaudeville for a few years; he was a dancer known for doing the "Charleston," "blackbottom," and "truckin'." In addition to his son William, Everett had two daughters, June and Hester. June had a degree in sociology and was a social worker, while her sister received training at a Brooklyn fashion institute and owned a hat store where she designed her own hats.

As Detroit was earning its nickname as the "Arsenal of Democracy" by building war equipment, Roxborough continued to manage Joe Louis, and Watson's insurance agency became the second black company in the country to sell U.S. war bonds after the Treasury Department designated it an issuing agency.[42] The first black company was Detroit's own Great Lakes Mutual Insurance Company. As Roxborough's trial was taking place in 1941, Joe Louis was asked by the U.S. Army and Navy to fight in a benefit to raise money for charities supporting soldiers. Louis's management team decided to allow him to fight a benefit fight for the navy and to donate all his earnings to them. At that time, the U.S. Navy had a reputation for barring blacks from its service and training centers. Roxborough's decision was met with both praise and criticism. John Roxborough stated that Joe Louis was only doing what he considered his patriotic duty and was seeking no glory for donating his entire earnings to the Navy Relief Society. Louis and Roxborough hoped that this deed would change the navy's attitude toward blacks.[43] Roxborough believed that if Louis had refused, he would have been stigmatized as un-American. He and Louis were fully aware of the navy's Jim Crow policy and felt that the fight would be the most effective way of exposing the navy's racial problems. Roxborough reasoned, "This might be just the time and just the spot for Louis to establish a splendid precedent that might help to break down anti-Negro sentiment in the United States Navy."[44] Although Louis put his championship on the line against Buddy Baer and donated his entire winnings, Baer did not. The black press's negative response to the proposed fight was not directed at Joe Louis or his management team but at the navy:

> The Navy's attitude toward Louis' people in war and in peace has been a constant reiteration of the age-old anti-Negro attitudes of the antebellum South. . . . The humiliation Negroes are confronted with when they attempt to enlist as American citizens—not Negroes—to help defend their country on the seas has been felt throughout the length and breadth of the land. Pearl Harbor, it was believed, would somehow change the bleak Naval conception of who has a right to fight on the ships for this country. It didn't. Instead, the barriers against black volunteers were built higher and the disciples of racial intolerance were more adamant than ever in demonstrating their conceptions of democracy to those anxious to serve.[45]

Before the fight, on January 9, 1942, Wendell Willkie entered the boxing ring and made a speech. Willkie thanked Joe Louis for his generosity in the name of the U.S. Navy and the American people.[46] Louis won the fight by knocking out Baer in the first round. Roxborough was proud of Louis, and that victory occurred just two days after he was sentenced for his role in the illegal numbers scandal.[47] A few days after the fight, sports writers honored Joe Louis at a dinner attended by army and navy officers, the former postmaster general, J. Edgar Hoover, the former mayor of New York, James Walker, and other dignitaries. Walker served as the speaker of the evening: "Joe, all the Negroes in the world are proud of you because you have given them reason to be proud. You never forgot your own people. You are an American gentleman. When you fought Buddy Baer and gave your purse to the Navy Relief Society, you took your title and your future and bet it all on patriotism and love of country. Joe Louis, that night you laid a rose on the grave of Abraham Lincoln."[48]

Joe Louis entered the U.S. Army in 1942 as heavyweight champion while Roxborough continued to appeal his conviction. While in the military, Louis would be credited with bringing unfair Jim Crow practices on military bases to an end. If he were not Joe Louis, the black American hero crafted by John Roxborough, he would not have had the clout to make this important difference for black Americans. Louis felt that he was an American fighting for his country, for a cause, which included freedom and equality. As such, he believed he had to stand up for blacks in the military and advocate to get them fair treatment. While in the army, he knew of blacks who had college degrees but were denied entry in the officer training program because they were black. When he learned about this, he used his political capital and spoke out about the unfairness of it. As a result, several blacks entered the officer training program, and all became lieutenants. When Jackie Robinson, who was in Louis's outfit, was denied the opportunity to play on an army baseball team, Louis again spoke out about it, which resulted in an order coming out of Washington, D.C., allowing blacks to play on any camp team regardless of their race.[49]

On another occasion while on a base in Alabama, Louis sat on a bench in front of a bus station when he was approached by an MP who told him he had to sit in the Jim Crow part of the station. When Louis refused to move to the back of the station, he and welterweight Ray Robinson, who was with him, were arrested and thrown into the stockade. After being admonished by a captain for not following the Jim Crow rules, his case made it to Washington, D.C. Again, orders came from D.C. ordering the end of Jim Crow buses in army camps everywhere. Louis would not speak or box at any camp that followed Jim Crow laws. Louis remembered, "I did not look for trouble in those camps. When I was outside a camp I obeyed Jim Crow, but I thought it wasn't American to have it in the army where all GIs were fighting for one cause."[50]

While awaiting the outcome of their appeal and free on bond, Roxborough and Watson entered into a venture to build a bowling alley in the heart of Paradise Valley for $100,000, which again was a source of pride for Detroit's black community.[51] The Paradise Bowl was lauded as one of America's most modern bowling establishments. It had a dining room and cocktail lounge, twenty lanes, a telescore system, check rooms, and the capacity to hold 300 people. Despite their convictions, Roxborough and Watson were still considered community leaders. When a local attorney ran for city council, both Roxborough and Watson were listed among the various community leaders that included men of the church, attorneys, doctors, and elected officials who endorsed the candidate.[52] Everett Watson continued to expand his business interests. The Paradise Valley Distributing Company he invested in was still operating and distributing Friar's Ale. According to an ad placed in the *Detroit Tribune* on September 6, 1941, the company, after operating at a loss for two years, had grown from two trucks and eight employees in 1937 to being the only beer distributing company in America owned and operated by blacks. By 1941, the company had a staff of thirty, and seven brand-new trucks were added to its fleet to serve nightclubs, taverns, and neighborhood stores.

Watson also purchased $1.5 million worth of property on the west side of Detroit to build 326 new houses for blacks in an area to be called Watson Park. The houses were to be simple, measuring 40 by 100 feet. He hoped this would help alleviate the congested housing situation for black Detroiters. According to Sunnie Wilson, "Mr. Watson was the first black I knew who owned a housing project. Some called him a numbers-man, but I looked upon him as a builder and developer."[53] Prior to and immediately after World War II, the city of Detroit experienced a housing shortage as people migrated to the city. Although both white and black Detroiters needed housing, for blacks, the situation was even worse due to discriminatory housing practices and restrictive covenants, which prevented blacks from buying or living in white neighborhoods. During the 1940s, about 150,000 new Detroiters were black; they made up two-thirds of the city's population growth and there was little to no housing available. At least 10,000 units of housing for blacks were needed to address some of the housing issues, but in response, only 1,500 of the 186,000 houses constructed in the Detroit area were available to blacks during the 1940s.[54] In 1944 when Watson bought property on the west side of Detroit with dreams of building much-needed homes for blacks, whites living in the area objected to his proposed subdivision. To quell their objections, Watson bought nineteen homes occupied by whites for $125,000.[55] This did not end white opposition, however. Several whites formed the South Detroit Community League to prevent the subdivision from being built. One member of the organization, a white police officer, paid a paroled convict $85 to set fire to three of Watson's homes.[56] Shortly after this incident, Watson and Roxborough learned they had exhausted all of the legal appeals when the U.S. Supreme Court refused to hear their case. As a result, both men began serving their sentences at Jackson State Prison in December 1944.

With their incarceration, blacks in Detroit now controlled less than 50 percent of numbers operations.[57] Roxborough's numbers house, the Big Four, was still in operation, being run by his younger brother Claude. Apparently Claude did not take his 1942 pledge never to engage in the operation of any illegal enterprise seriously. By August, he was on trial for owning part of the $2 million business. Key evidence in the trial against him centered on the fact that the Big Four numbers house had made payments to the Michigan Unemployment Compensation Commission.[58] These payments confirmed that the numbers house was operating and employing people.

Although Roxborough was convicted and imprisoned for his illegal numbers operation, many never forgot what he did for Detroit's black community. He was known for his generosity and dignified image, which earned him respect, and for being a "race man" who used his money and influence to advance the black race. Former Tuskegee Airman Peter Cassey Jr., who was associated with Roxborough, recalled in 1983, "John was totally a businessman. He used to turn everything to his own advantage. He was a racketeer—in the numbers. He had the Superior Life Insurance Company. He was a quiet businessman, always looking to spend money that would benefit his brother. He financed education for others. There were no scholarships, especially for blacks. Everything was on a cash basis. He helped a lot of people because he had the cash. In the Depression, no one else had it. . . . John Roxborough did good for other people. I don't remember him doing harm. Numbers were a means to survive and thrive."[59]

11
Fuller Hit's Story

Growing up I remember I wanted to be a numbers banker. That was the dream of a lot of my friends. Numbers bankers were classy. They had the respect of the community because they were the community's problem solvers. They were wealthy and had power. Many were the pillars of the community, right up there with doctors, lawyers, undertakers, and ministers.

—Fuller Hit, December 12, 2012[1]

Not all Detroit numbers operators were taken down by the MacDonald scandal. One such person was Fuller Hit's uncle, who continued to run his numbers organization. Fuller has firsthand knowledge of numbers gambling because he grew up with it. He likes to remind everyone that he has "seen a lot of life and lived a lot more." At age eighty-seven, he is small of stature but possesses an abundance of charm. Some have described him as a knowledgeable historian, hence his nickname "Doctor." With a keen sense of fashion, it is not uncommon to see the dapper statesman wearing an ascot or a derby on his graying, thinning hair. Fuller was not born in Detroit; when he was a toddler, his family relocated to the city from Canada. Fuller described his father as an educated professional who ran his own business in Detroit and his mother as an educated housewife. His life was one of privilege. As a young child growing up during the Great Depression, he has no memories of experiencing hard times but was aware of others who did. His family was fortunate and lived in a "nice brick house," and he and his siblings attended Catholic schools. Church was very much a part of his upbringing, and as a child, Sundays consisted of attending church in the morning and going to the movies in the afternoon.

Some of Fuller's earliest memories are of Paradise Valley and Black Bottom. Although his family did not reside in either, their business (which he declined to name) catered to its residents. Fuller stressed that Black Bottom was the "residential" part of black Detroit on the east side, and Paradise

Valley was the "business and entertainment" section. He described the area in the late 1930s to early 1950s as vibrant and full of life. In his words, "It was a true melting pot. You had people from all walks of life living, working, and playing there. There were doctors and lawyers next to porters and factory workers, who associated with street hustlers." Street hustlers included prostitutes, peddlers, panhandlers, thieves, confidence men and women, and numbers runners or writers. Fuller equated the Black Bottom with poverty. For him, it was a slum area where the poor lived, mainly blacks, but some whites as well. Conversely, Paradise Valley was where every business imaginable for blacks was located. Paradise Valley offered nightclubs, bars, restaurants, hotels, a bowling alley, a skating rink, drugstores, theaters, grocery stores, cigar shops, tailors, poolrooms, laundries, coffee shops, and many other businesses that catered to blacks. Because blacks were restricted in terms of where they could conduct business, Paradise Valley was always bustling with activity. Fuller remembered being entertained simply by walking along the sidewalks and inhaling the smell of fish frying or barbeque on pits. As a teenager, Fuller recalled dancing at the Graystone Ballroom, where the likes of Duke Ellington and Count Basie performed.

Fuller's uncle, Charles, was a major numbers banker and was friends with numerous other numbers bankers, including the Mosley family and Everett Watson, whose nickname was "Monk." Fuller grew up respecting these men and viewed them as surrogate uncles. He recalled that like Charles, Watson was a self-made man. He knew Watson had earned his early wealth as a porter on the ships. With his savings he bought into the Waiters and Bellman's Club, which was a private club for blacks that served liquor and provided gambling. Watson had a natural head for business but gained more knowledge by listening to and observing the businessmen he served on the ships. According to Fuller, Charles was an educated man who was of average size and looks. As a young man, Charles worked a few jobs, saving as much as he possibly could. When Prohibition hit the city, Charles took his savings and invested it in illegal whiskey. Charles would sell the whiskey to clubs and bars, and as his profits grew, he began to invest his money in several business ventures. One such venture was a poolroom, which provided illegal liquor to patrons and several gambling games including poker and blackjack. Charles's poolroom would later serve as the headquarters for his numbers business. Charles had a reputation in the community for being a fair man who employed a few people in his poolroom and financed neighborhood parties. When he began his numbers business, his reputation continued to grow. Not only did he continue to hire people in the neighborhood who needed jobs, but he was honest. He ensured hits were paid off in a timely way (even when he was hit hard), and when his employees were arrested, he stepped in and helped them with their legal troubles. His numbers house was known to take care of everyone in the community. When someone died, he ensured flowers or food baskets were delivered. If someone had trouble paying for a burial, all they had to do was let him know. Charles ensured children and the elderly received medicine when they could not afford it, and many people's rent was paid by him. Charles took care of his community because his community took care of him. He knew that his success depended on the people who patronized his businesses and knew all too well the struggle of everyday living in Detroit. Fuller said that people played with Charles and his other uncles because they were strong, trustworthy black men who took care of their race and their community.

According to Fuller, people of all races and economic status played the numbers in Detroit. Many poor people played the numbers because it was a chance for them to live a little easier, if only for a short while. Fuller remembered that at first, when numbers operations were owned and operated by blacks, both whites and blacks patronized them; however, once whites began owning numbers operations, black players tended to patronize black numbers organizations, and whites patronized white-owned numbers houses, reflecting the segregation that was the norm in Detroit and black solidarity in numbers.

As Charles's fortune grew, he further invested his money in legal businesses. Charles purchased real estate throughout the county and acted as a loan institution for several blacks who dreamed of running their own businesses in Detroit. He provided the seed money for grocery stores and restaurants, funeral homes, nightclubs, and hat shops in the city. He sponsored many young people's educational expenses at a few local colleges and made sure the neighborhood children had enough to eat and presents at Christmas. Charles was a source of pride for blacks in the city. Many praised him for his honesty, work ethic, sense of humor, and business savvy. His wealth was never envied because he gave back and was generous. In addition, Charles never flaunted his wealth. He was a plain dresser, who drove an average car and lived in a nice but modest brick house on the near east side. Charles's wife did not work, and she, too, was modest in her appearance. Her time was spent working at the church and with several women's organizations that furthered a variety of black causes in the city. Although Charles was respected and liked by many, not everyone accepted him. Fuller recalled that many black people did not agree with how Charles had made his fortune because they did not approve of numbers gambling. For some, it went against their religious beliefs, while others thought it cast all blacks in a negative light. Some did not want blacks playing the numbers because it perpetuated the image of blacks as criminals and "lazy gambling fools"; however, no one would inform on a numbers operator in the community. As Fuller explained, all blacks, regardless of their income, education, or status, were viewed by their race first and foremost by whites.

Many of Detroit's black elite only tolerated Charles and the other numbers operators because they had wealth and did give back to the community. Fuller thought that the only numbers operators in Detroit who were truly accepted by the black elite were those born into black elite families like John Roxborough or were highly educated like Dr. Haley Bell. Bell was a prominent black dentist who had practices in Detroit and Hamtramck. He grew up in Savannah, Georgia, where he attended private schools. He graduated from Meharry Medical College in Tennessee. In 1923, he came to Detroit and opened a dental practice. He was also part of a numbers organization for a while in Hamtramck. Dr. Bell was indicted by Judge Homer Ferguson's one-man grand jury for providing payoffs to the mayor of Hamtramck. In return for these graft payments, numbers gambling could operate without police interference. Although he was indicted, the charges against Bell were later dismissed.[2] Years later Bell would be one of the founders of Detroit Memorial Park, a black cemetery, and became the first black person to build and own a radio station (WCHB) in the United States in 1955. Bell was known for his charity work in the community and was presented the key to the city of Detroit in 1958.

Fuller was proud of Charles for many reasons. Fuller admitted that, as a child, he had no idea exactly what Charles did to get his wealth. It was not talked about openly. When relatives, friends, and adults talked about Charles, they called him a businessman and discussed his legitimate businesses. Fuller remembers people talking about what a great man Charles was and how he donated money, space, or food to churches, the Urban League, and several other causes that benefited the community. Charles attended church with his wife regularly and was active in politics. He was not affiliated with a political party but instead used his resources to support whatever candidate he felt would help blacks. When one candidate he supported ran for office, Charles had his numbers writers deliver campaign literature as they wrote their numbers. Most people trusted Charles and his numbers writers, who usually were family, friends, or neighbors, and voted in line with them.

As Fuller grew older, he found himself listening in on private "adult" conversations. It was then that he learned Charles was a numbers banker. This knowledge did not change how Fuller viewed Charles; if anything, Fuller respected him even more. When Fuller discussed what he had learned about Charles with his friends, they were in awe. Numbers men were respected for their wealth: how they dressed, their jewelry, the cars they drove, and the houses they lived in. Charles was no longer just the "nice" businessman but one of *the* numbers men. When asked if any women were numbers operators during this time, Fuller laughed and said, "No, their role was to marry a numbers operator." Most women who were in the numbers business in Detroit at that time tended to have minor roles as either numbers writers or cashiers, reflecting the predominantly clerical roles women had in the formal economy.

Fuller was approximately twelve years old when Janet MacDonald murdered her daughter and committed suicide. He remembered the shock everyone felt that she would kill her daughter. The fact that she had earned her living from the numbers but caused thousands temporarily to lose their livelihood was not lost on those affected by her actions. According to Fuller, it was weeks before things were back to normal for the numbers men. The closure of their establishments meant a loss of income not only for numbers employees but also for those who relied on the numbers as a source of income. The tragedy was an overall loss for the community because fewer people were making purchases at restaurants and stores. When the indictments from Judge Homer Ferguson's one-man grand jury were coming down, Charles's family was worried that Charles would be named as a defendant; however, this did not happen and he avoided being questioned. Some of Fuller's other "uncles," however, were not so lucky.

Fuller recalled only one other incident that temporarily stopped the numbers from being played: the 1943 riot. On June 20, 1943, a hot night in the city, a rumor spread that white men had thrown a black woman and her baby off the Belle Isle Bridge. In the white community, a different rumor spread that black men had raped a white woman on Belle Isle. Neither

rumor was true, and though the source of the rumors could never be pin-
pointed, the results were deadly. Rioting continued until June 22, when
federal troops arrived to restore order. By the end of the riot, thirty-four
people were killed, hundreds injured, and two million dollars in property
damage incurred. Of the thirty-four people killed, twenty-five were black,
and the police killed twelve of the twenty-five.[3] The riot silenced Paradise
Valley. Numbers playing, like everything else in the "Valley," ceased when a
state of emergency was declared in the city. Under the watchful eye of police
and federal troops, the state of emergency meant all bars were closed, mass
meetings and gatherings were prohibited, and a curfew from 10:00 p.m. to
6:00 a.m. was established. During the riot, looters destroyed several white-
owned businesses in Paradise Valley. Although bad for the white business
owners, it brought some fortune to black business owners who operated
grocery stores, butcher shops, pharmacies, and dry goods stores. Before
the riot, two black grocery stores were barely able to exist; after the riot,
business picked up so much they struggled to keep up. Although fewer
stores were open, customers reported they were paying less for goods after
the riots.[4] It did not go unnoticed that some blacks in Paradise Valley did
not support black businesses prior to the riot. One paper noted, "The fact
that Negro merchants in Detroit had to wait until a violent race riot came
in order to get their opportunity to sell to Negro people in strictly Negro
neighborhoods, is a sad commentary upon the pride and self-interests of
the Negro consumers. And the usual tale about the white merchant's ice
being colder and sugar sweeter than the Negro merchant's cannot hold
water here."[5]

Numbers playing ceased as people dealt with the devastating effects of
the riot. Fuller said he could still in his mind's eye see the smoke billowing
from cars on fire and hear the rumble of military jeeps screaming up and
down Woodward Avenue. Fuller's parents kept him as sheltered and as far
away from most of the violence as it occurred, but they could not shield
him from the devastation to Black Bottom and Paradise Valley. According to Fuller, Charles and other numbers operators stepped up to help
rebuild the black community by providing resources for food, clothing,
and shelter. Fuller recalled numerous people coming to Charles asking
for assistance with bail, medical bills, and funeral costs. Once again, it
was the numbers men who provided seed money for new businesses and
to the impacted ones.

Shortly after the 1943 riots, Charles completely retired from operating a numbers organization. He sold his interest to another numbers operator and slowly sold off his other real estate interests and businesses before eventually retiring to a farm where he died. Fuller at one point wanted to go into the numbers business like Charles but was quickly discouraged from doing so by his mother and father, who let him know the expectation was for him to obtain an education; however, Charles was the one who ultimately swayed him away from the business. Charles told Fuller it would be a sin against God not to use the gifts given to him simply to chase a dollar. With the stern lecture from Charles, Fuller would go on to get a college degree and use "those God-given talents."

The exit of Charles and the other original numbers bankers marked the end of the first phase of numbers gambling in Detroit.

12
The Aftermath

Judge Arthur Gordon's holding 17 gambling conspiracy defendants for trial in Recorder's Court may surprise people who thought that the O'Hara-Ferguson grand jury had put gamblers out of business in Detroit forever. The grand jury did not attempt the impossible. Gambling is an ancient institution. The public's only protection is an honest police force backed by incorruptible officials. A dishonest minority in the Detroit Police Department, with the connivance of venal City and County officials, took money from the gamblers and let them operate. The jury's job was to investigate this conspiracy and indict public servants guilty of betraying their trust. Gambling will not be abolished, as long as fools and their money are soon parted.

—*Detroit Free Press*, August 26, 1944

Life for many of the major players involved in the MacDonald scandal changed drastically after serving their time in Jackson Prison. The people closest to former Detroit superintendent Fred Frahm felt his downfall was a result of his magnetic personality. Frahm was popular among Detroit's movers and shakers and frequently associated and socialized with the rich and powerful. Frahm wanted their wealth and the lifestyle it provided. His friends believed it was these desires that led him to accept graft payments. After Frahm served his sentence, he returned home to a quiet life very different from his former life; he was rarely seen in public. Frahm became head of security for Pfeiffer Brewing. While on the job, on August 24, 1948, he collapsed and eventually died of a heart attack. He was sixty-two years old.[1]

Former Wayne County sheriff Thomas Wilcox, when released from prison on September 5, 1946, did not immediately gain freedom. He was sentenced to serve five years in federal prison for income tax evasion. Eventually, Wilcox was released and happily visited his old friends at the county jail once more before quietly retiring to his second home in Wisconsin.[2]

Former prosecutor Duncan McCrea, when released from Jackson Prison in 1946 after serving more than three years, promptly built a fortune in the lumber business in Michigan. McCrea had been disbarred for life in 1944, but this did not stop him from trying to get his law license reinstated in 1949. When this failed, he again tried to enter Detroit politics, this time as Detroit councilman; he was unsuccessful. In 1951, McCrea was involved in the construction of a drive-in theater near Mio, Michigan, when he had a heart attack and later died at the age of sixty-six years old.[3] McCrea's memory lives on daily at the Wayne County Prosecutor's Office. On the day he was indicted and arrested, he allegedly left his office so fast that he did not have a chance to grab his Fifth Avenue straw Panama hat from his office closet. The hat remained there for years. It was there in 1967 when Prosecutor William Cahalan entered office. For Cahalan, the hat "was always kind of a reminder that when you left office, it was probably a good idea if you had time to put your hat on first." Cahalan bought a clear plastic case for the hat, and when the prosecutor's office moved, it moved with him. The next prosecutor, John O'Hair, received the hat when he entered office. Cahalan told him the story, stressing the importance of leaving office with pride and dignity.[4] Today, the hat remains in the clear plastic case, mounted on a wall outside of the Wayne County Prosecutor's Office with the story for all to read as they pass by.

Former Detroit mayor Richard Reading was paroled on February 13, 1947, after serving a little more than three years of his sentence. He was released early due to poor health resulting from a heart ailment. After being released from prison, he went to his summer home in White Lake, Michigan, to live with his wife. A year later, Reading was still in trouble with the federal government for income tax evasion. Seriously ill and suffering from high blood pressure, he appeared before a federal judge to face a criminal income tax evasion charge. With a weak smile and described as broken, the man who was formerly known for his gregarious personality pled guilty, refusing to defend himself. The judge fined him $10,000 and gave him thirty days to sell some property to pay the fine. It took Reading ninety days to get the money; however, he was still not out of trouble. He was assessed a $17,026 fine by the Treasury Department in a civil action that resulted from his income tax delinquency.[5] In November 1949, he finally paid the $18,228 that was due.[6] After this, Reading faded from public life in White Lake. His son, Richard Reading Jr., who served less than a year of his sentence in Jackson Prison, suddenly died on November 30, 1951, of a heart attack in a northern Michigan hunting lodge.[7] Nine short months later, Reading's wife, Blanch, died on August 27, 1952. At the age of seventy, on December 5, 1952, Reading suffered a heart attack and was admitted to a hospital in Brighton. Unconscious, he was placed in an oxygen tent and was near death.[8] As always, his son Clarence remained by his father's side, and on December 9 at 9:17 a.m., Reading died.

Everett Watson was paroled to his wife, Ida, just down the road from Jackson Prison to their Grass Lake, Michigan, estate on October 4, 1946. For years Ida had managed many of Watson's business interests. She was accused of running the Yellow Dog numbers house and had even been arrested for her part before charges against her were dropped in 1940. While Watson was in prison, she continued to run his realty company and ensured three hundred houses were built on the southwest side of Detroit for blacks. Not only were the houses built, but Ida ensured all were sold, and the residents were peacefully living in their homes by the time Watson was released from prison.[9] The million-dollar subdivision was slated to be named "The Ida Watson Subdivision" in honor of her, but she refused. She wanted the development named after her husband and stated, "I want my husband's name to live forever." As a compromise, the subdivision was named "Watson Subdivision."[10] By 1948, Watson severed ties with the Paradise Valley Distributing Company and took over ownership of a jukebox business, Ray Music Company. In 1952, *Jet* magazine reported that Ida Watson was managing the Watsons' $2 million business interests.[11] At this point, Ida rarely left the Cherokee Farms estate, where she collected china and books and had an extensive wine collection. Three years later, on August 4, 1955, Ida, who had been battling ovarian cancer, died. She was buried at her beloved Cherokee Farms on a knoll overlooking a lake on the property on August 8, 1955, with hundreds of family and friends attending her funeral. Her burial site was not marked, and as a result, in June 2013, a construction crew building houses on the property stumbled upon her remains. When no relatives were located, her body was buried in a nearby cemetery. After her death, Watson, who had been dealing with arthritis since 1954, continued to run various businesses quietly in Paradise Valley. For five years, he would drive into Detroit to visit his various businesses and to reminisce with his Paradise Valley friends about the good old days.[12] A year before his death, Watson sold a large portion of his Grass Lake property to the state of Michigan.[13] The land was used by the state for an expressway and a state park. Watson died in Detroit on January 18, 1960, at the age of seventy-five after battling a yearlong illness. He was survived by a daughter and two grandsons.[14] He is buried in an unmarked grave at the Detroit Memorial Park cemetery.

Like Watson, John Roxborough was paroled from prison on October 4, 1946. After serving eighteen months in the Jackson Prison, he was freed on a Friday morning. At a little before 8:30 a.m., Roxborough's wife, Wilhelmina, arrived outside the prison gates. Wearing dark sunglasses, she refused to

Figure 17. John Roxborough leaving Jackson Prison on October 4, 1946. Reproduced by permission from the *Detroit Free Press*.

answer reporters' questions. With a smile on her face and her eyes fixed on the prison gates, she waited inside her huge vehicle with her brother for two hours before Roxborough emerged. As he left the prison, he appeared to be nervous but showed signs of relief and happiness. He looked much older than his years. He had noticeably lost weight, and his thinning hair was now more gray than brown. When questioned by reporters, he advised he had no official statement to make about his future until he spoke to Joe Louis. After all, it was Louis into whose custody he was paroled. Roxborough did chat with friends and members of the press he knew but warned them all his remarks were off the record. Right before leaving the prison for good, he shook hands with the prison chaplain before bidding him farewell. As he neared his wife, she continued to smile and greeted him with a kiss before whisking him away from the prison, photographers, and newspaper reporters.[15] Although Joe Louis wanted to throw a large party for his manager, Roxborough declined and opted instead for a quiet dinner at home with him, Wilhelmina, and a few

Figure 18. From left to right: entertainer Romaine Johns, trainer Mannie Seamon, heavyweight champion Joe Louis, John Roxborough, and bodyguard George Webber having dinner sometime after Roxborough was released from prison.

friends. Roxborough declared, "I just want to take it easy for about a week." When asked if he was still Louis's manager, Roxborough affirmed, "I've never been anything else. I'll just pick up where I left off."[16]

And for a while he did just that. Shortly after his release from prison, Roxborough and Louis began a business venture to sell Joe Louis Punch, a soft drink. There were big plans for the beverage, which was sold in thirty-one cities and South America; however, like other Joe Louis ventures, it ended in failure after a few short years. The soft drink allegedly had an awful taste, could not maintain its color, and had no fizzle. In 1946, the pair sold their Utica, Michigan, dude ranch called Spring Hill Farm to the state of Michigan. The more than four-hundred-acre farm, which was once a stop on the Underground Railroad, was purchased in 1939 by Roxborough and Louis. The farm housed horses, a restaurant, a dance hall, and a riding academy. Louis, who loved horses, held several horse shows at the farm. He and Roxborough were credited with getting blacks interested in horses and riding, and as a result, a few black riding clubs formed. For a few years, Louis hosted several horse events at the location and donated the funds to various charities before it was sold.

By 1949, Roxborough stopped managing Louis and became the president of Superior Life Insurance. Roxborough had previously established the Superior Life Insurance Company in 1934.[17] As with numbers gambling, Roxborough operated a successful insurance company based on his reputation for being fair and honest. By 1956, Roxborough's second wife, Wilhelmina, divorced him and was awarded a settlement of $83,000 for repeated acts of extreme cruelty. She testified that she had little knowledge of her husband's finances and complained that in the previous five years he refused to take her out socially and was rarely at home.[18] It was revealed the Roxboroughs' combined property was valued at $208,000. At the age of sixty-seven in 1961, Roxborough was director of sales for Mammoth Life Accident Insurance Company, which had bought out Superior Life Insurance Company and retained his services. By this time, he had lost more of his wavy hair, but his brown eyes still sparkled when he was interviewed by Joe Louis's former secretary Russ Cowans. At this time, the unassuming Roxborough spent his leisure time watching sports, fishing, and smoking the cigars he had loved for years.[19] Five years later, at seventy-four, Roxborough was bald, and his eyesight would eventually fail him. His mind was still sharp, and he had cut down on smoking his much-loved cigars, from twelve per day to four to five. He blamed the twelve cigars per day on stress and revealed he had given up liquor when he developed an ulcer. Approximately twenty-five years after being convicted for his role in running an illegal numbers operation, when asked about it, he minimized his involvement and proclaimed, "I was just a loaner. Just lent the outfit money to get started."[20]

In 1970, Roxborough was honored by the Veteran Boxers Association as "the man who created the Joe Louis image that symbolized him as American as apple pie and ice cream."[21] Roxborough said, "I like to think of Joe as a symbol of the struggle of the Negro in this democracy of ours and what can be achieved by the humblest citizen. He is my ideal of the great American success story come to life and thrillingly realized."[22] The money Roxborough made in the numbers business is directly linked to Joe Louis. With those penny bets, Roxborough purposely developed and created Joe Louis. Louis brought pride to blacks, showed the world blacks could be successful, and helped improve race relations around the world. His story and what he accomplished is one of the most important examples of what the collective pennies from numbers gambling financed. Over his lifetime, Roxborough remained true to his promise to help blacks. He contributed to the Urban League, sent at least thirty students through the University of Michigan, and helped numerous individuals by paying their rent and providing food and coal during hard times.[23] Roxborough also ensured neighborhood playgrounds had equipment, and he frequently supported a number of sporting endeavors.[24] He sponsored softball and basketball teams at Detroit's Brewster Center and the Naval Armory, which gave underprivileged neighborhood children a chance to participate in organized team sports.[25] John Roxborough lived to see the legalization of the lottery but died alone at the age of eighty-three on December 13, 1975, after a lengthy illness. Two hundred people attended his funeral, and Reverend Canon F. Ricksford Meyers said, "His generosity was of tremendously varied dimensions. He was engaged in many enterprises which gave opportunity to young people, and he also gave a financial hand to the poor and needy." He further stated Roxborough's lifelong concern for others "will not escape the piercing eyes of heaven."[26] Although listed as a pallbearer, Joe Louis, Roxborough's surrogate son, did not attend his funeral. Through a spokesman of Caesar's Palace in Las Vegas where Louis was employed as a host, the world learned Louis could not attend his former mentor's funeral because he was away on a business trip. Roxborough never had any children of his own and is buried in a grave without a headstone at the Woodmere Cemetery in Detroit. Only a round stone marked with the number "198" shows where he is buried. In the 1940 version of *The Original Three Wise Men Dream Book*, "198" plays for "free." Roxborough's grave leaves no record of his accomplishments or his contributions to the black community and the city of Detroit.

13

A New Era in the Numbers Racket

Bomb-tossing hoodlums and the strong arm of the law are dethroning Negro racket kings. Huge profits lure organized crime bosses into the number game.

—*Color*, June 1951

When John Roxborough ceased operating his numbers business, he also relinquished control of the wire service to Detroit's Italian mafia. This meant blacks no longer chose the racetracks where the winning numbers were drawn, which resulted in a loss in power. In a sense, whoever controlled the wire service controlled the numbers racket; withholding it from a numbers operator could spell an end to their numbers business.[1] Although the mafia was increasingly taking over the larger numbers operations, a few major black numbers operators like John White still managed to hold on in the black community. This was not the case in Chicago. The year 1946 marked the beginning of the end for black numbers men in that city to the Italian mafia. Edward Jones and his brothers, George and McKissack, started their policy business out of their tailor shop on the south side of Chicago sometime in the 1920s. Edward was head of the business and, over twenty-five years, generated $10–$30 million per year in the policy business.[2]

On January 30, 1941, Edward Jones was sentenced to twenty-eight months in a federal prison after he pled guilty to tax evasion. He was sent to Terre Haute, Indiana, to serve his prison sentence. While imprisoned, he met Sam Giancana, an Italian mobster who was part of the original Al Capone gang. Giancana, who was a low-level mobster at the time, was in prison on a four-year federal sentence for marketing illegal liquor. There he learned of Jones's policy operation on the south side of Chicago and how profitable it was. When Giancana was released from prison, he told the head of the mob that there was huge money to be made in the illegal lottery. Upon hearing this, the mob ordered Jones to be kidnapped.[3] On May 11, 1946, Jones was driving with his wife in Chicago when he was dragged from his car at an intersection. His brother George paid $100,000 to have his brother released on May 16, 1946. Eight hours after the ransom was paid, Edward was released.[4] Shortly after the kidnapping, the Jones brothers relinquished their policy business and moved to Mexico. Their "retirement" left only two other black policy operators in Chicago: Jim Martin on the west side of the city and the Joneses' former employee and partner, Theodore Roe. Martin hung on to his business until 1950, when he was targeted by the mob, who shot at him while he was driving in his Cadillac. After that incident, Martin retired, leaving only Theodore Roe against the mob.[5]

Theodore "Ted" Roe was the last standing black policy operator, who defied the mob on June 18, 1951, after the mob had conducted a series of bombings, shootings, and kidnappings to take over the racket.[6] On that summer day, four men attempted to either abduct or kill him as he was driving in Chicago. Roe stated that a car that looked like a police cruiser pulled up beside him and the occupants shouted, "We're from the state attorney's office. Pull over!" Roe parked his vehicle and demanded the men show him identification. Three men then dragged him out of his vehicle before he was able to pull free. Roe then drew his .38 revolver and fired as the men fired one or two shots at him before fleeing. Roe shot one man, later identified as mobster Leonard Calfano, in the head, killing him. Police concluded the attack against Roe was an attempt by a west-side mob to "muscle in" on Roe's policy operation.[7] After the incident, Roe stated his fight against the syndicate was a single-handed fight. Roe said, "I never have and I never will hide from the hoods. I'm a law abiding citizen, and I intend to stay."[8] Roe was arrested and held without bond for some time before eventually being granted bail and beating the murder charge against him on grounds of self-defense. On August 4, 1952, as he walked from his south-side apartment toward his vehicle, he was shot twice in the chest and once in the neck at close range with a shotgun. His death marked the end of blacks controlling the policy game in Chicago.[9]

Meanwhile in Detroit, blacks were still in charge of numbers gambling in the black community, and the largest numbers operator at that time was John White. John Judson White was born in 1909 in Columbus, Ohio. After his mother died in 1916, a great-aunt raised White, his older brother, and younger sister. He first came to Detroit in 1925 as a teenager. Sometime in his early life, White contracted tuberculosis, and after he recovered he was given a job by John Roxborough.[10] White later moved to San Diego, where he ran an illegal handbook for two years and had a reputation for not paying his customers or the owners he worked for in a timely manner.[11] Back in Detroit, John White was hired by numbers operator Thomas Hammonds in 1937. Hammonds owned a six-chair barbershop, two policy houses, Alabama and Georgia, as well as the Reno and St. Louis, and various real estate interests. At that time, White was paid $100 per week for "secretarial work," which included keeping the books and paying the thirty-one office employees who worked for the policy houses.[12] By 1938, White had a reputation for being exceptional at calculating figures: "Johnny White of Detroit, who is very smart on figures, never uses an adding machine to pay off his customers regardless of how long the line is," and he became known as the bookmaker.[13] By 1940, White was earning $200 per week working for Hammonds and numbers operator Irving Roane.[14]

Three short years later, in November 1943, White went from working for Roane to partnering with his employer to purchase the Gotham Hotel for $250,000.[15] The nine-story, twin-towered Gotham Hotel was located outside of Paradise Valley at 111 Orchestra Place and at the time of its purchase was owned by white businessman Albert Hartz. The fact that a white businessman would sell to blacks was a rarity. When Hartz sold the hotel, assessed at $200,000, to Roane and White, blacks were not allowed nor welcomed as guests. The 200-room hotel was elegant, and at the time of purchase, white guests occupied the entire hotel. Soon after the sale, white guests were given the option to stay in the hotel but decided to vacate. It then became open for black occupancy. Local gossip contended that Hartz sold the hotel to fair-skinned John White not knowing he was a black man.[16] At the time, it was rumored that because White was able to "pass" as a white man, Irving Roane used him as a front man for the purchase of the hotel; however, another explanation for the sale of the hotel could be tied to the fact that the infamous 1943 riots had just occurred in Detroit, and some whites were fleeing from its aftermath.

Racism at this time dictated where blacks lived, worked, played, learned, and shopped. Black Detroiters, regardless of wealth or education level, were discriminated against and treated unfairly. The segregated police department could be cruel and brutal in its treatment of blacks. Black Detroit police officers were only allowed to walk the beat, usually in black areas only, and were prohibited from riding in patrol cars until after World War II. When this ban was lifted, only one patrol car was allocated for black officers' use. This meant that for three shifts, only six black police officers could patrol in a vehicle over the course of a day. There were quota systems in place that restricted the hiring of black officers as well.[17] Very few blacks held positions of authority or command. After former mayor Richard Reading's scandal was exposed in 1940, the city charter established a merit system for promotions. This new system was subjective and allowed for discrimination against blacks.[18] This ensured the police department did not reflect the community it policed and added to Detroit's racial tensions. Several white police officers were responsible for numerous violent racial clashes, while others harassed and were prejudiced in their treatment of black Detroiters. In 1948, Ernest Goodman, a famous Detroit lawyer, summed up the plight of blacks in Detroit: "No white person who has not been intimately associated with at least a few of the numerous instances of discrimination against the Negro people can properly understand and appreciate the subtle and overt indignities under which Negro people live in our community. This prejudice manifests itself most sharply and in its most brutal form when expressed by policemen. For the policeman, in his person, represents the symbol of authority by which discrimination is frequently maintained."[19]

Part of the department's problem stemmed from the fact that many Detroit police officers were recruited from the South. They were rarely prosecuted for their brutal attacks on blacks. Little justice could be found in the court of law for black Detroiters either. It was common for black lawyers, their clients, and witnesses to be treated unfairly and shown disrespect by white judges and lawyers. Regardless of their age or title, white judges would commonly address all blacks by their first name or by a derogatory term. For example, on November 18, 1940, Judge Arthur Gordon, while hearing a case against numbers operator Thomas Hammonds, referred to the sixty-six-year-old Hammonds as a "chap" and called him "Brother Hammonds."[20] Predictably, blacks were also unfairly singled out by Detroit newspapers. Gloster B. Current, executive secretary of the NAACP, wrote a letter to Detroit's editors denouncing such discrimination: "The NAACP again protests the continued use of racial designation in crime news reporting. We have long contended that this practice does irreparable harm to race relations; that it stigmatizes an entire racial group. The daily papers, whenever amateur sleuths imagine a Negro is involved in a crime, without waiting for evidence, proceed to write stories which infer that the crime has racial significance. We have long pointed out that to refer to criminals by race, especially since this practice is confined to the Negro race, continues to give credence to the unscientific belief that one racial group is more prone to criminality than others."[21] Sadly, this practice still takes place today.

Amid this oppressive racial environment, Irving Roane and John White purchased the Gotham Hotel, planning to turn it into a social and business center for blacks who were prohibited from staying in white hotels. The hotel purchase occurred at a time when the city was rebuilding after the destructive riots. Many viewed the purchase of the Gotham Hotel as a much-needed example of blacks breaking the color barrier in Detroit. As such, the Gotham Hotel was advertised as being "A Monument to Our Race."[22] The hotel was in an excellent location, approximately one mile outside of Paradise Valley in what many considered an upscale and refined neighborhood. Its location meant guests had easy access to shopping establishments, theaters, movie houses, and nightclubs that offered the finest musical entertainment in the country at the time. With this in mind, Roane and White ensured the Gotham was a top-notch hotel that featured excellent accommodations and was known for its elegance. At a time when black hotels were few and far between, the Gotham boasted that it offered private bathrooms, telephones, televisions, radios, and air conditioning in every suite.[23] The hotel featured its own laundry services, barbershop, valet shop, flower shop, drugstore, haberdashery, and women's gift shop.[24] The Ebony Room, its prized restaurant, was decorated at a cost of $60,000. It was known for its African wood-carvings, featured a top-notch chef, and was the pride of black Detroit.[25] Music played through the sound system in the hotel's lobby, which was adorned with fresh flowers and hand-painted oil portraits of famous black Detroiters, such as Congressman Charles Diggs Jr., Judge Wade McCree, middleweight boxing champion Sugar Ray Robinson, and drugstore owner Sidney Barthwell. Along with those prominent black Detroiters were portraits of the numbers men John Roxborough, Everett Watson, and Thomas Hammonds.[26]

Many famous black Americans like Sammy Davis Jr., Joe Louis, Dinah Washington, Cab Calloway, Billie Holliday, and Miles Davis stayed at the Gotham Hotel. Ernest Borden, the nephew of John White, said that people from all over the country came to Detroit just to stay at the Gotham. Supreme Court Justice Thurgood Marshall "traveled over 70,000 miles, but

found the Gotham Hotel the most exquisite place to stay."[27] Actress Marla
Gibbs, who at one point worked as a switchboard operator at the Gotham,
recalled that no other black-owned hotel had the class and social standing
of the Gotham, which hosted the who's who of black society.[28] Langston
Hughes wrote an article about the Gotham Hotel in 1945, in which he told

Figure 19. John White in 1954. Reproduced by permission from the *Detroit Free Press.*

of "a kind of minor miracle" occurring in Detroit whereby the elegant and well-run Gotham was owned, managed, and staffed by blacks.[29] One guest of the Gotham indicated "the gentlemen running the Gotham deserve great credit for having furnished for the first time, real hotel service for Negroes."[30] In 1949 John White and Irving Roane announced plans to develop another

GOTHAM HOTEL, John R. St. and Orchestra Place, Detroit, Mich.

Figure 20. The Gotham Hotel owned by Irving Roane and John White. Author's collection.

upscale venue for blacks, a mile-long resort on Lake St. Clair in Canada. The resort would be located near Stoney Point, three miles east of Belle River, Ontario, and was to be known as the "Canadian Riviera."[31] In addition to White and Roane, numbers operator Eddie Cummings and several other prominent Detroit businessmen invested in what would later feature the Surf Club, which wealthy and famous blacks frequented in the 1950s.

John White's employees recognized the influential role he played in their lives. White's employee and secretary from 1951 to 1955, Beatrice Buck, credited White with teaching her half of everything she knew. White generously paid for Buck's college tuition. According to Buck, White was a huge proponent of black pride. He required all employees to belong to the NAACP and to be registered voters.[32] He reportedly kept someone sitting in the lobby of the Gotham to register visitors and guests to vote as they came into the hotel.[33] In addition, White gave generously to the NAACP. Judge Damon J. Keith, who worked as an attorney during the early 1950s, did civil rights work for Detroit's NAACP, which at the time was described as a financial mess. Keith remembered that when there was not enough money to pay operating expenses or salaries, John White provided the funds to keep the Detroit office afloat.[34]

John Dancy, executive director of the Detroit Urban League from 1918 to 1960, recalled that White was highly esteemed in the black community. Dancy found White to be generous in supporting a number of charitable causes, including the Urban League.[35] Although Dancy knew John Roxborough socially and took money from White and other numbers men, they were barred from the Urban League's grounds.[36] When Dancy was called to testify before Judge Homer Ferguson during his one-man grand jury investigation in 1940, he recalled being asked by Ferguson if he had solicited the numbers men for donations and confirmed he had: "I solicited them for the United Foundation and they gave handsomely to the cause." When asked if he had questioned where and how the numbers men made their money, Dancy indicated he had not asked. Dancy's personal view concerning numbers gambling was that it was silly. People who gambled would lose out in the end; however, he felt that gambling was only one of many minor troubles affecting the black community, and he preferred focusing on larger issues.[37]

In addition to providing superior accommodations, the Gotham Hotel also served as the headquarters for some of Detroit's black numbers bankers.

This is not surprising; many of the Gotham's key players had a history with the numbers. John White, Irving Roane, and the hotel manager, William H. Robinson, all had been involved with numbers gambling. Roane pled guilty in 1941 to operating a policy house, and Robinson was found guilty during the same trial as Everett Watson and John Roxborough. White previously worked as an office manager and bookkeeper for Thomas Hammonds and Irving Roane's policy houses in the 1930s and 1940s. In 1940, he testified before Judge Homer Ferguson's one-man grand jury and managed to avoid being prosecuted for his numbers activities.

These respected businessmen, who were a part of the bourgeois black society and derived part of their income from the numbers racket, brought respectability to this type of gambling.[38] In addition to powerful black businessmen, a number of well-regarded "religious figures" made considerable money by selling so-called winning numbers to players. In Detroit, there were many prophets and ministers who sold numbers to their parishioners, but Prophet James Jones arguably was the richest and best known.

Prophet Jones was from Alabama and claimed as a six-year-old boy to have been called to preach by God. Jones came to Detroit an unknown in 1938 but within six years gained popularity. He would go on to be the head of Triumph, the Church and Kingdom, and later the Dominion Ruler of the Church of the Universal Triumph.[39] Jones, who was tall and slim in the 1940s and 1950s, was known for his gold tooth, elaborate wardrobe of 200 suits, $12,000 white mink coat, and over-the-top jewelry, which included an enormous Topaz earring he wore in his left ear. Prophet Jones wore a robe valued at $20,000 while preaching to his flock, on whom he bestowed royal titles such as lady, lord, sir, princess, and prince. He lived in two mansions that he called his castles in the most affluent parts of Detroit. Prophet Jones was able to live such an ostentatious lifestyle because members of his church were generous and regularly bestowed monetary gifts upon him for his so-called healing powers and life-changing prophecies. Prophet Jones also charged people to receive advice, blessings, and special numbers to play in the illegal numbers game. The Charles H. Wright Museum of African American History's exhibit featuring a barbershop from Detroit's Black Bottom tells visitors of Prophet Jones's advice and numbers lines. Patrons could get into Jones's $5 line for thirty seconds, $10 line for one minute, or $20 line to receive numbers or advice. Jones had a radio program, which aired on Sunday mornings and evenings and allegedly reached 100,000 listeners. His radio sermons usually stressed patriotism, and every show began with the singing of "The Star-Spangled Banner" and reciting the Pledge of Allegiance.[40] He told his followers if they obeyed his decrees, all men would become immortal in 2000, ending illness and death. His decrees mainly centered on popularly held beliefs of the time that focused on morality, health, and cleanliness.[41] In spite of these decrees, Prophet Jones had no problem selling numbers to numbers players. His wealth and over-the-top beliefs were featured in *Jet*, *Life*, *Time*, *Newsweek*, and the *Saturday Evening Post*.

Not everyone was taken in by Prophet Jones, and many of Detroit's elite considered him a shyster who took advantage of the poor and superstitious. He was no stranger to law enforcement: in 1956 he was charged with gross indecency for allegedly attempting to engage a young male (who was really an undercover police officer) in a sexual act; and in 1958 he was arrested for possession of 860 numbers slips.[42] In spite of his troubles, many believed Jones could foresee the future, and there are numerous tales of people hitting the numbers after receiving their lucky number from him.

As more and more whites owned and operated illegal numbers businesses in Detroit, the benefits the black community received from the numbers game changed. White numbers operators did not reside in the communities where they conducted business and were not charitable to the community that patronized them. For example, the Polish Bank was a white numbers organization owned by Stanley Brynski, Henry Sobczak, and Edward Kowalski. Brynski owned Boat Center Inc., which sold, stored, and repaired boats. The business was made up of several buildings located on East Jefferson in Detroit; however, Brynski lived in New Baltimore, Michigan. For thirteen months beginning in 1949, Brynski was observed by police officers who gathered evidence of numbers gambling with movie cameras. According to evidence provided during his trial, Brynski's legitimate business also served as the headquarters for his numbers operation. It was believed the Polish Bank grossed $10 million per year.[43] Although the Polish Bank made millions of dollars in black Detroit communities, there is no evidence that the numbers operators were supportive of the black communities they conducted business in.

Although people of all races played the numbers, the belief that only blacks played was *still* prevalent. In response to this false narrative, a columnist wrote a piece called "Numbers and Negroes." The columnist stated:

I'm calling this one Numbers and Negroes because so many policemen and white people would have you believe that ONLY Negroes
gamble this way. The fact is that Americans white and black, gamble
hard and heavy. It is a part of our way of life. . . . But people WILL
gamble. How can they dismiss the get rich quick idea in a nation
where so many of the guys and gals whose names appear in the
SOCIAL REGISTER are themselves, or are the offspring of, pirates,
thugs, thieves and gamblers. . . . Numbers and Negroes might be titled
Numbers and people, because after all when people, regardless of race,
are confronted with the struggle for existence as it hits you in this
country you need to play or fight something.[44]

A 1958 study found that the numbers racket was an economic rather than a
race problem: "It appeals to low income groups because it gives them
a chance to share in the age old mania for gambling without risking large
sums at any one time."[45] Despite all the evidence to the contrary, most people
believed that the majority of numbers gamblers were uneducated blacks.
One Detroit magazine continued to report numbers gambling as a "black"
activity even though whites played as well. Not only did this magazine report
it as a black activity but once again slandered a whole race with sweeping
claims that most blacks played the numbers. The magazine wrote that the
poor odds in the numbers racket were a reflection of the lack of education of
the people who played the numbers and that better-educated, wealthy, and
middle-class people generally did not play the numbers: "the vast majority
of blacks waste much of their meager income playing this generally hopeless
game. Many justify their losses with the argument that it's worth foregoing
a necessity for the chance of gaining a luxury."[46] The Italian mafia knew that
everyone, regardless of race, played the numbers and expanded the numbers
game in the Detroit area. Whereas blacks were restricted in where they could
live and conduct business, race was not an obstacle for the mafia. Mobster
Peter Licavoli, a Grosse Pointe resident and Prohibition-era chieftain, diver-
sified his business interests and became prominent in Detroit's numbers
racket in the late 1940s.

Peter Licavoli was born in 1902 to Sicilian immigrants. He had little
formal education and was purportedly involved in various criminal activities while steadily rising in the ranks before becoming the head of Detroit's
mafia for several years. Licavoli provided hired hoodlums for union busting

throughout the 1930s for the Ford Motor Company.[47] It was alleged he was involved in illegal liquor crimes, gambling, narcotics, prostitution, extortion, murder for hire, and a number of other rackets for years in Detroit. Over his lifetime, he was charged thirty-eight times for crimes including armed robbery, murder, bootlegging, bribing a law enforcement officer, kidnapping, theft, extortion, income tax evasion, and contempt of Congress for refusing to answer questions at a Senate rackets investigation. Tennessee senator Estes Kefauver, known for chairing the United States Senate Special Committee to Investigate Crime in Interstate Commerce, better known as the Kefauver Committee, in 1950 and 1951, described Licavoli as "one of the most cold blooded and contemptuous characters to appear before our committee."[48]

The purpose of the Kefauver Committee was to investigate and expose organized crime across the United States. It did this in part by holding hearings, many of which were nationally televised live in fourteen cities across the country, including Detroit. When the committee held its hearings in Detroit on February 8, 1951, local television station WJBK-TV Channel 2 preempted the regularly scheduled broadcast to televise the proceedings. The next day, WWJ-TV Channel 4 picked up the coverage as well. During the two days of hearings in Detroit, thirty-six witnesses testified about organized crime. The witnesses included members of law enforcement, prosecutors, accused members of the mafia, numbers operators, members from private companies, Detroit's mayor, Michigan's governor, union officials, attorneys, and people from various levels of government. When Peter Licavoli, described as Detroit's top racketeer, was called to testify, he refused to answer most questions posed to him over a two-hour session, including those relating to his occupation, income tax returns, criminal record, and ties to the Detroit crime syndicate.[49] By March 1951, when the committee was conducting hearings in New York, WWJ-TV Channel 4 and WXYZ-TV Channel 7 televised those hearings. As many as thirty million people across the county tuned in to watch the hearings. Fifteen months later, when the hearings ended, they confirmed what the public already knew: that organized crime and corruption existed at various levels, and law enforcement needed to better address these rackets. In its final report, the committee declared it had served as a "powerful searchlight" that exposed widespread national and local crime to the public, and as a result, their efforts had a significant effect on law enforcement.[50]

At this time, Licavoli owned at least two numbers businesses, the Mexico and Villa House and the Chesterfield House, which was described as the largest in Detroit at the time. He also controlled the service, which relayed the winning number daily to numbers operators throughout the state for $15 per week.[51] In addition, Licavoli earned income from the printing of the green sheet, which was a tip sheet sold to numbers gamblers.[52] The green sheet was unique to Detroit numbers gambling. It was printed and distributed by the Detroit Italian mafia, who sold the four-page handbill to numbers operators. The going rate in 1953 was $30 for a thousand copies. Numbers operators either sold or gave the green sheet to numbers gamblers containing "lucky numbers" for players to play.[53] How often those suggested lucky numbers actually fell is unknown, but it is safe to say if they were played heavily they did not fall often. At this time, it was believed numbers gambling generated about $25 million per year in the city of Detroit.[54]

As numbers gambling continued to spread throughout the city, the Detroit Police Department began to use new methods of investigation. Lieutenant Clayton Nowlin, the head of the vice squad, began using movie cameras and photography to capture violators in the act. At the time, this new technology allowed law enforcement to close several numbers organizations, which were earning a million dollars annually. The use of movie cameras and photography was credited with the arrest of 1,500 people, $275,650 generated in court fines, 213 vehicles confiscated, and a quarter of a million dollars seized.[55]

On November 1, 1951, the federal government enacted a law requiring all gamblers to file their names with the Bureau of Internal Revenue. In addition to filing their name, gamblers, including numbers operators, were required to pay $50 for a gambling-tax stamp and a 10 percent excise tax on their annual gross bets to the federal government. Once numbers operators filed their names and paid the fee, they were issued a federal gambling stamp or license and were required to hang the license in their establishment or keep it on their person. Numbers operators in Detroit predicted they would go out of business; they felt after "paying commissions, hits, bonuses, and others for protection, we won't have a horse to ride on." One numbers operator predicted it would be cheaper for him to work for the government if he could be hired to supervise the numbers operation. Another numbers operator wondered how any numbers operators would be able to operate when their names and information would be available to police and prosecutors.

As a result, some Detroit pick-up men advised players they would no longer be able to pick up their numbers due to the impending closure of their
numbers organizations.[56] Even though numbers operators feared the new
federal law would force them to close, this was not the case. Instead, in the
law's first year, 125 people registered as gambling operators in Michigan and
reported they earned $1,048,860 and paid $104,886 in taxes.[57]

As expected, not all numbers operators abided by this new law. John
White refused to purchase the gambling-tax stamp and found himself
involved in another scandal involving numbers gambling and corruption
in the city. In May 1954, White once again was called to testify before a
one-man grand jury. This time, Judge John O'Hara served as the jurist. In
this scandal, more than sixty-five police officers were accused of associating with or taking bribes from a small, newly formed numbers operation.
When questioned, White refused to answer any of the forty-one questions
posed to him concerning his possible involvement in and knowledge of
numbers gambling in Detroit without his attorney present. Judge O'Hara
not only took exception to White's refusal to answer questions but did not
like his defiant attitude. O'Hara noted, "There is one thing the record does
not show, and that was Mr. White's attitude, and I must say that his attitude
was almost insolent in the manner in which he answered questions and his
attitude upon the witness stand. Not only was the personal attitude insolent,
but it was defiant, and I want to put that on the record." White was found
in contempt of court by Judge O'Hara and sentenced to ninety days in jail
and a $250 fine.[58]

Although arrested seven times previously for various crimes involving
gambling, this was the first time White was convicted. White appealed his
sentence all the way to the U.S. Supreme Court on the grounds that Judge
O'Hara did not have the right to deny him counsel and did not have the
authority to both cite and try him. The Supreme Court reversed both
the Michigan State Supreme Court's and Judge O'Hara's decisions by ruling
O'Hara did not have the authority to sentence White for the contempt of
court charge. White was retried for contempt of court in 1956 and was found
guilty by another judge, who sentenced him to sixty days or a $1,000 fine.
White paid the fine. Eventually, forty-seven police officers were suspended
and twenty-one fired. None was prosecuted when the lone witness refused
to testify.[59] Unlike the successful 1940 Ferguson grand jury, O'Hara's was a
disappointing failure and had little impact on numbers gambling. In 1955,

White was called in for questioning when $168,000 was discovered in his safe deposit box in Windsor, Ontario. The money was believed to be from his numbers operation; however, no Canadian laws were broken.[60] Later, White and other black numbers operators extended their numbers operations to "Night Numbers." Night Numbers was an additional numbers game whereby the winning numbers were derived from the night harness races. An FBI report noted, "Informant advised that during the time of year when the night harness tracks are running around the Detroit area there exists in Detroit a gambling operation known as 'night numbers.' Informant stated that the Detroit Italian syndicate has nothing whatsoever to do with 'night numbers,' in Detroit. He added that the payoff in 'night numbers' is still the same, 500–1, however, there is only one winning number each night and this number is taken from harness race results each Monday through Saturday evenings at Hazel Park, Wolverine, Northville and Jackson Park Harness tracks."[61]

Playing the numbers was changing at the same time the neighborhoods of Detroit were undergoing transition as well.

14

The Destruction of Black Numbers and Neighborhoods

However, as to location, the Inner City has many desirable attributes. It is situated in proximity to work places, to the cultural center, to the theatres and shops and public buildings of the downtown civic center. The city's freeways which converge on the Inner City offer fast, safe routes to the corners of the city.

—*Detroit: The New City, Summary Report*
Detroit Community Renewal Program

As the face of numbers gambling changed after the heyday of the 1940s into the 1950s and 1960s, so did the city. Time marched on in Detroit, and houses, buildings, and other structures began to deteriorate throughout the city. This was devastating to a city already dealing with overcrowding and housing shortages. People moved from downtown Detroit to other parts of the city and flocked to the suburbs in a desire to obtain better housing. Most factories in Detroit were built before 1929, and as technology improved and the demand for goods increased, the need for land to update and expand these factories increased as well. Factories, like the city's residents, began to flee the city in favor of the open suburbs. By the 1940s, one-third of the structures in the central or downtown area were considered blighted. In an effort to address this, Detroit mayor Edward Jeffries in 1946 unveiled his "Detroit Plan." Under this plan, the city of Detroit acted as a real estate broker for commercial entities and earmarked several areas in the city for redevelopment. Structures and land located in these redevelopment areas were condemned, acquired, demolished, and sold by the city to land developers. The city's goal was to compete with the suburbs and attract developers back into the city.[1] The Detroit Plan also ambitiously wanted to eradicate overcrowded and unsanitary conditions in densely populated black neighborhoods like Black Bottom, Paradise Valley, and the lower east side. In their place, new modern high-rise projects, hospitals, and other civic institutions replaced the close-knit neighborhoods.[2]

The once vibrant Paradise Valley had begun to feel the stress of aging and overcrowding due to neglect. In 1940, there were approximately 87,000 black residents in Paradise Valley; by 1950, the population had ballooned to about 140,000. No new construction or renovation was undertaken in Paradise Valley once the Detroit Plan revealed the area was being targeted for urban renewal, which also meant owners could not sell their property. This caused Paradise Valley and the surrounding area to be declared the worst slum area in the city.[3] Despite these problems, Detroit led the nation in black-owned businesses.

In 1953, despite the fact that black businesses were unable to buy or rent property outside of black neighborhoods and had difficulty obtaining capital from banks, they flourished in the areas the city deemed "slum." Detroit's black businesses included ten insurance firms, a chain of ten Barthwell drugstores (which earned approximately $2 million per year), five cab companies, seventeen clothing stores, two business schools, a loan company, several manufacturing companies, two machine shops, five wholesale meat companies, two dairies, one fruit and produce company, eighty grocery and meat companies, 150 gasoline and service stations, three furniture stores, twenty florists, 275 dry cleaners and tailor shops, fifteen privately owned hospitals, one new car dealership, two used car dealerships, 150 restaurants, four weekly newspapers, and a number of trade associations that developed their own standards for conducting business. It was estimated in 1951 that 350,000 blacks resided in Detroit, and their total spending potential was about $250 million.[4]

Black Bottom and Paradise Valley were in an area identified as "The Inner City" by city officials, and the city made it clear it had its eyes on the desired land. The area consisted of 10,000 acres of land, and most of the homes, stores, and businesses there were built before 1900. A large portion of the homes were frame construction and did not have central heating or other modern amenities. Detroit was home to ninety-four ethnic groups, and at one point, the inner city was recognized as being a melting pot where a number of groups settled while adapting to American culture. By the

1950s, however, the area was primarily occupied by non-white and lower-income groups. Most of the residents did not own their homes, and those who did generally lacked the means to renovate their homes. The city determined that most of the area was unsuitable for conservation treatment.[5] As such, the city moved forward with aggressive urban renewal projects and proclaimed them "Detroit's success story." Mayor Jerome Cavanagh wrote, "We are witnessing the growth of a magnificent, new inner city. . . . The greatest beneficiaries are the thousands of families that have been relocated from slum housing to decent, clean surroundings."[6] This was not the case, however; many residents found themselves displaced. Exasperated black Detroit homeowners who vehemently disagreed with the mayor began to refer to urban renewal as "nigger removal."[7]

One such Detroiter who felt that way was "Grandma Minerva." Born in Tupelo, Mississippi, in 1911, she grew up poor in the country where community and family ties were strong. As a young adult, she noticed a longtime friend suddenly had money. When she inquired how and where her friend came about her windfall, her friend took her to a nightclub and revealed she was a burlesque dancer. Grandma Minerva, who was an outgoing social butterfly, thought, "What the hell, I might as well!" With beautiful dark skin, a smile that lit up dreary rooms, and an easy laugh, she became a fan dancer in the black Shake Rag community. A sturdy woman who loved to socialize, Grandma Minerva had a reputation as a wild child but made friends wherever she went. Although considered the life of the party, she also had the reputation for being a straight shooter who did not mince words. As she aged, she eventually became a waitress serving drinks and laughs. It was there she met her husband "Ralph" and they married in 1942. Two years later "Winnie" was born in 1944.

Like many other blacks from Mississippi, it was work and opportunity for a better life that called the small family to Detroit in 1946. Ralph was a skilled mason and the booming construction in Detroit was a good fit for him. While he worked, Grandma Minerva became a stay-at-home mother and housewife in Detroit's Black Bottom. She took pride in caring for her family and home, but she struggled with adjusting to Detroit. She felt the city was too fast-paced, and she missed her family and friends, as well as the feel of the much smaller Shake Rag community in Tupelo. Slowly, she adjusted to Black Bottom—to the many people, sounds, and activity. The sense of belonging and community returned. Just as she loved listening to jazz and the blues in Mississippi, she found Detroit offered great music too. Detroit also offered something else: a chance to play numbers. It was playing the numbers that helped her become part of her Black Bottom community. Her numbers writer, "Tony," would sit with her for hours on her front porch. They would talk about everything, from music to neighborhood gossip and of course numbers. Other numbers players would join in, first talking about what number fell and who hit and missed before talking about other things. Slowly, over time, playing the numbers became Grandma Minerva's habit that brought her much joy. She loved how numbers occupied her mind. She loved memorizing dream books and her favorite was *The Original Three Wise Men Dream Book*. It was not uncommon for people to tell her about their dreams and ask her what they played for. When dreams were not enough, she went to almanacs for inspiration and tried to develop systems for picking the next winning number. And then one day, Grandma Minerva's settled life was ripped away by urban renewal. Her small family was forced to vacate their well-kept home in the name of progress.

The small, solid, middle-class family moved from Black Bottom to a home a few miles east sometime in the late 1950s. They were lucky to find housing. At that time, there was still a housing shortage and they were restricted from living in certain areas because of their race. Years later, Winnie noted that the government never built anything on the plot of land where their home was located. To this day, the plot of land is an overgrown field of weeds. Again, Grandma Minerva had to adjust to losing friends and community. For her, urban renewal was personal. It felt targeted because of her race. Its ramifications were great as families, communities, and businesses were lost. This second move was easier because her friend and numbers writer, Tony, moved nearby. He seemed to know everyone, even in this new location, and having that relationship helped. It was one of the few businesses that she remembered from the old neighborhood that survived. Her friendship with Tony, her numbers writer and confidant, lasted for about forty-five years until his death in 1991.

Upon his death, "Josephine" picked up his business of writing numbers for her and the neighborhood, although it was never the same. Josephine did not pay out as well as Tony and did not spend long periods of time on the porch socializing. For the next twenty years until Grandma Minerva's death, she was simply the woman who came daily to pick up Grandma Minerva's $20 a day bets. Her husband, Ralph, died in 1993, and the thrill of playing the numbers helped brighten dark days. Winnie was a grown woman with a child of her own, "Jessie." Jessie, her only grandchild, became Grandma Minerva's world and their relationship grew stronger as Grandma Minerva aged. It was to Jessie and her grandson-in-law that she reminisced about the old days, playing the numbers, and the pain of urban renewal.

While blacks were dealing with the destruction of their communities, they also had to deal with continued racism involving the Detroit police. In the 1950s, blacks made up only 3 percent of the 4,200 officers of the Detroit Police Department.[8] By 1956, black officers were still not allowed to ride in the same patrol car as whites, walked segregated beats, and were prohibited from arresting white criminals. Fred Williams, a black Detroit police officer, recalled that "in those days, the police force was like an occupying white army in the black community. It was domination and fear rather than respect." The police were hated and feared by Detroit's black communities, who expected white police officers to call them offensive names and mistreat them.[9] As if this were not enough, black Detroiters also faced issues due to economic decline, namely, high unemployment rates. One in five Detroit adults in 1950 either did not work at all or worked in the informal economy. This number would continue to grow into the 1960s.[10] Again, numbers gambling provided a sense of hope to those trying to survive.

Under these conditions in 1961, Jerome Cavanagh was elected as Detroit's sixty-fourth mayor, and when he took office in 1962, he appointed George Edwards as Detroit police commissioner. Edwards was an attorney who had previously been a Wayne County and Michigan Supreme Court judge. He had the reputation of being a liberal, and one of his goals was to reform the Detroit Police Department. He believed in the importance of ensuring everyone was afforded equal civil rights regardless of race. Many blacks supported his attitudes toward race relations; however, many whites resented his views. Some of Edwards's strongest critics were Detroit police officers. Many had the attitude that since Edwards was pro-black, any advance for blacks was a loss for whites. They also felt that because he had a record of being a staunch civil rights advocate, this proved he was anti–law enforcement. Edwards believed that improving race relations would essentially improve overall community relations, and he wanted "to maintain vigorous law enforcement while implementing reforms geared towards racial justice."[11] Edwards made it clear he did not believe that crime was a racial problem, rather "the existence of suspicion and distrust between law enforcement officials and the Negro community certainly is."[12] Further, he wanted to promote and safeguard the notion that the law was for everyone regardless of race. These views only added to the distrust that some members of the white community and police department had concerning Edwards and fueled outright mutiny within the department's ranks. For example, several command officers within the police department made it their mission to discredit him and undermine all his efforts at police reform in Detroit.[13]

To gain the trust of blacks and improve police relations, Edwards attended several meetings with black civic and religious groups at which he repeatedly heard complaints concerning gambling in neighborhoods. At one such meeting, one man's concerns struck a chord with Edwards. He wanted to know how he could teach his children to be supportive of law enforcement when the Gotham Hotel operated the numbers racket in plain view. Edwards learned that in addition to the Gotham being an upscale hotel, John White rented space to numbers operators. With this knowledge, Edwards believed that ending gambling at the Gotham was a must for the reputation of the city, the police department, and him. Edwards assumed that by closing the Gotham, members of the black community would see that the police department was serious about eradicating vice from their neighborhoods.[14]

Edwards's opportunity to take down the Gotham Hotel came with the help of Detroit's urban renewal project. John White's Gotham Hotel, just outside of Paradise Valley, was first impacted by integration and later became a victim of urban renewal. Hotels owned by whites slowly began to integrate and allowed black lodgers, and as a result, blacks began to patronize those hotels instead of the Gotham.[15] The Detroit Medical Center had plans to expand, and the Gotham's location fell within its path. In September 1962, the hotel was forcibly and officially closed to make room for this new project. Once White had exhausted all of his appeals to the city in an effort to prevent the Gotham from being demolished, residents of the hotel were forced to vacate. The Gotham's last official day hosting guests was September 8, 1962. On that day, a farewell party was hosted for White. He was presented with a plaque by City Councilman William Patrick and praised for his charitable deeds over the years. Patrick noted the closing of the hotel was the end of an era.[16] Although the hotel was officially closed for occupancy, this did not mean it was closed to numbers operations. Two months after it was closed, on November 9, 1962, the Gotham Hotel was raided by 112 members of the Detroit Police Department, the Michigan State Police, and agents from the Internal Revenue Service in what federal agents called the largest and most successful gambling raid at the time.[17]

On the day of the planned raid, there was some concern that John White would be notified of the impending raid on the Gotham. To prevent this, most of the law enforcement officers had no idea what their assignment would be for the day. They arrived at the Gotham at 5:00 p.m. on Detroit Street Railway buses. The time coincided with the time numbers workers would be counting receipts. The Gotham was considered immune from police activity and was known as "The Fortress" because of the difficulty officers had in obtaining warrants to halt the illegal gambling activities that took place within its walls.[18] The Gotham's security measures were considered daunting. Lookouts were placed throughout the hotel to sound an alarm if police officers entered the hotel. A closed-circuit television was in the lobby to forewarn operators of police activity, and as an added measure, numbers offices were frequently moved within the hotel.[19]

On the day of the raid, an undercover federal agent was placed inside the hotel to prevent the lookouts from activating the alarm system. Although the agent was able to prevent the lookouts from alerting White and the other occupants, a hotel employee managed to shut down the elevator to give them a chance to lock up or destroy evidence. Once law enforcement agents were inside the Gotham, they proceeded to open every door in the hotel with an ax. John White and other infamous numbers operators were arrested and federally charged with tax evasion and failing to obtain a gambling-tax stamp; however, not every numbers operator was arrested on that day. Eddie Wingate, another well-known numbers operator whose numbers headquarters was located in the Gotham, was not present and avoided arrest.[20] Wingate frequented the Gotham Hotel on a regular basis, and at the time of the raid was considered one of Detroit's top numbers operators. Shortly after the Gotham was raided, Wingate left Detroit for Miami, Florida.[21] In total, forty-one people were arrested. White was arrested in his penthouse suite. He and a few other gamblers were gathered around a billiard table shooting dice. On the billiard table was $3,500 in cash. Raiding officers found at least one numbers office on every floor of the Gotham. These offices contained work stations equipped with adding machines, and the windows were covered to prevent anyone from observing what was occurring in the room. The linen closets did not contain linen; rather, they contained copious boxes of coin wrappers. Overall, the Gotham gave the appearance of what it was, a numbers factory.[22]

The search of the Gotham took twenty-four hours to complete; all told, 160,000 bet slips, $60,000 in cash, various records, thirty-three adding machines, eleven safes, and other gambling paraphernalia including playing cards and dice were seized.[23] Examination of the seized records revealed the Gotham grossed $15 million per year, and an investigation of the playing cards and dice revealed the cards were marked and the dice were crooked. Information was also found on-site that showed the winning numbers were frequently fixed against heavily played numbers, which prevented high payoffs.[24]

After being released on a $10,000 bond, John White went to black newspapers to tell his side of the story. White stated that the raid was needless and uncalled for because there was no evidence of illegal numbers operations. After all, he declared, no one was actually caught in the act. White claimed the law enforcement officers broke into his hotel "like members of the Notre Dame football team" armed with axes and sledgehammers that they used to break down every door in his hotel.[25] White alleged the law enforcement officers, while in his hotel for twenty-four hours, drank up all of his personal whiskey, milk, and soft drinks and ate all of his food.[26] He was upset with one particular black Internal Revenue Agent named "Brown" who was an integral part of the hotel raid. White felt that much of the damage was done by the Treasury agents who were trying to get promoted, specifically Agent Brown.[27]

When White complained to law enforcement authorities about the damage done to his hotel, he was told the damage was of no concern to him because the building was being taken over by the Detroit Medical Center. In spite of this claim, White was still the owner of the hotel and had not received any money from the Detroit Medical Center for its purchase.[28] As to the charges concerning crooked cards and dice, White stated, "Making all that show about crooked cards and dice over the television and employing a professional card manipulator to show how things were done was might cheap and dramatic for a man of the Commissioner's stature."[29] Edwards was pleased with the results of the raid, and in the "Personals" of the *Detroit Free Press* placed an ad that said, "TO ANY Anonymous Correspondents of 1962—Thank You! Keep writing!" When questioned about his ad, Edwards stated that an anonymous letter led to the raid on the Gotham Hotel. He said, "We had about 20 letters last year that proved valuable, and so we wanted to thank the people."[30]

The raid also revealed the connection between John White and Detroit's mafia when law enforcement found the private phone numbers of mafia members Anthony Giacalone and Peter Licavoli in White's office. White refused to comment when asked if he was affiliated with the syndicate. He also refused to comment on having any knowledge concerning the "fixing" of numbers.[31] Law enforcement authorities believed that White and other black numbers operators ran their own operations but were affiliated with the mafia for a few services. For example, they depended on the mafia for the daily winning number combinations, protection from law enforcement, and the printing of number paraphernalia like green sheets and "K" books. Green sheets were used by number players as a guide, and "K" books were used by numbers writers to record bets.[32]

An FBI informant revealed that the mafia had previously issued strict business protocols as to who could sell numbers and where numbers could be sold. No numbers could be sold in John White's territory or in Peter Licavoli's Murphy House territory. A month after the raid, black numbers operators, including White, met with Detroit's Italian mafia leaders Peter Licavoli, Mike Rubino, and Anthony Giacalone. According to the FBI, Eddie Wingate was also at the meeting that took place on December 26, 1962.[33] Giacalone, the enforcer for the Detroit mafia, worked for Licavoli. Like Licavoli, Giacalone had an extensive arrest record, which included car theft, rape, armed robbery, assault, illegal gambling, bribery of a police officer, income tax evasion, loan sharking, and fraud.[34] On August 9, 1954, he was arrested for bribery when he approached a Detroit police officer and offered to pay him $200 per month for information on any future gambling raids. As a result of this, he was charged, convicted, fined $500, and sentenced to eight months in the Detroit House of Corrections.[35]

The meeting between John White and the mafia took place at a Detroit restaurant to repair a rift between the two groups. The goal of the meeting was to cement relations between the members of the Italian mafia and the major black numbers bankers.[36] The Italian syndicate at that time still controlled how and what winning numbers were announced. The black numbers operators were infuriated that the mafia at times changed the winning numbers to avoid high payoffs. Changing the number contradicted the image the black operators had of being honest and operating a fair game. How the winning number was determined at this point was not at all straightforward. The two winning three-digit numbers were picked by using the figures in horse-race payoffs for winning bets at a selected track. The numbers were derived from the prices paid for win, place, and show in the first four races at a selected track, which were then added together. The third digit from the right in this total became the first digit of the first winning number for the day. The second and third digits were obtained by similar manipulations involving the fifth and sixth races at the selected track. The second daily winning number was found by using the last digit of the first race number plus adding in the pari-mutuel totals for the seventh and eighth races at the selected track.[37] This complicated formula made it easy for the mafia to make adjustments if a number was heavily played. As a result of the meeting, the mafia agreed always to publish the correct winning number and no longer change it for profit.[38]

In January 1957, the U.S. Senate established the Select Committee on Improper Activities in Labor and Management, chaired by Senator John McClellan of Arkansas. The purpose of the committee, also known as the McClellan Committee and the Senate Rackets Committee, was to establish the relationship between organized crime and labor-management. Attorney General Robert Kennedy was the committee's chief counsel and the raid on the Gotham caught the committee's attention. In a statement given on September 25, 1963, to the Subcommittee on Investigations of the Senate Government Operations Committee, Kennedy said that the raid on the Gotham was an example of "dedicated, honest and courageous police action."[39] A month later, Police Commissioner George Edwards testified before the McClellan Committee's hearing on organized crime that Peter Licavoli was one of five mafia heads of illegal enterprises that grossed a total of $150 million a year.[40] Prior to Edwards's testimony on Friday, October 25, 1963, the Detroit Italian mafia numbers houses closed down. They were no longer in the numbers racket. Police were not sure why but believed the mafia feared local prosecution, which could stem from Edwards's testimony. The *Atlanta Daily World* reported that "for the first time in 40 years, the numbers racket here, conducted for the most part by Negroes, and which at one time grossed more than $21 million dollars in annual business went 'completely dead' for four days last week. Why the sudden shutdown? There were reports that the La Cosa Nostra crime syndicate, which reportedly had moved in to finance the numbers operation with big money, had ordered the clamp down because of pressure from law enforcement agencies."[41] Another report claimed that on October 25, 1963, Detroit's top mafia boss ordered his organization out of the business of collecting numbers bets, although the mafia still controlled how the winning number was chosen. The mafia's only role was to sell the winning number to black numbers bankers for a monthly percentage. At that time, it was reported again that the Detroit numbers were fixed by the mafia; however, a second winning number called the Pontiac number was fair and honest. Many years later, it was revealed this was true, and mafia member Rip Koury was responsible for choosing the Detroit number. Detroit bankers would call each evening to report the numbers that were heavily played with how much they would lose if the number fell. Koury would then choose a winning number that would not "break" the bank, while still ensuring some won. "We gotta have winners," Rip said, "or people don't play. We just don't gotta have *big* winners."[42]

While awaiting trial, John White procured a suite at the Mark Twain Hotel to continue operating his numbers business. He had a suite on the first floor to conduct his business, and hotel owner Sunnie Wilson recalled seeing white numbers operators coming to see White and giving him money. In July 1963, the Gotham was demolished. On the day it was torn down, Wilson drove White to the site so he could witness the wreckage; the scene brought White to tears.[43] As the 4,800-pound wrecking ball hit the hotel, old checks, hotel registration forms, bet slips, and money wrappers floated to the ground.[44] While the hotel was being demolished, the wife of the original owner of the thirty-nine-year-old hotel, Alice Hartz, recalled that when her husband first had the hotel built, it offered quiet residential accommodations to the city's leading artists and musicians, namely members of the Arts & Crafts Society of Detroit and the symphony orchestra. Hartz indicated after nineteen years, her husband had to sell the hotel because of other business interests, and shortly after, the hotel became known as a gambling mecca. As it was for White, for Hartz the demolition was emotional; she could barely watch it being torn down.[45] Many were saddened to see the Gotham demolished, and some felt it was a personal attack on the black community. William Hines, a Detroit resident, recalled, "I remember the destroying of the Gotham Hotel, which surpassed all black-owned businesses at the time as the number one hotel in America, even superseding New York's. This was entirely Class A. Harper Hospital fought us over getting a liquor license so we could have a beautiful lounge. They did everything to stop us. Sure, every black was aware that that was the resting place for the numbers. That's when the officials discovered how much money was in the black community, and they proceeded to destroy it when they discovered it."[46] For Detroit's black community, the Gotham was more than just a hotel or the headquarters for numbers gambling. It was the place where dreams were made for many. It was where political campaigns were planned and launched and where financial deals were sealed for blacks who were shut out of opportunities from mainstream financial institutions.[47]

A year later, on July 8, 1964, while awaiting trial, John White died at the age of fifty-five of a heart ailment. He had been hospitalized three times since the raid on the Gotham. Some believed that the loss of the Gotham triggered White's death. At his funeral, hundreds paid their respects to a man who was credited with being a benefactor of many worthy causes, including financing the education of many of Detroit's young people.[48] Reverend Otis Saunders made the following remarks concerning White: "[He was] a man who has a lot of people 'searching themselves' and if they do a thorough job, they may (and I'm sure they will) find something that could have kept John White on this earth." In a popular newspaper column read by many black Detroiters, White was commended for bringing about a new community for blacks when he bought the Gotham. He was praised as "a man who couldn't say no to anyone who needed a helping hand; a man who, regardless of his prolonged illness, took time out to shelter others; a man who decided to go 'upstairs' to lighten the load of a few cowards who turned their backs on him when he needed them most . . . John White was one who loved to wager. They called him a gambler. We all are in a world of chance, but I would like to set the record straight. John was honest and had he been the type of man whom an Ohio judge and few others would have you believe, he would have been twice a millionaire."[49]

The Gotham Hotel was such a source of pride for blacks in the United States, the Charles H. Wright Museum of African American History in Detroit has a small exhibit featuring it. In 2009, the images of numbers operators John White and Irving Roane were immortalized in stone at Detroit's Paradise Valley Park. The memorial park was created to pay tribute to the once thriving black entertainment district and to honor the men and women who made it possible.

With the closing of the Gotham Hotel, the face of playing the numbers changed again, opening the door for the Italian mafia to take a larger portion of the numbers racket in Detroit.

15
Big Ed and Detroit's Italian Mafia

WINGATE reportedly remains in control of Negro numbers operation in Detroit, Mich., with actual operation believed to be handled by close relatives and associates. Investigation indicates possible violation of ITAR—GAMBLING Statute on part of Wingate and associates. Separate case being investigated.

—Federal Bureau of Investigation, May 14, 1964

The destruction of the Gotham Hotel did not end numbers gambling in the city. It simply meant black numbers operators like Eddie Wingate relocated their operations. Wingate was the oldest child of Eddie Sr. and Esther "Eaddy" Wingate, born on November 13, 1919, in Moultrie, Georgia. He had six siblings and was in the eighth grade when his father, a farmer and later barber, became ill. As a result of his father's illness, Wingate dropped out of school to care for his family. According to one source, he picked cotton and worked in a slaughterhouse before eventually heading north to Detroit sometime in the 1930s to work at the Ford Motor Company. While at Ford, shrewd Eddie Wingate Jr. saved his money and began to branch out into other ventures, including owning and operating his own cleaners, barbershop, and restaurant.[1] On June 23, 1942, Wingate married Ethel, and eventually co-owned City Cab. At some point, Ethel handled the operations of the taxicab business. Wingate dabbled in the talent business and became the owner and executive director of Standard Theatrical Enterprises, a talent agency whose motto was "The House That Builds Stars."[2] Eventually, Wingate became a numbers operator.

Exactly when he became engaged in the numbers business is unclear, but the FBI believed he began in 1950 and by 1952 had made it big.[3] According to his FBI file, Wingate was arrested on February 7, 1958, for conspiracy to violate the state of Michigan's gambling law, and charges were dismissed on April 15, 1958. Two months later, on June 2, 1958, Wingate was arrested for operating a numbers house, but charges were dropped the next day. In July of that year, *Jet* magazine reported that Wingate was Detroit's "new numbers banker" who spent "money like crazy."[4] Wingate's FBI file also contained information concerning his alleged girlfriends.[5] In March 1959, an FBI agent reported that Eddie Wingate was attempting to buy $50,000 in

Figure 21. Ed Wingate. Artwork by Avery Sky.

stock in a company being formed by numbers kings Irving Roane and John White. Roane and White were negotiating for the purchase of a rubber plantation in Liberia, and Wingate wanted in.[6] At 6'2" and weighing 245 pounds, "Big Ed," who it was rumored had come to Detroit on a freight train and built a numbers empire by at times not making payoffs, had finally arrived.

In 1962, Wingate formed and operated Golden World Records on the west side of Detroit. He hoped to cash in on the recording industry after witnessing the success of Motown Records. Wingate ran the record label with Joanne Bratton. He bought the company's first recording equipment and set it up in the basement of Joanne's mother's house. Later, Wingate built a recording studio that was second to none on Davison Avenue on the city's west side. He gained a reputation as a big spender with the musicians, and it was not uncommon for him to pay them in cash for their services. Some affectionately called him "Uncle Ed," while others at Golden World felt it was ridiculous to call him uncle. Rather, they remembered him as a cold and unfeeling gangster.[7]

Wingate wanted a recording company that was professional and would be known for its high-end recording studio. He accomplished just that, and soon enough, Wingate's Golden World Records put out several records that were commercial successes. As a result, Golden World was competing with Motown Records; Berry Gordy bought Golden World Records from Wingate in 1966.[8]

Although Wingate had a few legitimate businesses, he successfully continued to run his numbers business. An FBI informant in June 1963 reported that Wingate had more numbers businesses than anyone else in Detroit. He accomplished this by paying pick-up men more money than anyone else. This move ensured he took the lion's share of Detroit's numbers. He effectively took John White's place as Detroit's number one numbers operator. His business tactics so infuriated the mafia that they shot at him on two occasions in 1959 and 1962. At that time, it was estimated Wingate's numbers operation was doing a daily business of $40,000 to $50,000. Again, it was rumored that police were being paid for protection.[9]

No longer operating out of the demolished Gotham Hotel, Wingate was operating his numbers business out of the Algiers Motel, of which he was part owner by 1964.[10] The Algiers Motel, located on Woodward Avenue in Detroit, became infamous during Detroit's 1967 riot. On July 26, 1967, three young black men were murdered inside the motel by three white police officers. The investigation of the homicides and subsequent trials of the accused gained national attention, and eventually the police officers were acquitted. Due to the national attention, the city of Detroit took a hard look at the motel and concluded it was a public nuisance; it was considered a haven for lewdness and prostitution. As a result, the county prosecutor filed suit against Eddie Wingate and the other owners of the motel requesting it be abated.[11] By this time, Wingate had already moved his numbers operation to his newly built Twenty Grand Motel located at West Warren Avenue and 14th Street on the city's west side. Like the Gotham Hotel, the Twenty Grand Motel served other purposes.

Wingate and his business partner, Ernest Mackey, built the Twenty Grand Motel for approximately $500,000. The two-story structure had fifty-two units and included a penthouse. At the time of its grand opening on July 31, 1966, it was called one of the city's plushest and was adjacent to the 20 Grand, a famous nightclub, which was not owned by Wingate. Each room in the motel had "its own theme and personality, with wall-to-wall carpeting, modern paintings and king-size beds."[12] When the 1967 riots broke out nearby, it was rumored that Wingate put employees armed with shotguns on the roof of the hotel, and as a result, no one dared damage his property.

By 1968, the Detroit Italian mafia was reportedly back in the numbers business and not just providing the winning number. They set out to take over as much of the numbers market as they could and successfully ran some black numbers operators out of business by financially ruining them and enticing their numbers writers to work for them. Exactly how they did this was revealed in a *Detroit Free Press* three-part article on the numbers racket. The author, Tom Ricke, indicated he spent over a month with numbers runners to gather information for his article. One of the people Ricke interviewed was a black numbers operator known as "Joe." Joe fell victim to the mafia's strategy. He claimed the mafia would have men "load up" or place many bets on the Detroit number. The mafia fixed the number to "bust" the other numbers bankers, who would be unable to make all the payoffs. Joe claimed that on July 19, 1968, they made the winning number 788, and as a result, he had to pay out one of their men $20,000 when the number fell. A few months later, they again fixed the number, 824, and Joe lost $28,000 that month. To add insult to injury, two years later, Joe stated he placed a $40 bet on 747 that fell. To keep from paying him, the mafia changed the winning number. As a result, Joe learned he could not fight the mafia and greatly reduced the amount of his business, and as a result, the mafia then left him alone. What the mafia did to Joe was not uncommon. The Italian mafia often changed a number and ensured that their people hit big with independent numbers operators. This in turn would bankrupt the independent numbers operators who could not afford to pay off the winning number.[13]

"James," another man interviewed by Ricke, ran numbers for more than thirty years. During that period, he had been taken to police headquarters more than two hundred times for numbers running. He reported it was harder for him and other old-time numbers writers who were smaller operators.[14] James felt the biggest change and problem with Detroit's numbers gambling at that time was the Italian mafia. He said they took the numbers business away from several blacks and ran what was widely believed to be a fixed game whereby it was simply impossible to win. The fix was in for two reasons: it ensured the mafia generated the largest profit possible for them and kept out any independent numbers operator from running their business.[15] As telephones became more readily available, this too impacted the numbers business. Not all numbers writers went door to door. People simply and conveniently called in their numbers, and this spelled the end for many numbers writers.

Another blow to black numbers operations occurred when the mafia began to lure their numbers writers and pick-up men and women away from their organizations by offering more money, which included 25 percent of the profits and $50 per-week expense money as an incentive. At this time, numbers writers and pick-up men and women were the heart and soul of a numbers operation. Detroit's black community knew their numbers writers. They trusted them and had relationships with writers who often were part of the community. Simply put, the Italian mafia was not part of the community and would not be accepted. For the mafia to keep the business in these close-knit communities, it was imperative they put the black numbers writers and pick-up men and women on their payroll. As the writers and pick-up men and women left the black organizations, they took their clients and business with them. For the black numbers operators who were able to keep their operations going, they ended up sharing their profits 50–50 with the mafia.[16]

With the influx of the mafia into numbers gambling, older black numbers runners lambasted the new numbers game. They felt it was no longer run by respected black community leaders but by the dishonest Italian mafia who ensured no one could surmount the impossible odds and win: "The numbers man is no longer a community leader. He and the minister used to hold the respect of their neighborhoods. Families on welfare who placed their nickel bets with the numbers man everyday got free turkeys on Thanksgiving if they couldn't afford them."[17] The *Detroit Free Press* reported the business of selling money dreams via crooked numbers had become sophisticated with the upper tier making all the money, while the poor remained poor. The masses, who could only dream of getting rich, continued to buy dream books, lucky incense, and oils while praying and holding out hope that their big payday would come someday.[18]

Even in the underground economy, race and socioeconomic status played major roles in the lives of the have-nots. Like mainstream society, the underworld played its part in keeping the oppressed, specifically blacks, beleaguered. In 1969, *Detroit Scope Magazine* reported that organized crime was one of the most important factors in keeping people in poverty. They estimated that 30 percent of all money that organized crime made came from "ghetto dwellers." The article went on to say that the mafia derived a great deal of money from the numbers racket, gambling, prostitution, and narcotics. They further noted, "The Mafia benefits from the continuation of poverty and racial oppression, because poor, uneducated, economically weak people are the easiest prey for its vicious activities, which in turn help keep its victims enslaved in poverty. Throughout the last decade, the Mafia has operated to an increasing extent as an equal opportunity employer, hiring black hoodlums and permitting blacks to run numbers and bookie operations. But, like many organizations in the world of legitimate businesses, the Mafia does not permit blacks into upper echelon executive positions—mostly because that is a matter of family and nationality."[19]

Although the face of numbers gambling was changing, law enforcement continued to go after the racket. On May 11, 1970, law enforcement staged the largest gambling raid in American history when three hundred FBI agents arrested fifty-eight people at thirty-six locations throughout the metropolitan Detroit area. Those arrested were middle-level to upper-level managers of the numbers racket. With the raids and arrests, FBI director J. Edgar Hoover declared that the mafia-controlled numbers racket had been eradicated in Detroit, and this meant that twelve to fourteen thousand people who worked for numbers operators were unemployed. The FBI shut down numbers operations that they believed took $94 million per year in bets by putting wiretaps on the operations' telephones.[20] Law enforcement realized the telephone had changed how numbers operations ran and, in response to this, changed their tactics by eavesdropping on telephone calls made to and from numbers establishments. With these wiretaps, law enforcement learned that the numbers were in fact rigged to ensure that heavily played numbers did not fall. The FBI reported that the Detroit Italian mafia made $18,000 per month from simply supplying the winning numbers to independent numbers operators in the city and an additional $10,000 per month for protection. Those named in profiting from this were Anthony Giacalone and Louis "Rip" Koury.[21] By this time, it was estimated that 30,000 Detroiters played the numbers, and when including the Detroit suburbs, estimates reached 150,000. Most bets were for one dollar, but many players played $10 to $20 per bet.[22] Although the FBI touted they had eradicated numbers gambling in Detroit, it was reported their big bust was in fact a bust. The day after their raids, the numbers game was back in operation.[23] The *Afro-American* reported that the raid was an unsuccessful attempt to quash the mafia-dominated numbers racket in the Detroit area.[24]

Figure 22. Louis Koury (*left*) and Anthony Giacalone (*right*) in court in February 1969. Photo courtesy of *Detroit News*.

Just two years later, law enforcement would again stage raids and arrest numbers operators. At this time, the importance of race and socioeconomic status in the numbers racket was noticed not only by Detroit's black community but also by the judicial system. Detroit Judge George Crockett Jr. declared, "There seems to be a tendency for the law to work one way for the poor and the Black and another for the wealthy and the white." When the arrested numbers workers came before Judge Crockett, their defense attorneys presented a motion questioning the lawfulness of the arrests, while the prosecution vacillated on charges. In response, Judge Crockett ordered all the arrested released. He further told prosecutors not to bring in any more similar cases unless they were prepared to go to the suburbs and arrest the people who really profited from the numbers game.[25]

In March 1972, the Michigan legislature passed a proposal that was slated to go before the voters to legalize the lottery. Judge Crockett stated, "Maybe this will get rid of the numbers business and make gambling a state monopoly; then the proceeds, hopefully, will be to underwrite projects for social change, such as hospitals, schools and recreational facilities."[26] Many argued that Detroit's black numbers operators of the past had done just what Judge Crockett hoped a state-run lottery would do.

At this point, the Detroit Police Department estimated that about 100,000 people or one in fifteen Detroiters played the numbers every day, many of whom were black and lived in the ghetto. One reporter wrote that numbers started in the ghetto and was still there. Further, he reported, numbers was the only way for many to get money, was a habit for others, and for still others was a way to buy dreams to get them through empty days. For the price of a ticket, many purchased a thought. They purchased the right to dream all day about what they would do with the money if they won.[27]

By October 1972, Wingate's Twenty Grand Motel was raided by federal, state, and local law enforcement agencies as part of a four-month investigation into numbers gambling. The motel was considered the primary headquarters for the $11 million per year operation and "the largest volume of daily business of any illegal gambling setup in recent times."[28] As always, Wingate, known for his ability to stay one step ahead of law enforcement, again avoided prosecution. This was the cost of doing business and was a minor inconvenience. He and other numbers operators now had to contend with a bigger inconvenience: the legal numbers man—the state of Michigan.

16
What about the Women?

Fannie Davis, a Detroit Numbers Queen

Fred Astaire was great, but don't forget that Ginger Rogers did everything
he did, backwards . . . and in high heels.

—Bob Thaves, *Frank and Ernest*, 1982

Most of this book has focused on numbers men, but women were major
players as well. These women maintained respectability, cared for their families, and ran a numbers operation. When Fuller Hit (chapter 11) was asked
about the role of women in numbers gambling, he laughed and said their
role was to marry a numbers operator. The story of gun-wielding Ida Watson
told a different tale. In 1936, Ida fought off armed robbers to keep them from
accosting her husband at their home. In 1941, at least two people testified
that she was the "boss" of Everett Watson's numbers organization in his
absence, and at one point, she was responsible for running her husband's
real estate company, jukebox corporation, and approximately $2 million
worth of assets. Ida challenged gender and race norms at a time when it was
unheard of for a black woman to have such power and independence. Not
only did she literally participate in community building by being the driving
force behind much-needed homes being constructed for blacks, but she was
active in numerous Detroit charity organizations raising money for various
causes including the NAACP and the Detroit Community Fund Campaign.
As Elizabeth Schroeder Schlabach noted when discussing black women in
Chicago's policy game, Ida was able to be a part of an illegal business while
at the same time maintaining respectability in the community.[1]

Fannie Davis is another example of a woman who independently operated her own numbers business in Detroit and still commanded respectability in her community. "A friend to many," "kind," "generous," "intelligent,"
and "classy" were used repeatedly to describe Fannie Davis.[2] She was born the
ninth of ten children some time in 1928 in Nashville, Tennessee. Fannie, at
eighteen and a high school graduate, married in 1946 and would eventually
have five children. In 1955, like many other blacks, Fannie and her husband
made the migration north to Detroit, dreaming of relief from the South's Jim
Crow laws and praying for a better life, which would include a good-paying
job in one of Detroit's many factories. General Motors hired her husband,
and their family settled on the west side of Detroit. At that time, more and
more middle-class blacks were moving to the west side, also called "the best
side" by many west-side blacks. Blacks who managed to escape to the
west side considered it an oasis because of its well-kept homes and land-
scaped yards. Two-parent homes were the norm there, which offered better housing and schools for children. Mothers tended to be respectable
homemakers and fathers were the sole breadwinners. One resident, Sue-
setta McCree, felt that the families of the west side had similar values. She
explained black families shared a belief in God, in following the law, in having a strong work ethic, and in valuing education.[3] The west side for many
blacks became symbolic of finally having arrived in middle-class America.

While Fannie Davis's husband worked on the assembly line, she was a
homemaker who epitomized what it meant to be a respectable middle-class
black woman. Fannie was more than this, however; she worked on the side
as a numbers writer. Fannie had played the numbers in Nashville and had a
brother who was a numbers pick-up man. When she came to Detroit,
numbers gambling was nothing new to her, and she started, like most, as a numbers writer who turned in the numbers she wrote to a numbers operator.
For her efforts, Fannie was paid the standard percentage for the numbers
she wrote and at one point wrote numbers for Ed Wingate. According to
Fannie's daughter Bridgett Davis, it is unclear how her mother met or began
working for Wingate, but she may have met him through her brother, who
was a horse trainer who had dealings with Wingate because of Wingate's love
of horse racing. At the time Fannie worked for Wingate, he was one of the
biggest numbers operators in Detroit. While working for Wingate, Fannie,
who by all accounts was considered lucky because she hit the numbers often,
put a nice sum of money on a number and won a substantial amount of

money from him. This windfall allowed her to realize a part of her American dream: to purchase a home for her family. But more importantly, it allowed her to end writing numbers for Wingate. According to Fannie's daughter, her mother bought a house on the northwest side of Detroit prior to white flight. Fannie wanted to live where white Detroiters lived because that was where good basic services like schools, decent grocery stores, street lights, and regular trash collections were available. Homeownership meant greater security and freedom. An article in the *Detroit Free Press* in 1951 noted there was no greater stabilizing factor for a family than owning a home. Homeownership meant satisfaction, happiness, and enhanced standing in the community. It also marked the homeowner as a good citizen and provided "an anchor in a storm—a roof over one's head in times of adversity."[4] Fannie's windfall also made her an independent numbers operator by the late 1950s.

It was during this time that a new black society emerged as well as a new attitude concerning playing the numbers: "With the emergence of the new Negro 'society,' playing the 'numbers' has become respectable. This is not strange, since some members of 'society' derive their incomes from the 'numbers.'"[5] In other words, playing the numbers was no longer considered the pastime of lower-class gamblers. Fannie's father had been a businessman in the South and she witnessed how he was treated by whites. Fannie knew that if she wanted to be successful, she had to operate and control her own business and depend on black clients. She had no desire to work for whites, nor wanted to be a part of the black bourgeoisie. Bridgett remembered the numbers business was a good match for her mother because of her natural business skills and her personality. In addition, Fannie was a stay-at-home mother, and the operation allowed her to care for her family and run her own business from her home. Fannie believed in and loved beauty, and the numbers allowed her the resources to indulge. Bridgett stated, "She traveled, she dressed beautifully, she gave her children good educations, trips, creature comforts, a feeling of being cared for and safe, and most of all—a sense of entitlement. She preached self-worth."

Fannie was happy she no longer worked for Wingate and felt that being the "middleman," as a numbers writer, would never allow her to access the real profits of the numbers business. She knew that running her own numbers business meant taking on risk but she was willing to do so. Fannie had figured out the key to running a successful numbers business "was to be lucky enough to not get hit for a certain amount of time; after that, for the most part your customers will pay for each other's hits." By 1960 or 1961, her business was thriving. At its height, she had ten to fifteen people who wrote numbers for her. The number of people that the writers took numbers from varied. Fannie also took numbers directly from special customers. She obtained these customers via word of mouth from friends of friends, and they sought her out because she had a reputation for being honest, fair, and likable. Her numbers organization was known for being reliable, organized, and very well managed. She was seen as successful, and some interpreted that as her being a lucky person. People wanted to be around her success in the hope that her luck and success would somehow rub off on them. She took customers' numbers at the same time every day, collected from her writers at the same time each week, and paid off winnings immediately. She never accepted or required a "tip" from people who had a winning number and was known to let people play on credit.

Her business was mainly a family business where her husband and children worked and were paid. Fannie's five children had varying roles; some wrote numbers from customers who called via telephone or called customers to report the winning numbers. Others created the records that showed what customers owed minus their hits, and the two oldest had customers of their own for whom they wrote numbers. Fannie's spouse at one point collected money from customers and paid out their hits; however, Fannie was always in charge because it was *her* business. Concerning her father's role in her mother's business, Bridgett recalled in the beginning her father helped collect the tickets and money because of the risks involved, including being arrested or robbed. Her father had no problem with her mother running her numbers business and it became a very important part of the family's livelihood after he became disabled and could not work. Her parents eventually divorced and her mother remarried in 1969. Fannie's new husband, like her first husband, supported her in her business. Only once did Fannie get in trouble with law enforcement, and when this occurred, her husband confessed and took the blame. He felt that as a man, it was his job to "do the time" because jail was no place for a woman.

Although Fannie owned her own business, she had a relationship with a black Detroit numbers operator named "Mr. Taylor." Mr. Taylor was a large numbers operator and would act as her cover bank. In other words, he would take over her business or cover winning bets if there were too many winning hits. When this occurred, Fannie would draw on a percentage of her business until she could build her capital up and then again independently run her business. Fannie found relationships and networking necessary in her line of work. In addition to Mr. Taylor, Fannie had relationships with bank managers and a check-cashing establishment. These relationships were necessary because they ensured she could deposit third-party checks from customers without difficulty and afforded her a line of credit for cash she could borrow to pay off hits if necessary. Bridgett remembered the check-cashing establishment was owned by a husband and wife, and her mother was best friends with "Miss Lula," the wife. Fannie would go to Miss Lula and get large sums of cash to pay off a hit. Miss Lula knew Fannie would quickly repay it, and they trusted each another. According to Bridgett, their relationship was an important resource for her mother because it meant reliable access to cash. Similar to what LaShawn Harris noted in her work on black female numbers runners in New York, Fannie's network made it possible for her to navigate the difficulties of running an informal business.[6]

Fannie's numbers business ensured her family had a chance at the American Dream. Numbers gambling allowed Fannie, over the course of thirty-five years, to purchase two homes, raise five children and a grandson, and send four of them to college. The numbers allowed her to purchase rental properties and new cars for herself and her children, and it supported what some considered a lavish lifestyle at the time. Fannie was able to travel extensively; buy expensive clothing, furniture, and jewelry; and help establish her adult children financially. Her numbers business enabled her to help a lot of people who were not related to her. Fannie gave money to people who were incarcerated, to college students, to churches, and to young people trying to make a start in life. Bridgett recalled, "She was a philanthropist. And she employed a handful of young men in her business too. These were men with few other options." It was not uncommon for Fannie to pay for trips to Las Vegas and Miami Beach for friends or to feed and clothe the needy. She would take the neighborhood children to the circus and amusement parks. Because she ran her business from home, Fannie would babysit young mothers' children so they could work or attend school, and when she saw a young person in need of money, she would generously give it to them without expecting to be repaid.

Fannie was very familiar with the Bible and periodically went to church. She had no tolerance for so-called prophets, charlatans, and ministers who lived high off of poor people's donations. Fannie gave generous donations to the church by placing them into the donation basket during service. She was not beholden to church rules nor did she worry about sinning. Bridgett stated her mother "fundamentally believed that 'God helps those who help themselves,' so she felt no contradiction between her livelihood and her love of God. She would have *never* discussed her livelihood with her pastor and members of the church. If it was an open secret, folks knew not to ask her about it. This was true for everyone who wasn't a customer or friend. People talked, sure, but my mother did not discuss her business with outsiders. She trained all her children to do likewise."

Although numbers gambling provided a solid middle-class existence for Fannie and her family, there were downsides to the business. She found it a hard business to be in because, at times, she had to deal with people who resented her success. Occasionally, customers did not want to pay what they owed or had unreasonable expectations with regard to her availability. When a winning number was heavily played or someone hit for a large sum of money, operating the business could be especially stressful because Fannie had to ensure she had the money to cover the winnings. Bridgett never heard her mother discuss the challenges of being a woman in the numbers business. Fannie relished knowing she was in charge of her business and could spend her money as she saw fit. She knew the numbers business was hard and understood the pitfalls of having large payouts and people potentially cheating her. She did, however, occasionally talk about the stress that accompanied being the family's breadwinner.

Men and women held Fannie in high regard for being a woman running a numbers business. Major male numbers operators like Mr. Taylor and Ed Wingate respected her, and she had solid relationships with them. People knew they could not take advantage of her and were in awe of her. The fact that she commanded such respect played a major role in why she was a successful numbers operator. She used to say, "Nobody is gonna just walk all over me." Fannie had a reputation for being aboveboard: she paid her hits quickly and was trusted. People also admired her because she was fair, generous, and supportive. She genuinely liked to see other people do well too. Bridgett stated that everyone she talked to about her mother thought what Fannie did was extraordinary as a black woman.

Although running a numbers operation was hard to deal with at times, Fannie never wished she had done anything else or ever expressed regrets. She knew that operating her own numbers business was the best she could do at that time due to her education level, gender, and race. Fannie never felt as if she were taking advantage of the people who played numbers with her. Bridgett recounted:

My mother *never* felt bad about folks playing numbers with her. Think about it: that's like the party store owner feeling bad about selling you a lottery ticket, or the blackjack dealer at a casino feeling bad about taking your chips, or a racetrack ticket operator feeling bad about taking your bet on a horse. For her, it was a legitimate business that happened to be illegal. She used to tell the story of Joseph Kennedy, who supposedly got his start as a bootlegger. No one cared that he got his seed money that way for the fortune he built. She'd say, "Why was it okay for him? Because he was a white man? Hell, liquor became legal anyway." My mother felt she was helping folks get a shot at making the kind of money their jobs would never pay; she felt she was giving them hope; and to be clear, she often paid out big sums of money, so she wasn't just on the receiving end.

Fannie knew that playing the numbers allowed her and a lot of other black people the means to "make a way out of no way." According to Bridgett, Fannie would never let someone play with her who was unable to pay their bill or take care of themselves and their family. She knew her customers and was friendly if not friends with many of them, so she refused to take numbers from someone if it seemed they could not afford to play. Bridgett remembered Fannie was neither "cutthroat nor desperate for a dollar by any means; that is a cliché of gamblers and numbers runners. She was an ethical businesswoman who believed that the odds were in her favor but that the chances were good enough for a customer to feel it worth their while to play. If they didn't hit, she made money; it they hit, she paid it out with no grudges. 'People play numbers to hit, so you can't be mad when they do,' she said. To her, it was an above-the-board arrangement, with risks and potential gains on both sides. She also understood that her risks were higher, so her potential gain should be higher." Bridgett never saw any one of her mother's customers, in the twenty-five years she watched Fannie do business, who looked like a victim. What she did see was joy. She felt playing numbers gave people joy. Bridgett did hear her mother "speak of the rare folks who'd choose to stop turning in their numbers to her because they felt like she was doing too well—as if she'd made her money off of them—and other folks who turned in with her specifically because she was doing well; some people, she explained, liked to know you were doing well, because it made them feel you were lucky, and luck attracts luck."

Fannie Davis successfully managed her numbers business for thirty-five years. She did this during a time when women were expected to be homemakers and not business leaders. In the numbers business, the norm was for women to be numbers writers or collectors, not operators. Fannie overcame not just being a woman but being a black woman who successfully managed her own numbers business. She continued to manage her numbers business successfully even after the state legalized the lottery in 1972. The state of Michigan's legalization of the lottery managed only to change how the winning number was chosen for her and other numbers operators. Fannie was a numbers operator until her death. Bridgett stated, "I want to be clear: 'the pursuit of Happiness' is something she took seriously in the Declaration of Independence; she was a black woman born in 1928; she was clear-eyed about her American right to have the same opportunities and resources as any white person, *and* the racist tactics and policies used to keep those things from her. She absolutely understood that money was the key to that right. And she was happier when money was flowing—because it gave her the freedom to do what she loved: live well and share the wealth. We all learned, thanks to her, that we deserved—that we were entitled to—the American Dream too."

17

The State of Michigan

The Legal Numbers Man

Of course the ultimate white takeover was the state lottery.

—Anthony Shafton, *Dream Singers: The African American Way with Dreams*

The public, the media, and even legislators questioned whether the lottery should be legal beginning in the 1930s. In 1937, a state legislator, John Hamilton, introduced two bills. One proposed to legalize all types of gambling, and the other proposed licensing bookmakers and operators of sports pools. Neither bill was passed, and Hamilton again presented a bill to legalize gambling in 1939 with negative results.[1] In 1939, the black weekly, the *Michigan Chronicle*, published an article titled "Should the Numbers Racket Be Legalized?" The author of the piece, a former newspaper editor, indicated he thought it should; otherwise, half the population would be in jail for playing the numbers. His thinking was that people have been motivated to gamble for pleasure or profit from the beginning of time. He further argued it was common knowledge that numbers gambling occurred in all large cities, and the police could not prevent people from playing the numbers, just as they could not prevent people from drinking during Prohibition. The legalization of numbers gambling would end police and government corruption, remove the stigma that numbers bankers faced, and generate tax revenue.[2] A year later, following Judge Homer Ferguson's one-man grand jury, the *Detroit Free Press* polled Detroiters to see whether they favored legalizing gambling. Their poll showed that, for a variety of reasons, 57 percent of Detroiters did. One person indicated, "People are going to gamble no matter what . . . so you might as well make it legal and let the state get some money." Another person remarked, "Gambling is human nature so why not recognize it."[3] In

1949, the *Michigan Chronicle* posed nearly the same question it had ten years earlier: "Should the Numbers Game Be Legalized?" Letters poured in to the paper in response. One indicated that if the numbers game were legalized, the government should be obligated to the numbers men who had built the game from a simple pastime into a major business. The writer predicted that if the numbers were legalized it would "be a boon to our people because they know the business inside and out and it would mean bringing one of our means of livelihood out of the racket class into the realm of business also on the side of the law where it rightfully belongs also too long the numbers and the people running them have been a source of sordid display for politicians seeking office." Another reader felt that numbers should be legalized to allow those who worked for the illegal numbers an opportunity finally to use their business skills without guilt and remorse. Still others felt the legalization of the numbers would provide employment and revenue for the state while ending corruption in the police department.[4]

Three years later, Michigan state representative Charlene White of Detroit introduced a bill to the state legislature to legalize numbers gambling. She was the only black woman in the state legislature at the time and proposed the bill under the guise that the revenue generated from it would curtail the state's deficit, balance the budget, increase revenue for senior citizen benefits, and strengthen the school fund. Her plan called for numbers operators to pay a $2,500 fee for a license and 5 percent of their monthly gross to the state.[5] Several people in Detroit's black community had strong opinions about the proposed bill. An attorney for the NAACP felt that numbers should not be legalized because it was a vice and it "shattered the moral fibers of our civilization for profit" from poor people, who could least afford to gamble.[6] Another black Detroit attorney, however, felt that the numbers should be legalized because it was in the best interest of society; people were going to gamble anyway and legalization would at least mean government control.[7] Representative White's dream of legalization of the numbers game would not come to fruition. At Michigan's 1961 Constitutional Convention, another attempt was made by lawmakers to legalize the lottery, but all proposals put forth were vetoed.

Over the years, twenty-nine attempts were made to end Michigan's lottery ban without success.[8] Finally, on March 15, 1972, the Michigan House voted 82 to 10 to put the lottery issue on the May 16, 1972, ballot for voters to decide whether Michigan's lottery ban would be lifted. Those who opposed legalization argued that the lottery would cause more crime and would attract those who could least afford to lose to play. In addition, some saw legalization as an erosion of decency and viewed the lottery as unwholesome. Those in favor of legalization argued that the lottery would generate much-needed revenue for the state of Michigan and allow people to enjoy wagering legally.

The voters of Michigan overwhelmingly voiced their desire to legalize the lottery when they voted by a three to one margin to amend the state constitution on May 16, 1972. This vote ended the 137-year ban on lotteries. Approximately 80 percent of blue-collar Detroit suburbs, which were mostly white, voted for the creation of a state lottery, as did a large number of both white and black Detroiters.[9] Almost every county in the state voted to legalize the lottery including rural counties, which had been expected to vote against lifting the lottery ban. Overall, 73 percent of Michigan's voters supported the lottery. This flew in the face of the stereotype that only poor blacks played the numbers and would be interested in a lottery. After the ban was lifted, a bill was proposed to create a state lottery and allocate $1.5 million in seed money.[10]

When the lottery was first set up, it was modeled after the state of New Jersey's lottery. The director of New Jersey's lottery stated, "Our goals were to make the tickets readily available and affordable—and to set up a prize structure that would substantially alter the average person's mode of living while including a scattering of small prizes."[11] New Jersey's lottery had been in operation for sixteen months and generated $69 million in one year with weekly ticket sales of about $2 million. The state of Michigan had estimated they would bring in as much as $60 million per year.[12] Michigan planned to sell lottery tickets for fifty cents apiece through retail agents throughout the state. The drawings for the winning prizes were held weekly, with first prize being $50,000.[13]

By August 1, 1972, Governor William Milliken signed the McCauley-Traxler-Law-Bowman-McNeely Lottery Act, or Act 239, into law. The act mandated several things as it pertained to the lottery. It created the bureau of the state lottery and the position of lottery commissioner. Per the act, the lottery commissioner would be appointed by the governor of Michigan and would report directly to him to ensure accountability and integrity of the office. The role of the commissioner was to initiate, establish, and operate the state lottery. The commissioner had the power to decide what games would be offered to the public and the cost associated with playing. The lottery's intent was to "produce the maximum amount of net revenues for the state consonant with the general welfare of the people."[14] The lottery act also mandated, when practicable, that at least 45 percent of the total annual revenue from the sale of lottery tickets or shares be paid out in prizes. Money generated from the Michigan state lottery was to be used for paying out winnings and for operating costs, and the remaining amount would be deposited in the state school fund.[15] Finally, on the day the governor signed the act into law, he appointed Gus Harrison as the first lottery commissioner. Harrison, a former state corrections director, after being in office for one month predicted "the lottery would put something of a dent in the state's number racket."[16] By October, however, he had changed his tune. Harrison stated the state lottery was not trying to compete with the daily numbers business. He admitted that he was concerned that "people in the inner city may look upon the lottery as a white man's game and not play it. We don't know whether or not it will be a problem yet, but, for example if we don't get a representative number of applications for licenses to sell tickets from black businesses, we will send men into the city to get them."[17] The irony was the state actively sought the business of blacks whom they once categorized as poor, ignorant criminals.

The numbers bankers at this point did not see the lottery as a threat. One west-side banker felt that many of the people who played the numbers would not want to give their name to the government if they won due to taxes. He felt people would view the lottery like the Irish Sweepstakes and would perhaps buy a ticket, but they would not give up playing the daily numbers. Numbers were more than a betting game for most people who played; it was a lifelong habit. In his view, the Michigan lottery could not replace that feeling of euphoria of placing a bet on a three-digit number in the morning, and then dreaming and hoping of winning all day long. The thrill of picking your own number and having a hand in your destiny was lost if you bought a Michigan lottery ticket, because the number was out of the player's control.[18]

Law enforcement officials also felt that the new game would not be competition for the numbers racket. They agreed that, unless the lottery became a daily drawing, they would not be able to compete with the illegal numbers games: "If they had action every day, they might run the numbers into the ground. At least they would have an effect. You would have to pay federal taxes, but you wouldn't have to worry about the payoff man keeping your money and leaving town or worry about the number changing all the time."[19]

One month before the lottery was officially to begin, the illegal numbers were still functioning. On October 27, forty-two state and local law enforcement officials conducted a raid on Ed Wingate's Twenty Grand Motel in Detroit. The state police alleged the motel functioned as the headquarters for a $9 million per year numbers operation. During the raid, seven men and five women were arrested and $3,000 was confiscated, along with guns, narcotics, six cars, adding machines, bet slips, and gambling records. The gambling records would reveal that only 5 percent of the money was returned to gamblers in winnings because the numbers were fixed.[20] Just a few short weeks later, the Michigan state lottery was up and running.

Roughly 7,800 agents were granted the right to sell lottery tickets for the state in 1972. According to the state's annual report for 1973 virtually everyone who was a "licensable" business or organization and who submitted an application for a license was granted one to avoid charges of favoritism.[21] Some blacks viewed the legalization of the lottery as an attack

Figure 23. Lottery player shows off her lottery tickets on December 5, 1972. Photo courtesy of *Detroit News*.

on blacks and the ultimate takeover of what they considered a black game. In order to show their diversity, the state ensured they reported that the first agents to receive their license were "a Detroit bar owner, a black Lansing businessman, a Grand Rapids chain store operator, and a Bay City business proprietor."[22] When granted a license, the agent had to pay an annual fee of $10 and received a 5 percent sales commission or 2.5 cents per ticket sold.

Figure 24. One of Michigan's first lottery agents, November 4, 1972. Photo courtesy of *Detroit News*.

In addition, the agents received a bonus ranging from $50 to $5,000 based on the sale of a major prize ticket.[23]

The first fifty-cent green game lottery ticket for the "World's Richest Lottery" went on sale November 13, 1972, for the first drawing held on November 24, 1972. Buyers of the fifty-cent ticket could not choose their lottery number; their number was assigned with the purchase of the ticket. The Michigan Lottery decided to use the slogan "World's Richest Lottery" because Michigan's lottery would award 4,004 prizes per million tickets, which was twice as many as other lotteries. This meant the vast majority of prizes were small, but it also increased the number of ticket buyers who could win.[24] This allowed the Michigan Lottery to create more winners in a shorter period of time, similar to what John Roxborough did during the Great Depression with ticket buyers. Before the first drawing, the *Detroit Free Press* noted that the state-run lottery was a better bet for players because the state returned more money to players as opposed to illegal numbers. The newspaper also stressed that the state-run lottery was "above board" and players knew the odds, as opposed to numbers rackets where the number was rigged. Finally, the newspaper pointed out that profits from the illegal numbers supported organized crime.[25]

The first drawing, which took place at Cobo Arena in Detroit in conjunction with the Detroit Auto Show, was filled with pomp and circumstance. The drawing was open to the public and was free of charge, and a number of state officials, including the governor, participated.[26] A few weeks prior to the first drawing, Lottery Commissioner Gus Harrison announced that the drawing would have a circus-like atmosphere with entertainers, clowns, short-skirted girls, and other celebrities present. The purpose of the atmosphere was to make people feel good about the drawing.[27] With new cars as the backdrop, pretty "lottery ladies" in elegant dresses selected the winning numbers. Lottery ladies first mixed 1,000 large colored balls, each of which was printed with a three-digit number ranging from 000 to 999, in a giant drum by turning a wheel attached to the drum. Once the balls were mixed, the drum was tipped over to allow ten random balls to fall into ten numbered cups. Next, the lottery ladies stepped to a clear globe containing ten envelopes. Each envelope contained a number from one to ten, which corresponded with the winning positions of horse races run in Michigan tracks on a particular day.[28] The state was required by federal regulation to tie the selection of the winning numbers to horse racing to avoid paying a 10 percent federal tax on all proceedings.[29] Once the envelopes were mixed, one envelope was selected and opened. Once the number inside was revealed, the lottery ladies went to the cup matching the number from the envelope and revealed the number of the ball inside of the cup. For example, if an envelope contained the number three, the cup with the number three on it would be opened and the ball inside placed on a stand.[30] On November 24, 4,000 people witnessed the first ball selected from the cup, which was number 130. The process was repeated with a second envelope and the second number, 544, was revealed. The winning numbers were 130 and 544. Winners included people who had either 130 as the first three digits of their six-digit number or 544 as the last three.

A total of 23,612 people won $25 each and a chance in the state's million-dollar grand prize (after thirty million tickets were sold). Eleven people won the chance to enter the state's "superprize" drawing: first prize was $200,000, second prize was $50,000, and third prize was $10,000. Unlike the illegal numbers where winners were paid in cash immediately, the winners of the $25 prize had to wait for payment. They first had to go to the secretary of state office and present their winning ticket for verification. The secretary of state office then sent winners' information to the Bureau of State Lottery in Lansing, and then two weeks later, winners received a

Figure 25. The state of Michigan's first lottery drawing, November 24, 1972. Photo courtesy of *Detroit News*.

check in the mail. The state of Michigan proclaimed the first drawing a success. In one week's time, 5,886,191 fifty-cent tickets were sold, grossing $2,843,096. Of that amount, the state netted $1,510,189 and $1,324,393 was paid in prizes.[31]

The state lottery claimed "every ticket has an equal chance to win, whether it is purchased in Dollar Bay, Dansville, Dowagiac or Detroit," in an effort to reassure those living outside the Detroit area. What they did not understand was most tickets were sold to residents of this area, thus accounting for the large number of winners from those counties. In order to overcome this perception, the Michigan Lottery ensured the first year that weekly drawings took place in every area of the state, which also gave the public the chance to observe the drawing themselves.[32] Ironically, years later, residents of Detroit would feel that the majority of winning tickets came from suburbs and rural areas. The Michigan Lottery ensured stories of all its winners were published to prove the lottery was fair and to encourage ticket sales. Each winner had their story featured. For example, Herman Millsaps was Michigan's first million-dollar lottery winner and was described as "an excellent winner." He worked for Chrysler and his first purchase was a new Chrysler sedan. Greek immigrant Christeen Ferizis, at forty-seven years of age, became Michigan's second million-dollar winner. Ferizis spoke no English and had been in the United States for eight years with her husband before hitting it big. According to their story, they had come to America to get rich. When the state legalized the "World's Richest Lottery," it changed the narrative or perception concerning numbers gambling. No longer was it a fraudulent evil played by black, ignorant people; rather, it became legitimate entertainment for everyday people and operated with integrity and dignity. It was now a valid vehicle to the American Dream.

In its first year of operation, the state lottery indicated it was successful despite advertising limitations. Federal laws prohibited the lottery from using the U.S. mail for distribution of advertisements or promotional materials. The Federal Communications Commission also banned advertising or promoting lotteries on radio and television. These laws had previously been put in place to prevent illegal numbers games from operating and ironically curtailed the state-sanctioned legal lottery. The state found the laws to be antiquated and unfair for their modern-day lottery.[33]

By the end of the first year, experts claimed the Michigan Lottery was the most successful of all state lotteries, partly because it was allowed to operate as a business with integrity and dignity.[34] Michigan newspapers were also credited with helping the lottery achieve success because of their unprecedented coverage and support. Another key to the lottery's success was the winners themselves, whom the public were able to identify with.[35] By the end of the first year, the Michigan Lottery had sold 271,380,471 tickets, which represented $135,690,235 in gross sales. Strong sales took place all over the state, including rural counties like Berrien, Ingham, Jackson, Kent, Monroe, Saginaw, St. Clair, and Washtenaw, with the strongest ticket sales coming from the more populated counties of Wayne, Macomb, Oakland, and Genesee.[36] Even with those strong numbers, the state knew that their weekly lottery was no competition for the numbers racket. Knowing it could not compete, the state admitted it was looking into the possibility of a daily game that could. The state lottery stressed that although they hoped to eradicate the illegal lottery, their main objective was to generate revenue.[37]

As predicted, the illegal numbers racket was still doing strong business in 1975 when Detroit mafia member Louis "Rip" Koury testified before a federal gambling commission. Koury admitted to being in the illegal numbers business for fifty years and told the commission that the illegal numbers game generated about $1.2 million per week within the metropolitan Detroit area. He stated that legalized lotteries did not hurt the numbers racket; rather, they helped it by introducing new bettors to the game.[38] Koury indicated that anyone who had the desire could get into the numbers racket.[39] He estimated that forty to fifty people ran numbers gambling games in the metropolitan Detroit area, and approximately 250,000 people played every day. He further admitted that the illegal gambling organizations communicated with each other about the amount of money that was bet on certain numbers to ensure minimal losses. Koury confessed that the Detroit number was decided by the mutual agreement of the largest and most powerful numbers operators. Allegedly, there were no threats or extortion involved in deciding the winning numbers and the various organizations banded together for mutual protection.[40]

Although Lottery Commissioner Guy Harrison in 1972 stated that he and other lottery officials were giving serious consideration to having a daily game that would compete with the illegal numbers game, it took five more years before the Michigan Lottery offered a daily lottery that allowed players to choose the numbers they wanted to play. On June 6, 1977, Michigan's newest lottery game, called the "Daily," went on sale at three hundred computerized sales terminals, all within a ninety-mile radius of Detroit. The Daily was almost a carbon copy of the illegal numbers gambling game, and the state proclaimed it was starting a numbers game to compete with the illegal numbers game. A player at this point was finally able to select his or her own three-digit number, and numbers were drawn Monday through Saturday. This appealed to numbers players who liked the freedom of playing their own special numbers.

Unlike the illegal numbers game, which could be played for as little as a nickel, the state-sanctioned Daily required gamblers to wager from fifty cents to six dollars on their three-digit number. The Daily, like the illegal numbers, allowed wagers to play straight and box bets. To win with a straight wager, the number had to be played exactly as it was drawn; however, boxing a number allowed for several chances to win if the three numbers chosen were drawn. The payouts were 500 to 1, with a straight wager for fifty cents netting the winner $250. The Daily also took a page from illegal numbers and allowed winners to cash in the same day their number fell for winnings up to $550 at several Daily sales locations. Winners who won over $550 were required to complete a claim form and their winnings were mailed to them. The winning number was broadcast live on WWJ-TV Channel 4 and released to additional news outlets throughout the state.[41]

The Michigan Lottery heavily promoted its new Daily game in newspapers. It advised players, "Now, you pick your own 3-digit number. Play your birthdate, telephone number, bowling score or street address. It's your choice."[42] By the second day of the new Daily game, the state understood what it was like for numbers operators who were hit hard when a number was heavily played. On June 7, 1977, "137" was drawn after a sales agent advised a newspaper that was the number he was playing, and 2,236 people played it with him and won. People liked playing the number "317" and boxing it because it translated to March 17, St. Patrick's Day. The 2,236 people played "137" for $216,219 and caused the state to pay out $242,166 in winnings, which left the state with a net loss of $25,947. The payoff was 112 percent and would be the highest one for the year. The Michigan Lottery took the loss in stride, "There are going to be days when popular numbers will come up and the customers will come out ahead, a little or a lot. And there will be days when unpopular numbers come up and we'll come out ahead, a little or a lot." Overall, the Michigan Lottery estimated it would average a profit of 40 percent.[43] The legal lottery would be competing with two illegal daily numbers games. According to a Michigan FBI agent, at that time in the Detroit area, there were two major daily numbers games, one run by white numbers operators and one by black numbers operators.[44]

During its first year, the Daily averaged sales of $1.3 million per week and the average payoff for winnings was 45 percent. The state continued to expand sales terminals throughout the year, eventually covering the whole state.[45] A year later, the Daily weekly sales increased to $3.4 million and produced 41 percent of the Michigan Lottery's total sales. The Michigan Lottery soon began crediting the Daily with creating hundreds of new jobs because of the need for agents across the state.[46]

Lottery players soon became loyal to the Daily and certain establishments. For example, the Chene Trombley Market located on the east side of Detroit, one of the first to be licensed by the state, soon gained a following and a reputation with hardcore players for selling winning tickets. At this time, the Daily was known as the state-sanctioned version of the numbers racket. One player noted, "This place is a winner man. I play 30 bucks a week."[47] The amount he played amounted to 10 percent of his weekly paycheck, but he, like thousands of others, was convinced that the store was lucky and was where winners purchased their lottery tickets. Another reason that the Chene Trombley Market was popular was its location. It was near the expressway, and suburbanites who were too embarrassed to play at their neighborhood stores found the location beneficial. It was far enough away from where they lived but easily accessible.[48] In 1979, roughly 6,000 people played at the store, and it sold about $1 million worth of lottery tickets and paid out $868,922. The sales generated $50,000 for the store owner.[49]

For others, the Daily was a nightmare that led to an addiction. Valerie Kaczor's newfound lottery addiction changed her life. In 1985, Kaczor, thirty-two years old and a former nurse, was a married mother of two living the American Dream as a housewife in suburban Detroit. She and her family lived in a tri-level house equipped with the latest appliances and entertainment systems. For her, the game transformed her from a loving mother and responsible housewife to a suicidal felon.[50] Kaczor claimed that her family became burdened with $30,000 in medical bills because of her deceased mother-in-law's illness. Kaczor did not want her husband to worry about the outstanding debt and instead turned to the Michigan State Lottery for financial help. Kaczor, an educated woman, said the pressure of the debt made her think about the lottery after hearing her neighbors talking about it. She decided if the lottery could help her neighbors, maybe it was her answer and would help her as well. Initially, she invested $100 in lottery tickets and won $1,000. In less than a month's time, Kaczor was spending $700 a day with the state lottery on numbers gambling, hoping to hit the big one. At one point, Kaczor was wagering $1,000 a day with the state lottery. To finance her lottery habit, she wrote approximately $500,000 in bad checks and altered money orders. For a while this worked, and she bragged that she several times managed to be only $15,000 in the hole. The end came when she began to be investigated by the FBI. She was arrested, and in order to be released on a $55,000 cash bond, her family had to sacrifice their snowmobiles, cars, trailers, children's coin collections, and wedding rings. After being arrested, Kaczor admitted herself into a hospital for treatment and was diagnosed as being "hooked on the numbers." After being released from the hospital, Kaczor said, "I don't intend to go back to that lifestyle, no matter how broke I get."[51] In spite of this, Kaczor was convicted on several felony counts for fraud and forgery for her nine-month lottery spree and sentenced to four consecutive prison terms of three to fourteen years.[52]

The creation of the new Daily game once again did not end illegal numbers playing. This was supported by the Commission on the Review of the National Policy Toward Gambling. The commission in a report noted, "FBI intelligence shows that an organized crime family is active in Detroit and that it controls illegal gambling in Michigan, with the exception of the black numbers traffic."[53] In October 1977, Vito Giacalone was indicted for running a multimillion-dollar numbers racket in Detroit. Tied into this indictment was Eddie Wingate. Just a month prior to Giacalone's indictment, Wingate was arrested with seven other men for running a $100,000 per day off-track horse-betting ring out of the Twenty Grand Motel.[54] In addition to his numbers organization and various other businesses, Wingate had a passion for race horses. He owned several thoroughbreds around the country and bred, trained, and raced them. Again, this arrest would not yield a conviction. It was rumored Wingate was always able to stay one step ahead of law enforcement because he had a few high-ranking officials on his payroll who would tip him off concerning raids and investigations. During Giacalone's indictment, it was revealed Wingate used that valuable information to tip off the Italian mobster concerning the FBI's investigation into Detroit's gambling operations.[55]

Vito "Billy Jack" Giacalone would be acquitted by a jury on charges he masterminded Detroit's multimillion-dollar numbers racket. In 1982, five years after the Daily Three was introduced, law enforcement officers again raided a large numbers operation. Twenty-one locations in Detroit and the suburbs were found to be part of a $60 to $80 million per year numbers organization owned and operated by the Detroit mafia.[56]

Although the lottery was legalized and illegal numbers operations continued to decrease, they did not disappear. Instead, many numbers operations had a loyal customer base. In Detroit, in August 1989, the *Detroit News* reported that the old numbers underground game was still in existence. It survived and flourished after the Daily Three was introduced because the drawn Daily Three number was used for the daily illegal number. Players knew when they won because they watched the numbers being drawn on television and obtained the number instantly. State lottery officials knew the illegal numbers were still thriving in plants and other areas but admitted they were powerless to stop it. The assistant prosecutor in charge of an organized crime task force in Wayne County noted the illegal numbers games continued to operate in offices, factories, stores, and homes and cut across racial, ethnic, and geographic lines.[57] The legalized lottery not only helped the illegal numbers game in assuring players the winning number was not fixed but also diminished public perception that playing the illegal numbers was wrong.[58]

Numbers players indicated they continued to play the illegal numbers for several reasons, including the following:

- Winners were paid off at rates that were six to one or even seven to one compared to the state lottery scale of five to one.
- Numbers runners offered credit to their trustworthy and loyal customers who at times had little ready cash while awaiting pension or welfare checks. These customers were allowed to pay at the end of a week or month and could use their winnings to settle their unpaid debts.
- Players could bet as little as a nickel unlike the minimum required by the state-run lottery.
- Winnings were unreported and tax-free. For example, a two-dollar bet on a straight three number could net a winner $1,000 or more under the table with the cash being paid the next day.

Finally, the social component of playing the numbers contributed to its lon-gevity. Playing the numbers meant socializing, bonding, drinking, eating, and swapping stories and memories. It allowed people who felt shut out of the regular economy to rebel—and so they played underground.[59] The illegal lottery also thrived in Detroit-area plants.

18

Playing the Numbers in the Plant

Even after it was legalized there are still street numbers.

—Big Will, September 27, 2012

Even after the state lottery was introduced, illegal numbers continued. Numbers gambling was prevalent in Detroit neighborhoods for years, so it is no wonder that it could be found where people worked, particularly the automotive plants. Like neighborhoods, automotive plants are communities. Because of the long work hours, plant employees tend to spend more time with each other than with family, and the plant community often offers as many amenities within its confines as can be found outside of it.

Ford Motor Company's Rouge plant was notorious for numbers gambling. In 1942, a raid on a Detroit neighborhood revealed that numbers gambling was taking place within the plant. Numbers writers were Ford employees who on the side wrote numbers for neighborhood numbers organizations.[1] By the end of World War II, investigations into numbers gambling in ten war plants, including the Ford Rouge plant, determined employees were wagering $25,000 per day. The investigation revealed that the numbers organization drew its customers exclusively from the plants and employed hundreds of numbers writers in each plant.[2] In spite of the investigation, which resulted in several arrests, numbers gambling continued in many plants. The Rouge plant continued to have problems with numbers gambling in 1947 and after a yearlong investigation fired twenty-three employees who were part of a $15,000 per day numbers gambling ring.[3] The investigation was initiated after a number of wives complained that their husbands were losing money from betting and bringing home reduced pay.[4]

In 1948 a survey of gambling in seven factories across the United States, including Detroit, revealed that of the $75 million per year spent on gambling in Detroit, $20 million came from auto plants.[5] According to its findings, there were few plants in Detroit employing 100 or more people that did not have some form of gambling, and plants with 1,000 or more employees tended to have at least three or four numbers writers.[6] In addition, just as many white employees played the numbers as black employees. Number writers worked for both the Detroit mafia and independent numbers operators both inside and outside plants. The numbers writers tended to have a designated time and location where people could come to play their numbers. Pick-up men collected the bets during plant hours in different ways. Some employees, like truck drivers who had scheduled access to the plant, also did double duty as collectors, while some numbers writers would simply wrap the numbers slips and money in packages and drop them from plant windows to the collector who waited outside the plant on the sidewalk.[7] Management at the plants generally did not approve of gambling but did not invite law enforcement to investigate or arrest employees on its premises. If an employee was found gambling at the plant, they were usually fired. In spite of management's views, local police departments generally arrested one or two people per week at large plants.[8] The same year that the survey was completed, it was estimated that approximately twenty-five numbers rings including the Murphy and Alabama and Georgia Houses of Detroit, with 250 numbers writers, operated within the Ford Rouge plant.[9] These numbers operations generated between $5 and $10 million per year.[10]

One black numbers operator, Edward Hester, who was also a Ford employee and UAW committee man, decided to seek police protection for his numbers operation at the Ford Rouge plant in 1948.[11] Hester had hoped that police, in addition to offering him protection, would arrest his competitors. After giving the Dearborn chief of police $100 at a meeting Hester stated, "It's worth $50,000 a year to me to have the mayor, police chief, and Vice Squad let me run in the Rouge plant." Hester's plan was to pay $2,000 to $5,000 per month to city officials in Dearborn to run his numbers organization, called the Beason House, unmolested.[12] At the time, approximately 69,000 people were employed at the plant. The Ford Rouge plant encompassed 1,212 acres and had within its boundaries a bus system that operated on 26 miles of roadway, 106 miles of railroad track, and over one mile of docks. Ninety-nine buildings of more than 15,000,000 square feet of floor space housed 120 miles of conveyors. During a regular 24-hour period, a total of 49,000 vehicles, 148,000 people, and 468 trains passed through the Ford Rouge's gates.[13]

Within this huge and busy plant, gambling took place virtually every-where. Numbers writers would take numbers out of closets or rooms, and the employees who had counters would openly take bets. Crane operators would roll their equipment between buildings and allow bettors to place their bets and money inside a lowered bucket.[14] Hester, as a union committeeman, unlike most employees at the plant, had access to the entire plant. His job as a union committeeman was to represent other employees if they violated company policies or had grievances. Because of this, he was not tied down to one location and could move about freely visiting various employees. On one occasion while meeting with Labor Relations, Hester turned in seven rival numbers writers. Ford's labor relations representative turned the infor-mation over to local law enforcement, which then promptly investigated and arrested the men.[15] It was shortly after Hester turned in his rivals that he attempted to bribe the chief of police and subsequently was arrested. Upon further investigation, it was learned that Hester had 180 numbers writers working for him, and his headquarters was located in the Fairbairn Hotel, formerly owned by Walter Norwood and located in Detroit's Black Bottom.[16] Hester became infamous when he was subpoenaed to testify on February 9, 1951, before the Kefauver Committee in Detroit. The committee questioned Gordon L. Walker, the manager of Ford Motor Company's securities and communications department, concerning illegal numbers gambling in its plants. The committee wanted to know about large-scale gambling in plants and chose Ford's Rouge plant to study because at the time it was the largest plant in the country. Detroiters witnessed Hester on the televised hearing, wearing dark sunglasses, answer a limited number of questions concerning his employment with Ford and his participation in illegal gambling at the plant. When the committee asked him questions concerning his attempt to bribe Dearborn's chief of police, he refused to answer.[17]

Gambling was not just confined to Ford Motor Company, and it was not confined to men. For example, in 1955, seven women who worked at the Ternstedt Division of General Motors were convicted and sentenced to six months' probation and assessed a $75 fine each for operating a numbers ring. Like these women, Janice Markovich was part of a numbers ring in a General Motors plant. Janice, a black woman whose youthful beauty belies the fact she is in her early sixties, was born in Pontiac, Michigan. At the age of ten, her family moved to the west side of Detroit where she grew up. Her mother was a day worker and her father, like so many others, worked in the plant, and neither played the numbers. Janice's father was very strict and would frequently say he ruled his home like "Hitler ruled Germany." In her household, she was expected to help care for her six brothers and sisters, which she did. Janice graduated from high school, married, had two children, and eventually obtained her bachelor's degree. She became a widow at an early age and found herself working at a General Motors plant because

Figure 26. Edward Hester testifying on February 9, 1951, before the Kefauver Committee in Detroit concerning numbers gambling in the Ford Rouge plant. Photo courtesy of *Detroit News*.

it paid well. While at GM, she had a few jobs from working on the line, to supervising, and finally driving trucks because it gave her freedom. She would not play her first number until 1979, and as luck would have it, her number 497 was a winner. With that win, she became a numbers player, and since that time has hit the numbers many times. Her largest windfall was for $3,000. She found it impossible to tell how many times she has won. Although Janice feels she hits often, it is never for much money, and she knows that she has lost more than she has won over the years. When she wins, she always buys something that she wants and gives 10 percent of her winnings to God.

For her, playing the numbers became a habit—so much so she gave up smoking so she could afford to play the numbers. When asked why she enjoys playing the numbers, Janice said a group leader that worked for her in the plant years ago summed it up best: "It is the only place, only thing you can do to get some money and you do not have to fill out a long application and be rejected if you are lucky enough." To Janice that statement made perfect sense. Numbers did not discriminate. When you played the numbers, your gender, race, and socioeconomic status meant nothing. Numbers was truly an equal opportunist. She admitted her habit has its dark side. She stated, "At least with dope you got a high, if you don't hit, you ain't got shit. Numbers can be your biggest pimp baby. It can pimp man or woman."

Janice liked the challenge of trying to figure out what number would fall, was fascinated by what numbers in dream books symbolized, and believed there was a spiritual side to them. She believed that to play the numbers you must be focused and have a strategy to play, and this was another aspect she liked about the numbers. Janice, who believes in God and regularly goes to church, found that playing the numbers at times was relaxing, yet could be worse than having a drug habit. Janice's solution for her habit was to become a numbers writer in the plant, which allowed her to play numbers and maintain her lifestyle for herself and her children. She found that she loved being a numbers runner. It allowed her to escape the problems of everyday life. She indicated, "You had to have a brain to write numbers, you had to be focused." Numbers writing allowed her to put everything else out of her mind to accomplish all the tasks it took to write the numbers successfully. It also allowed her to meet fascinating people from all walks of life. Janice estimated that about 75 to 80 percent of the people in her plant played the numbers. They played because, if they hit, the winnings enabled them to buy little things outside of what a paycheck would allow. Most played illegal numbers because the payout was higher, and it allowed them to avoid taxes and other financial obligations such as court order default judgments and child support. Janice views the illegal numbers as a dying art because of the legal lottery and would hate to see it come to an end.

One of the most infamous cases of illegal numbers gambling in an automotive plant came out of the Ford Rouge plant in 1996, years after the legalization of the lottery. Ed Martin, a Ford electrician, was investigated by authorities for his relationship with student athletes at the University of Michigan. During a federal investigation into his activities in 1999, it was learned that Martin had operated an illegal numbers gambling ring from 1988 to 1999 out of his home in Detroit and at the Ford Rouge plant. Martin and his family would take bets from people at the Ford Rouge plant, as well as from all over the country, with the Ford plant being his primary source of bettors.[18]

Ed Martin was born sometime in the early 1930s and grew up in Georgia. In 1953, he moved to Detroit and landed a job with Ford as an apprentice electrician. In 1983, he was injured on the job and received disability compensation until he officially retired in 1998 from Ford. It is unclear when Martin began running his numbers operation, but he, with the help of his wife, son, and a friend, successfully ran it for numerous years at various Ford plants in metro Detroit. In addition to working at Ford and running a numbers operation, Martin, or "Big Money Ed" as he was known, considered himself a basketball fanatic who wanted to be a part of college and professional basketball.[19] As such, it was not uncommon for Martin to attend middle school and high school basketball games throughout the Detroit area. While attending the games, if Martin found a youth whom he felt had talent, he would befriend the youth and their family. Martin, as part of the established relationship, would bestow gifts and at times financial assistance to the student and/or their family. When Martin provided what he considered a large sum of money to a student or their family, it was with the understanding the money was a loan that was to be repaid once the student became a professional basketball player. This served two purposes for Martin: it allowed him to launder illegal numbers gambling money, and it served as a pension or social security system for him in later years. With the proceeds generated from his illegal numbers operation, Martin, from 1992 until 1999, loaned four University of Michigan student athletes or their families about $616,000.[20]

These young men became professional athletes, and one did in fact repay part of the money Martin loaned him. Martin's loans to the student athletes and their families, however, violated NCAA regulations. As a result, the University of Michigan was sanctioned for their relationship with Martin. As the story unfolded in the media, Martin was depicted as a predator who took advantage of talented students and their families. Martin's perspective was different; he felt he was a friend to those involved and had generously tried to help them. At the time, Martin felt the friendship went both ways; however, he later felt that the students and their families took advantage of his friendship and generosity.[21] Others, however, felt that Martin was a generous man who simply provided financial assistance to those in need. Martin was eventually charged federally and pled guilty to conspiracy to launder money. While awaiting sentencing in 2003, Martin died of a blood clot at Henry Ford Hospital in Detroit. His wife, Hilda, who helped run the numbers operation, was originally charged with her husband; however, as part of Ed Martin's plea agreement, charges against her were dropped. Hilda Martin died five months after her husband.

Illegal numbers operating at automotive plants would not end with Ed Martin. Others successfully ran their numbers operations out of other plants before and after Martin, primarily because the plant-run numbers was more lucrative to a player. At one Ford plant in the Detroit area, a numbers runner provided the rules of his plant in 2012:

- Winning numbers paid 600 to 1, which was more than the 500 to 1 paid by the Michigan Lottery.
- Bet amounts for the three-digit ranged from a nickel up to $20; the Michigan Lottery would not accept such small wages as a nickel. Their minimum bet is fifty cents. In addition, their maximum payout is $500.
- Bet amounts for the four-digit ranged from a nickel up to $10; again, the Michigan Lottery would not accept such small wages as a nickel. Their minimum bet is one dollar, and their maximum payout is $5,000.
- At this plant, certain numbers (for example 1010, 1028) could not be played. These were fancies that tended to be heavily played and the numbers operator did not want to take bets for these numbers.

- Players could conveniently play weekly or daily.
- Players could play numbers drawn from the Michigan or the Ohio State Lottery. This was important to some players who felt one lottery was better for their number than the other.
- Players could play on credit; if they hit, the numbers writer would automatically take 10 percent and what the player owed from their winnings.[22]

Although there are some benefits to playing the illegal numbers, there are also some disadvantages, namely, the inability to play certain numbers like "1010," which accounted for one of the highest payouts in Michigan's lottery history on January 29, 2010, when it fell. The payout for the number was $21,660,452, which amounted to 3,371.4 percent of the amount wagered that day.[23]

"Big Will" was another numbers operator who ran a successful operation for years in a plant. He retired from a metro Detroit General Motors plant in 2007, where he worked as a sweeper, and for years he ran his numbers business on the side at the plant. When he retired from his formal job as a sweeper, he also retired from his numbers business. These days, he spends his time doing what he loves most: playing golf with a few lifelong friends. Big Will enjoys golf because it makes you think all the time and it does not hurt that he has a good golf game. The golf course is where he feels most at ease, and it is where he told his story about his numbers business. Big Will is a quiet giant who is both tall and wide; he lumbers when he walks because of walking for many years on a concrete floor. Just looking at him, he appears intimidating, but once he begins to talk, you are struck by his easy manner. He possesses an unassuming intelligence that shines through in his description of his many life experiences.

Big Will was born and raised in South Carolina. It was there as a child that he developed his love for golf. His fondest memories are of caddying and then playing a round on a South Carolina golf course. As an adult seeking employment in 1964, Big Will left the South behind and headed to Detroit. He described himself as a country boy who arrived in the big city that was alive and full of excitement. He fell in love with Detroit because there was always something to do. He loved the restaurants, shopping, and entertainment. He recalled, at that time, Detroit was a place you wanted to live in. His first year in Detroit was spent becoming familiar with a new city, and he worked in a now closed plant for one year before going to work for General Motors in 1965. He would work forty-two years in various assignments before retiring. In 1966, Big Will married his childhood girlfriend, and in 2012 they celebrated their forty-sixth wedding anniversary. They had a son and a daughter.

Big Will first became involved in what he called "street numbers" as a source of extra income in 1969, a few years after the Ford Motor Company disclosed that a numbers organization took $4 million per year from its workers at just one of its plants. The investigation also revealed that employees, who were making $100 per week from Ford, were making up to $1,000 per week as numbers runners in the plant.[24] Similarly, Big Will would make more money running numbers than what he was paid by General Motors. Big Will knew people who were numbers writers and pick-up men. As he saw it, there was no hard work in writing or picking up numbers, and the extra money would go a long way. The first person he wrote and turned in numbers for was Ed Wingate, and he recalled taking one-cent, two-cent, nickel, and dime bets, which added up to big money. Once he became involved in writing and picking up numbers, he found the work was not hard but that it was stressful. The stress came from getting people whom he allowed to play on credit to pay.

Eventually, Big Will learned the ins and outs of the business and broke away from Wingate. He then became a hybrid numbers man whereby he had his own clients he wrote numbers for and was a pick-up man for a big numbers operator whom he never met. Big Will only knew that "Joe" was white. Big Will was able to write numbers for Joe because another pick-up man vouched for him. Every weekend, Joe would send someone to Big Will to pick up his money or to give Big Will the payout money. When Big Will's numbers operation began to turn a profit, he no longer cashed his paycheck from General Motors. Instead, his wife would take his check and hers and put it in a savings account. He began to invest in savings bonds with the profits from his numbers business in 1969 and once hit the numbers for a large sum. Big Will viewed the checks and savings bonds as the key to his retirement; his dream was to be able to retire and not have to work for anyone.

According to Big Will, everyone at his large plant knew that he ran a numbers operation. Some of his regular customers were management and employees from the labor relations department. The people who played the numbers with him were black and white, hourly workers and management, educated and uneducated, old, and young—in other words, there was no "type." He found that most of his customers, however, were white, and they were motivated to play illegal numbers to avoid paying taxes on winnings. His black customers, he felt, played the numbers because it was the thing to do; after all, most of them grew up with street numbers as a part of their life. Although numbers operators took money from the neighborhoods, they put it back in several ways, and this brought acceptance with black customers that played with him.

When a person placed a bet with Big Will, they put their number on a piece of paper, explained how they were playing it, and signed their name or code. Although Big Will took numbers bets personally from people in the plant, he also had twelve books or twelve people who wrote numbers for him. Each book or person had their own clients they took bets from. Big Will would pay his numbers writers, who were both black and white, the standard 25 percent, and if the numbers writer's client hit, they would deduct 10 percent of their winnings. Big Will only deducted 10 percent for his clients who played on credit; otherwise, he did not take any percentage of the winnings. Like in the old days, Big Will provided his numbers writers with books where they recorded their clients' bets and then were required to turn the slips in to him. Cut off time was 6:30 p.m., which allowed Big Will to call in the numbers to a woman who worked for him. In addition, his cut-off time allowed him to purchase lottery tickets from the Michigan Lottery if a number was heavily played. At one time, Big Will was considered the biggest numbers man in the area where his plant was located; this and his size are why he is nicknamed Big Will.

His freedom as a sweeper enabled him not only to collect numbers but also to call them in. Calling in the numbers at times posed a dilemma because he needed access to an office for privacy and a telephone. At times, he would use what he thought were empty offices on the plant floor, and on one such occasion he ran into a supervisor, "Tony," whom he later befriended. As Big Will recalled it, he was sitting inside Tony's locked office with his feet on the desk talking on the phone. As a sweeper or maintenance worker, Big Will literally had keys to most of the plant. Tony inquired who he was and why he was in his office. Their first meeting did not go well, and Big Will walked away thinking Tony was mean and would perhaps be a problem; however, after talking to him a few times, he realized Tony was simply a hardworking man who was about business. They would later learn they both had a love for golf and played at the same course with the same people. Big Will respected Tony for being a fair foreman, and Tony respected how Big Will took care of people within the plant. Tony knew Big Will was the numbers man, but if Big Will did his job, there was never a problem. Tony played a few numbers with Big Will, and Big Will remembered Tony's number because, like other numbers players, he played the same number that had personal significance to him. Tony was not a regular player, and Big Will would frequently ask, but Tony "sho' was tight." Tony was typical of most of management and the union; they knew of the numbers gambling at the plant and tolerated it; it had been around for years and was a part of plant life.

Big Will felt that he was successful as a numbers man because he was honest, people trusted him, and he paid out a lot of money. He credits his father with instilling in him as a young man the importance of trust and never stealing. Big Will told of one customer who hit for $15,000 with him. When Big Will realized the man hit the numbers and won, he attempted to contact him numerous times before discovering the man was on vacation for two weeks. He spoke with the man and offered to bring him his money, but the man advised him he trusted him and would wait to be paid upon his return to work. Big Will insisted his numbers writers also be trustworthy. Once, one of his numbers writers forgot to turn in a number for a customer who played the same number daily for years. Unfortunately for the writer, the day he did not turn in the number it fell, and the woman won. He at first refused to pay her because he had not turned in her number. She then went to Big Will and told him what had occurred. Big Will paid the woman her winnings and took the money out of his writer's profits. In addition to being trustworthy, Big Will had a reputation for being compassionate and helped many people over the years. For example, once someone owed him $30 for numbers played for the week but could not pay. The customer told Big Will he was having some family and money problems and was going to get his lights turned off. Big Will told him to keep the $30 and then gave him the money he needed for his electric bill. Big Will acted as the unofficial mayor of the plant, quashing conflicts along the way. As a sweeper, he had access to a lot of information from both management and the union, and like a town crier, he spread information and news around the plant.

Big Will also credited the success he had in numbers with a few other rules and advice he received when he first started out. Someone told him never to take a bet on more than he could pay out because, as Big Will indicated, a numbers man "can get tapped out especially on favorites and with the four-digits." Because of this rule, the most he would allow anyone to bet on a four-digit number was $3 and $30 for a three-digit number. The payout for hitting a three-digit straight for $30 or a four-digit straight for $3 was $15,000. Big Will made his cutoff $15,000 because he knew that if Joe reneged on paying the winning number, $15,000 was an amount he (Big Will) could easily afford to pay from his own money. The second piece of advice he received from a Jewish numbers man was to avoid certain fancies or favorites. Specifically, he told Big Will never to accept a bet for "123, no kind of way, 567, no kind of way, 962 no kind of way." When Big Will asked him why, the Jewish numbers man stated, "Black people dream too much!" Big Will quickly learned that several of his black customers' favorite numbers to play were 123, 456, 567, and 962, which did not fall much, but when they did, the payouts were massive.

He credits his aunt, Big Minnie, who died at 99½ years of age, with teaching him how to remember numbers and what the numbers meant in dream books. Numbers writing was a family affair; Big Minnie wrote numbers at the Dodge Main plant for over thirty years. His aunt memorized her dream books and had the ability to recall what dreams, or rows, corresponded to certain numbers. For example, 123 was called the car and water row, and 976 was the death row. Because of Big Minnie's ability to memorize numbers and what numbers played for, it was common for people to consult her about their dreams. Big Will found over the years mainly "old folks" used dream books, and they, like his aunt, tend to memorize its contents.

Big Will recalled two incidents where he feared legal action. The first occurred in 1997. For more than a year, a law enforcement officer worked undercover at his plant as an hourly employee and even played numbers with him. One day, as Big Will was coming to work, he noticed law enforcement officers were arresting people at the plant. He later learned that a raid of the plant had taken place. The undercover law enforcement officer had been placed in the plant to investigate widespread drug dealing, and eventually more than twenty people were arrested for dealing drugs. Although Big Will had worried that he would be targeted for his numbers gambling activities, he was ignored by law enforcement. He later realized the officer played numbers with him to "fit in" with the other employees.

The second incident occurred when a customer who occasionally played the numbers with him began to play cards. The man would lose his whole paycheck every week to the men he played with but told his wife he was losing his money playing the numbers. His wife became upset and called the plant to complain that her husband was losing his whole paycheck to the "numbers man." Big Will was questioned by management, who told him they had heard he was the big numbers man in the plant and because of him, people were not bringing their paycheck home. He denied he was a big numbers operator, and consequently, management called in the local police. Big Will was not arrested but instead was given a summons to appear in court. When he received the summons, he met with everyone who played numbers with him and told them to give him all their losing Michigan Lottery tickets, including scratch-offs. When he appeared in court with a famous high-powered attorney, Big Will brought two plastic grocery bags filled with the losing Michigan Lottery tickets. When his case was called, his attorney stepped up and introduced his argument; Big Will was in fact a bookie in the plant, but he had a massive gambling problem himself. His attorney presented the two plastic grocery bags containing over $280,000 in losing State of Michigan Lottery tickets as evidence. He told the judge that every penny Big Will earned or won was gambled and lost with the state of Michigan's lottery, and the $280,000 in lottery tickets represented his losses for the year. Upon hearing this, the judge slammed his gavel and dismissed the case. Big Will recalled the judge said, "I don't ever want to see this man down here for no bookie charge no more!" Big Will's take on the dismissal was that the judge had no other choice but to dismiss. If not, in his mind, the Michigan Lottery would have owed him $280,000 for being a legal bookie. Big Will stated, "Because he knew if he had charged me with that, they would have had to pay me, the state owed me $280,000 cash. Cause they were losing tickets. Case dropped." According to him, this defense kept him out of jail. Big Will's line of thinking was very similar to that of retired Wayne County Circuit Court Judge Edward Bell who, on June 24, 1975, testified before a federal commission on gambling that "the State should not run a legal lottery game and at the same time retain criminal sanctions against illegal numbers games."[25]

Big Will found numbers were good to him over the years. Not only did he earn a fortune from writing numbers and from having writers work for him, but he won a significant amount of money as well. Big Will one day dropped laundry off at the cleaners. His laundry claim ticket was "5816." He played this number straight on a hunch and won $85,000. With his winnings, he purchased land for his father in South Carolina and invested and purchased land for himself. He believed that if he had saved better when he was younger, he would have had $10 million in the bank at his retirement; however, when he was young, he found he spent money excessively on card games, where you had to buy your way in for $5,000 to $10,000 per game. In one ten-year period, Big Will estimated he wasted about a million dollars. Despite this, with age came wisdom, and Big Will was able to save and prosper. He credited numbers gambling, and not his legitimate work at GM, with allowing him to "make it." He is proud to note that he started out in an apartment, and today he has savings, property, land, and a home and his family is financially stable.

Over the years, Big Will has seen a change in both the city of Detroit and the numbers business. He believes that the Michigan Lottery has taken away a lot of business that he and other numbers men enjoyed for years. Young people, he feels, are more likely to gamble at the casino than play the numbers. Gone is the feeling of community that numbers brought. Although he has experienced and witnessed ups and downs over the years, he has no regrets for doing what he considered the key to his American Dream: street numbers.

19
Finis

In those days, gambling was so personal that the numbers people brought your winnings to your house. . . . Everybody in the 'hood played the numbers daily. . . . The numbers game was a blessing for many. . . . When the numbers "hit" it made everyone in the 'hood happy and there were joyful celebrations. The numbers men and women embodied high society, affluence and prominence. Many were well respected. In lean times, families were able to survive and raise their children by hitting the numbers and hosting pay the rent parties. . . . Truly the 'hood was the village that is so often spoken of today. . . . Still, something was lost when the numbers people crumpled up their pay-off envelopes and betting slips and many shut down.

—Betty DeRamus, *Detroit News*, April 10, 1999

The story of playing the numbers in Detroit's black communities has not been captured for posterity like it has been in other cities, such as New York and Chicago. Like Detroit, both New York and Chicago had numbers gambling operations that were run by blacks. In all three cities, the men and women who operated these numbers operations supported black communities both economically and socially. All locations had corruption in their respective police departments and other government agencies, which, for a price, turned a blind eye to their illegal activities. In all three locations, the mafia stepped in and to some extent took control of numbers gambling, but this differed in Detroit. In New York and Chicago, they did so violently, but there was no widespread violence in Detroit. When the Italian mafia broke into the numbers game in Detroit, they had a gentlemen's agreement with the black numbers operators not to encroach on each other's business.[1] Both black and white numbers operators worked independently of each other for a long period of time. It was the incarceration of John Roxborough, and not a violent overthrow, that opened the door for the mafia to take over the wire service. Even when the mafia did so, dictating what the winning number would be, they did not take business away from the black numbers men. A fee was paid for the service, and like society, a segregation of the races occurred. Initially, the mafia catered to white customers and utilized mostly white employees, while blacks took care of black customers with black employees. Race relations in Detroit were so segregated that blacks for the most part would not knowingly patronize the white-run numbers establishments. For years, white and black numbers operations coexisted. When the mafia decided they wanted a larger share of Detroit's numbers business, they obtained it with financial warfare. They changed winning numbers to enrich themselves and to bankrupt the black operators in a Wall Street–like hostile takeover.

The story of numbers gambling in Detroit tells of a time and place that is no longer in existence. It is a Detroit story that reveals how playing the numbers influenced and shaped these bygone communities. It is a story of innovation, hard work, faith, and hope. It is a story about heroes and villains and all of those in between. It is a story of shades of gray, where in some instances the game was credited with heroic feats and at other times with causing irreparable harm. It shows how, against the odds, some were able to obtain the American Dream while it remained elusive for others. The American Dream was about more than just financial success. It was at times about the dream of having an opportunity and numbers operators provided this. Some black numbers operators' success became a source of pride in the black community and proved that despite the odds against them, blacks could have success too. The story of Detroit numbers looks at race and how something as simplistic as a numbers game came to be used to vilify and degrade a race at one point, while also helping uplift it and creating racial solidarity. Numbers playing in Detroit and the black men and women who operated their establishments can take some pride in what they did directly or indirectly for race relations in Detroit and around the world. Who knew that the penny, nickel, and dime bets out of Detroit would impact how the world viewed black people? Those bets enriched the right people, who in turn ensured Joe Louis and others were in positions to effect positive change in race relations and desegregation and promoted positive black images that blacks needed and sought throughout the United States. The investment in Joe Louis is just one powerful example of how the profits from playing the numbers left a lasting positive legacy.

There are countless stories of how playing the numbers allowed many to be self-sufficient and promoted individuals' capacity for self-determination. The history of playing the numbers in Detroit demonstrates how both the formal and informal economies are linked and fuel each other. When the formal economy failed its citizens, the informal economy (numbers gambling) filled the void. When a number of black Detroiters could not find employment elsewhere, it was Detroit numbers that employed them in both professional and skilled jobs.[2] The numbers operators were businessmen (and women) and made large sums of money from those who played the numbers and put money back into the community in a number of different ways. When blacks were forced to deal with structural injustices in employment, housing, banking, and government, numbers operators filled the void. The money from Detroit numbers funded various businesses, newspapers, insurance agencies, loan offices, housing projects, prizefighters, baseball teams, scholarships, nightclubs, and cultural projects. At times, numbers operators provided for communities' basic needs of food and shelter, as well as the hope that was needed to survive, especially during the Great Depression. In 1934, W. C. Woodson, executive secretary of the "Colored" YMCA in Detroit, wrote, "These men have a deep sense of appreciation of the need among their group and it is rare that they refuse requests for help. The system of giving is not sound social work procedure, but they sustain the reputation of helping their supporters and friends who are in need."[3] Playing the numbers was illegal and its morality can be argued; however, it had its benefits—at times it was an "evil for good." One reverend in the 1930s captured this when he said, "The numbers is not an evil because the money is spent right in our own community and the bankers are our best charity givers."[4]

Numbers gambling established relationships and bonds within the community because it served to circulate and redistribute resources. As Sunnie Wilson explained, money would circulate for weeks in Detroit's black community, and that economic power helped the city flourish.[5] Numbers operators had a special relationship with the communities they served. They were enriched by their patrons who trusted them, by the community that allowed them to exist, and, as such, were obligated to support the communities they served. The numbers operators reciprocated by taking care of the community during holidays, acting as an informal department of social services for the poor, and providing funding to parks, youth activities, and scholarships. They even funded civic organizations like the Urban League and the NAACP. Their philanthropy solidified their reputation as trusted, respected, and revered race men and women. It increased their social capital and in the end may have increased their profitability. Playing the numbers was an exchange system that individuals and groups used to fulfill each other's needs. This form of economic exchange system, which acted as a system of "total services," was similar to what sociologist and anthropologist Marcel Mauss wrote about in his essay "The Gift," when studying gift giving via the Kula circle. This notion of giving back to the community by the numbers operators can also be viewed as corporate social responsibility, a business's response to issues beyond their economic and legal duties.[6] The study of corporate social responsibility can be traced back to the 1950s, but numbers operators were engaged in it well before then.

The story of Detroit numbers reveals what it means to be a community. Playing the numbers brought people within the community together by acting as an instrument for community solidarity and was a communal activity. The numbers game served as a common thread that caused people to gather, visit, drink, and talk about their numbers and dreams.[7] This communal aspect of playing the numbers slowly faded when the lottery was legalized and shut out the neighborhood numbers workers who were the catalysts for those times.

Some people played for entertainment, while others enjoyed the social aspect, and still others played to win. One player, "Brother D," a hardworking barber from Detroit, emphatically claimed he played to win. Brother D was his barbershop's intellectual philosopher and could be counted on to lend an ear and to always have a relevant life story to tell. He had an amazing memory and frequently showed it off by quickly rattling off various numbers he played and their significance to him. Brother D lived by the motto "You got to be in it to win it because when you lay off they pay off!" He felt that numbers called to him and believed fate at times stepped in to guide him to winning numbers. When asked what he said to naysayers, people who are against playing the numbers for moral reasons, or to those who point out the odds and call it a fool's game, he said, "I don't listen to holy rollers; they don't put money in my pocket! I am a grown man who pays the cost to be my own boss. I know the odds but I play because I want to. There have been situations where I would have been begging for money, if I had not played and hit. The small investment is worth it to me."

Even though people from all walks of life played the numbers, historically the poor have been targeted for the most criticism—they should not have the freedom to "waste" money on a luxury but should save their money for life's necessities. Anthropologist Judith Goode has indicated that blaming the poor for their state of poverty has a long history in Western capitalism: they are viewed as "flawed" people who need to be "reformed" or fixed by experts. Goode further notes, "One irony is that in trying to rebuild self-esteem into 'faulty' individuals, a great deal of paternalism and disrespect is manifested by individuals and bureaucratic organizations."[8] This blaming of the poor is also rooted in playing the numbers. Other arguments against playing the numbers have included that the poor are victimized and do not understand they are being taken advantage of. Ethnocentrism, or the tendency to judge or view other cultures according to the standards or viewpoint of one's own, can be problematic.[9] This Detroit story about playing the numbers is a different perspective. For some, playing the numbers was about taking control and having a feeling of self-worth—the opposite of being a victim. Playing the numbers for others was viewed as a small luxury, a moment of entertainment or fun that they could afford. It made life tolerable and brought joy in an otherwise tough existence. Regardless of socioeconomic status everyone deserves this choice.

Finally, Detroit's numbers operators' largest contributions can never be truly measured. There are countless stories of people who hit the number and because of their "blessing" were able to catch up on their rent, pay a bill, or simply eat for another month. Playing the numbers was a rational act for them. Even when a player did not hit, the numbers men and women provided hope for a brighter future for people who *felt* this powerful emotion when, for a few pennies, they placed their dreams and faith on a number.

Notes

Introduction

1   A. Friend, "The Life of Willie D. Mosley," *Detroit Tribune Independent*, 1 June 1935, 1.
2   "Mosleyes Invite Friends to Celebrate Birthday," *Chicago Defender*, 11 March 1933, 7.
3   "Greetings to the Public," *Detroit Tribune*, 14 April 1933, 8.
4   "Welcome to Our City," *Detroit Tribune*, 14 April 1933, 6.
5   "'Bill' Mosley Is the New Boss of Detroit Stars," *Pittsburgh Courier*, 1 July 1933, 14.
6   "Policy Baron Is Slain in Detroit," *Pittsburgh Courier*, 1 June 1935, 1.
7   "Moseley to Serve Free Xmas Meals," *Detroit Tribune*, 23 December 1933, 2.
8   "Plays Santa to 2,000 Kiddies," *Detroit Tribune*, 22 December 1934, 2.
9   "Body of Slain Policy King to Rest in State," *Detroit Times*, 26 May 1935, 3.
10 "Wm. Mosley Digit King Is Murdered," *Chicago Defender*, 1 June 1935, 2.
11 "Policy Baron Is Slain in Detroit."
12 "Body of Slain Policy King to Rest in State."
13 "Willie D. Mosley Is Laid to Rest," *Detroit Tribune Independent*, 1 June 1935, 4.
14 "2,000 Attend Connolly Services," *Detroit Times*, 27 May 1935, 3.
15 "7,000 at Rites of Policy King," *Detroit Times*, 29 May 1935, 3.
16 Ibid.
17 "Willie D. Mosley Is Laid to Rest," 8.
18 "Body of Slain Policy King to Rest in State."
19 "Policy King's Pals Cheer Death Charge," *Detroit Times*, 13 June 1935, 1.
20 "Mosley's Slayer Convicted," *Detroit Tribune*, 5 October 1935, 1.

21 "Policy Probe Witness Face[s] Perjury Charges," *Chicago Defender*, 1 November 1941, 3.

22 Justine Wylie, *Detroit's Near Eastsiders: A Journey of Excellence against the Odds, 1920s–1960s* (Detroit: Detroit Black Writers Guild for the Near Eastsiders, 2008), 97.

23 "Detroit Is Dynamite," *Life*, 17 August 1942, 17–19.

24 Earl Brown, *Why Race Riots? Lessons from Detroit* (New York: Public Affairs Committee, 1944), 24.

25 J. A. Bracey, A. Meier, and E. Rudwich, *Black Nationalism in America* (Indianapolis: Bobbs-Merrill, 1970), 26.

26 "Policy Racket Busters Kick Over Valley's Pot of Gold," *Detroit News*, 16 September 1938, 16.

27 Sunnie Wilson and John Cohassey, *Toast of the Town: The Life and Times of Sunnie Wilson* (Detroit: Wayne State University Press, 1998), 65–66.

28 Ibid., 66, 102.

29 Ibid., 66–67, 155.

30 Jayne Curnow, "Gambling in Flores, Indonesia: Not Such Risky Business," *Australian Journal of Anthropology* 23, no. 1 (April 2012): 101.

Chapter 1

1 Gustav Carlson, "A Study of a Culture Complex" (PhD diss., University of Michigan, 1940), 189.

2 Herbert Asbury, *Sucker's Progress: An Informal History of Gambling in America from the Colonies to Canfield* (New York: Thunder Mouth Press, 1938), 88.

3 Ibid., 89.

4 George Sullivan, *By Chance a Winner: The History of Lotteries* (New York: Dodd, Mead & Co., 1972), 3.

5 Ibid., 5–6.

6 John Samuel Ezell, *Fortune's Merry Wheel: The Lottery in America* (Cambridge, MA: Harvard University Press, 1960), 13–62.

7 Ibid., 81.

8 Asbury, *Sucker's Progress*, 76–77.

9 David G. Schwartz, *Roll the Bones: The History of Gambling* (New York: Gotham Books, 2006), 149.

10 Ibid., 148.

11 Ibid., 149.

12 Ibid., 150.

13 Ann Fabian, *Card Sharps, Dream Books, and Bucket Shops: Gambling in Nineteenth-Century America* (Ithaca: Cornell University Press, 1990), 107.

14 Schwartz, *Roll the Bones*, 148.

15 "Lotteries," *Detroit Free Press*, 8 March 1832, 2.

16 "A Story and a Warning," *Detroit Daily Free Press*, 5 September 1855, 2.

17 "Effect of Winning Lottery Prizes," *Detroit Daily Free Press*, 11 February 1857, 2.

18 Fabian, *Card Sharps, Dream Books, and Bucket Shops*, 8–11.

19 Asbury, *Sucker's Progress*, 91–92.

20 "A New Movement against the Lottery," *Detroit Free Press*, 3 December 1858, 1.

21 Fabian, *Card Sharps, Dream Books, and Bucket Shops*, 151.

22 Schwartz, *Roll the Bones*, 150.

23 "A New Movement against the Lottery."

24 Ezell, *Fortune's Merry Wheel*, 205–29.

25 Reven Brenner and Gabrielle Brenner, *A World of Chance: Betting on Religion, Games, Wall Street* (Cambridge: Cambridge University Press, 2008), 141.

Chapter 2

1 Olivier Zunz, *The Changing Face of Inequality: Urbanization, Industrial Development, and Immigrants in Detroit, 1880–1920* (Chicago: University of Chicago Press, 1982), 33.

2 David Katzman, *Before the Ghetto: Black Detroit in the Nineteenth Century* (Chicago: University of Chicago Press, 1973), 69–74.

3 "Keno! How It and Other Games Flourish in Detroit," *Detroit Free Press*, 3 December 1880, 1.

4 "Found Guilty," *Detroit Free Press*, 9 February 1884, 8.

5 "Playing Policy: Marvin Cleveland Held to the Recorder's Court for Running a Policy Shop," *Detroit Free Press*, 5 January 1889, 4.

6 John Philip Quinn, *Fools of Fortune; or, Gambling and Gamblers* (Chicago: G. L. Howe & Co., 1890), 186.

7 "M. Quad's Return," *Detroit Free Press*, 28 April 1895, 13.

8 Richard Kaplan, *Politics and the American Press: The Rise of Objectivity, 1856–1920* (New York: Cambridge University Press, 2002), 43–47.

9 Arthur Pound, *Detroit: Dynamic City* (New York: D. Appleton-Century, 1940), 217.

10 "M. Quad: A Sketch from Harper's Magazine," *Detroit Free Press*, 25 July 1886, 12.

11 "M. Quad, at 70: Still Our Most Prolific Humorist," *New York Times*, 11 February 1912, SM 10.

12 M. Quad, *Brother Gardner's Lime-Kiln Club* (Chicago: Belford, Clarke & Co., 1892), 17.

13 "The Stage: M. Quad Again to the Front with a Comedy," *Detroit Free Press*, 30 July 1882, 13.

14 "Bro. Gardner's Lime-Kiln Club," *Detroit Free Press*, 3 October 1880, 9.

15 "Policy," *Detroit Free Press*, 18 February 1881, 1.

16 "The Gamblers," *Detroit Free Press*, 22 April 1883, 1.

17 "No More Gambling," *Detroit Free Press*, 1 April 1882, 8.

18 "The Gamblers," *Detroit Free Press*, 21 May 1882, 1.

19 "Policy Shops," *Detroit Free Press*, 22 December 1882, 3.

20 "The Pool Selling Case," *Detroit Free Press*, 19 April 1883, 1.

21 "The Gamblers," *Detroit Free Press*, 22 April 1883, 13.

22 "56-52-44: How Mr. Merryweather Struck Policy for $50," *Detroit Free Press*, 30 March 1884, 17.

23 "Mr. Merryweather," *Detroit Free Press*, 13 April 1884, 23.

24 "To Suppress Policy Shops," *Detroit Free Press*, 31 March 1887, 5.

25 "The Black Lookout," *Detroit Free Press*, 19 April 1892, 8.

26 Ibid.

27 Katzman, *Before the Ghetto*, 93.

28 "Forty Policy 'Joints' Open," *Detroit Free Press*, 14 May 1902, 1.

29 "Policy Joints Were Closed," *Detroit Free Press*, 15 May 1902, 1, 10.

30 Ibid., 10.

31 Ann Fabian, *Card Sharps, Dream Books, and Bucket Shops: Gambling in Nineteenth-Century America* (Ithaca: Cornell University Press, 1990), 8–9.

32 "Policy Writers at Work," *Detroit Free Press*, 16 May 1902, 1.

33 George Haynes, *Negro Newcomers in Detroit* (New York: Arno Press, 1969), 21.

34 "Policy Playing Continues," *Detroit Free Press*, 30 March 1903, 4.

35 "Bad Phase of Policy Craze," *Detroit Free Press*, 2 April 1903, 5.

36 "Former Counterfeiter Accused of Conducting a Policy Game," *Detroit Free Press*, 22 August 1908, 12.

37 "Detroit Negroes on the Increase," *Detroit Free Press*, 20 August 1908, 10.

38 "Policy Game May Come Back," *Detroit Free Press*, 5 July 1908, 24.

Chapter 3

1 The epigraph comes from Gerald Astor, *And a Credit to His Race* (New York: Saturday Review Press, 1974), 33.

2 Ibid., 32.

3 Fred Hart Williams Papers, 1935–1957, Burton Historical Collection, Detroit Public Library.

4 Astor, *And a Credit to His Race*, 32.

5 "John W. Roxborough Mourned," *Michigan Chronicle*, 20 December 1975, 1.

6 "Lawyer Roxborough Dead," *Detroit Free Press*, 19 August 1908, 1, 4.

7 William Nunn and Chester Washington, "The Life of Joe Louis," *Pittsburgh Courier*, 13 April 1935, A5.

8 Russ Cowans, "Years Rest Lightly on Roxie," *Pittsburgh Courier*, 15 April 1961, 23.

9 Astor, *And a Credit to His Race*, 32–33.

10 Nunn and Washington, "The Life of Joe Louis."

11 Tony Langston, "Tony Langston's Drama and Movie Review," *Chicago Defender*, 8 December 1917, 4.

12 "The Trip," *Chicago Defender*, 25 September 1920, 5.

13 Elizabeth Martin, *Detroit and the Great Migration: 1916–1929* (Ann Arbor: University of Michigan Press, 1993), 47.

14 David Levine, *Internal Combustion: The Races in Detroit, 1915–1926* (Westport, CT: Greenwood Press, 1976), 86.

15 Martin, *Detroit and the Great Migration*, 5.

16 "Dress Well Club," Dress Well Club Brochure, 20 September 1917.

17 Martin, *Detroit and the Great Migration*, 5.

18 Justine Wylie, *Detroit's Near Eastsiders: A Journey of Excellence against the Odds, 1920s–1960s* (Detroit: Detroit Black Writers Guild for the Near Eastsiders, 2008), 4.

19 Martin, *Detroit and the Great Migration*, 41.

20 Wylie, *Detroit's Near Eastsiders*, 2–6.

21 "Jobs Scarce for Negroes," *Detroit News*, 27 April 1935, 15.

22 "Detroit Now in Danger of Jim Crowism," *Chicago Defender*, 29 July 1922, 1.

23 Astor, *And a Credit to His Race*, 33.

24 Gustav Carlson, "A Study of a Culture Complex" (PhD diss., University of Michigan, 1940), 16–17.

25 Ibid., 18.

26 Swanson Carter, "Numbers Gambling: The Negro's Illegal Response to Status Discrimination in American Society" (Master's thesis, Wayne State University, 1970), 47.

27 Ibid., 44.

28 Robert Conot, *American Odyssey: A Unique History of America Told through the Life of a Great City* (New York: William Morrow, 1974), 213.

29 Carter, "Numbers Gambling," 44.

30 Edward Coffey, "Detroit, Michigan," *Pittsburgh Courier*, 26 March 1927, B7.

31 City of Detroit Historic Designation Advisory Board, *Proposed East Kirby Avenue Historic District Final Report*, n.d., 2–3.

32 "Great Lakes Insurance Company Keeps ahead of the Times," *Detroit Tribune*, 14 April 1933, 1, 2.

33 Carter, "Numbers Gambling," 45.

34 Ibid., 44.

35 "Detroit Business Men Play Santa to Needy," *Pittsburgh Courier*, 31 December 1927, 9.

36 "Roxborough Escapes Fidelity Crash," *Detroit Tribune*, 24 December 1938, 1.

37 Brad Flory, "Correcting Faulty Local Wisdom on a 'Fabulous and Colorful Character' from Jackson County's Past," *Ann Arbor News*, 29 August 2013, 1.

38 Donna Barnes, "Industrialist Bus Watson Estate," *Jackson Citizen Patriot*, 29 April 1962, 11.

39 "Mystery House May Be Policy's Redwood Palace," *Detroit Free Press*, 10 September 1938, 1.

Chapter 4

1 Swanson Carter, "Numbers Gambling: The Negro's Illegal Response to Status Discrimination in American Society" (Master's thesis, Wayne State University, 1970), 47.

2   Shane White, Stephen Garton, Stephen Robertson, and Graham White, *Playing the Numbers: Gambling in Harlem between the Wars* (Cambridge, MA: Harvard University Press, 2010), 150, 151.

3   J. Saunders Redding, "Playing the Number," *North American Review* 238 (December 1934): 533–42.

4   Gustav Carlson, "A Study of a Culture Complex" (PhD diss., University of Michigan, 1940), 8–10.

5   Carter, "Numbers Gambling," 31.

6   Jim Bankes, *The Pittsburgh Crawfords* (Jefferson, NC: McFarland, 2001), 19–23.

7   Lena Horne and Richard Schickel, *Lena* (New York: Doubleday, 1965), 5–35.

8   Ibid., 77.

9   "Spiritualists Doing Thriving Business," *Pittsburgh Courier*, 15 December 1928, 12.

10   Drake St. Clair and Horace Cayton, *Black Metropolis: A Study of Negro Life in a Northern City* (New York: Harcourt, Brace and Company, 1945), 474.

11   John Carlisle, "Chancy Games People Play," *Detroit News*, 12 May 1970, 6C.

12   Tom Ricke, "Numbers Golden Era Fades," *Detroit Free Press*, 6 March 1972, 1A, 8A.

13   Anthony Shafton, *Dream Singers: The African American Way with Dreams* (New York: John Wiley, 2002), 74.

14   Anthony Comstock, *Traps for the Young* (New York: Funk & Wagnalls, 1883), 77.

15   Mark Mellen, "Numbers Racket," *Easy Money* (September/October 1936): 21.

16   George McCall, "Symbiosis: The Case of Hoodoo and the Numbers Racket," *Social Problems* 10 (1963): 361–71.

17   Catherine Yronwode, "Hoodoo in Theory and Practice," www.luckymojo.com/auntsallys.html.

18   Professor Zonite, *The Original Three Wise Men Dream Book* (Detroit, 1940), 1.

19   Herbert Gladstone Parris, *The Lucky Star Dream Book* (New York, 1928), 4.

20   "Dream Book Editor Wins Suit," *Detroit Tribune*, 7 December 1940, 1.

21   "Dream Book Publisher Sues for $40,000," *Afro-American*, 26 March 1938, 2.

22 Ibid., 1.

23 Ibid., 2.

24 "Dream Book Editor Wins Suit."

25 "Numbers Fans Make Killing on 263 Times Tip," *Detroit Times*, 16 March 1938, 3.

26 Carter, "Numbers Gambling," 48.

27 Bill Gibson, "John Roxborough, Louis's Manager, Is Detroit's Santa," *Afro-American*, 22 June 1935, 20.

28 "Suspended Police Inspector Says Reading Took $18,000 in Nine Months as Share of Graft from Policy Houses," *Detroit Free Press*, 5 May 1940, 1, 4.

29 "Detroit Plays $50,000 Daily on Digits," *Afro-American*, 10 January 1931, 1, 16.

30 Carter, "Numbers Gambling," 44.

31 Coleman Young and Lonnie Wheeler, *Hard Stuff: The Autobiography of Mayor Coleman Young* (New York: Viking, 1994), 20.

32 "McCarthy Suspended from Racket Squad after Woman's Suicide Note Told of Graft," *Detroit News*, 24 April 1940, 14.

33 Carlson, "A Study of a Culture Complex," 50.

34 Ibid., 51.

35 Ibid., 51–52.

36 Ibid., 53.

37 Carter, "Numbers Gambling," 33.

38 Ibid., 33–34.

39 "Records Show McCrea-Block Deal for $5,000," *Detroit Free Press*, 12 April 1940, 1, 13.

40 Carlson, "A Study of a Culture Complex," 53.

41 "Police Renew Quiz after Racket Diary Vanishes Strangely," *Detroit Free Press*, 9 August 1939, 5.

42 "The Great Black Strip," *Detroit Free Press*, 24 July 1973, 103.

43 "Bookies to Lose Phones at Grand Jury's Orders," *Detroit Free Press*, 2 February 1940, 1, 10.

44 "Holstein Seized by Bandits! Kept 3 Days, Bound, Blindfolded and Gagged," *New York Age*, 29 September 1928, 1.

45 "Seabury Probing Harlem Murders," *Brooklyn Times Union*, 16 March 1931, 4.

46 "Numbers Queen Fears Schultz'll Put Her on Spot," *Daily News*, 17 September 1932, 3.

47 "Policy Racket Crown Studded with Bullets and Prison Bars," *Daily News*, 8 February 1938, 16.

Chapter 5

1 Robert Conot, *American Odyssey: A Unique History of America Told through the Life of a Great City* (New York: William Morrow, 1974), 265.

2 Sunnie Wilson and John Cohassey, *Toast of the Town: The Life and Times of Sunnie Wilson* (Detroit: Wayne State University Press, 1998), 67.

3 "Detroit Launches Fight on 'Policy' Gambling," *Chicago Defender*, 22 September 1928, 1.

4 Mark Haller, "Bootleggers and American Gambling, 1920–1950," in *Final Report of the US Commission on the Review of the National Policy towards Gambling* (Washington, DC: GPO, 1976), 120.

5 "Numbers Rise Told by Gambler," *Detroit News*, 12 September 1938, 1.

6 "Detroit 'Policy' Racketeers Defy Police Clean-up," *Chicago Defender*, 22 December 1928, 1.

7 "Minsters Lag in Fight on Vice," *Chicago Defender*, 2 February 1929, 1, 2.

8 People of the State of Michigan vs. Walter Norwood et al., Testimony of Percy Miles–Walter Norwood, July 12, 1940, p. 132, RG 2011–37, Box 915, Folder A24008, Michigan History Center, Archives of Michigan.

9 Ibid., 98.

10 Ibid., 101.

11 Ibid., 106.

12 Ibid., 110–12.

13 Ibid., 113.

14 "Detroit Launches Fight on 'Policy,'" *Chicago Defender*, 1 September 1928, 1.

15 "Detroit Wars on 'Policy' Gambling," *Chicago Defender*, 15 December 1928, 1.

16 "Detroit 'Policy' Racketeers Defy Police Clean-up."

17 "'Policy' Toll $50,000 a Day Here," *Detroit News*, 9 December 1928, 2.

18 Ibid., 1.

19 Ibid.

20 Swanson Carter, "Numbers Gambling: The Negro's Illegal Response to Status Discrimination in American Society" (Master's thesis, Wayne State University, 1970), 48.

21 James Peyton, "Detroit News," *Chicago Defender*, 8 September 1928, A4.

22 "Detroit Launches Fight on 'Policy.'"

23 "Detroit 'Numbers' Game Cause of War," *Afro-American*, 1 June 1929, 3.

24 Russ Cowans, "I Cover the Town," *Michigan Chronicle*, 9 December 1944, 20.

25 Russ Cowans, "'Valley' Pioneer Succumbs," *Michigan Chronicle*, 23 January 1960, 1, 5.

26 "Young Chicagoan Elected to Board of Insurance Co.," *Pittsburgh Courier*, 9 March 1929, 3.

27 "Detroit Men on Mortgage Company BD," *Pittsburgh Courier*, 20 July 1929, 2.

28 "$20,000 in Jewels Taken in Police Raid," *Detroit News*, 23 June 1929, 3.

29 The People vs. Everett Watson before Honorable Charles Bartlett, Judge of the Recorder's Court, September 16, 1929, Michigan History Center, Archives of Michigan.

30 Conot, *American Odyssey*, 259.

31 "Ku Klux Clan Issue in Detroit Politics," *Pittsburgh Courier*, 2 November 1929, 4.

32 Kenneth T. Jackson, *The Ku Klux Klan in the City, 1915–1930* (Oxford: Oxford University Press, 1967), 128.

33 Ibid., 128–29.

34 Ibid., 273.

35 Ibid., 132.

36 Ibid., 135.

37 Ibid., 134–35.

38 Ibid., 135.

39 Ibid., 136.

40 "Fiery Cross Burns as Detroit Voters End Hot Campaign," *Washington Post*, 3 November 1925, 5.

41 "Smith Winning in Detroit," *New York Times*, 4 November 1925, 4.

42 "Detroit Mayoralty Fight in Spotlight," *Chicago Defender*, 5 October 1929, 4.

43 "Detroit Elects Bowles Mayor in Close Race," *Chicago Daily Tribune*, 6 November 1929, 2.

44 Cash Asher, *Sacred Cows: A Story of the Recall of Mayor Bowles* (Detroit: Self-published, 1931), 35–40.

45 The People vs. John Roxborough and John Doe alias Wilson Examination before Honorable Henry S. Sweeny, Judge of the Recorder's Court, February 24, 1930, Michigan History Center, Archives of Michigan.

46 "Bowles' Recall Is Asked: Petitions Are Being Circulated," *Detroit Free Press*, 22 May 1930, 1.

47 "125,000 Voters Sign to Recall Detroit's Mayor," *Chicago Daily Tribune*, 17 June 1930, 11.

48 "Bowles' Recall Is Asked."

49 "Emmons' Vice Charge Is Denied by Mayor," *Detroit News*, 26 May 1930, 1, 38.

50 Carter, "Numbers Gambling," 50–51.

51 Morgan Oates, "Law Mixed with Fun? Tom-Tom Was the Man," *Parade, Detroit Free Press*, 22 January 1961, 2.

52 "Emmons' Vice Charge Is Denied by Mayor," 1.

53 "125,000 Voters Sign to Recall Detroit's Mayor," 1–4.

54 "Detroit Is Rushed into City Election," *New York Times*, 27 July 1930, 49.

55 "Killing of Buckley Arouses Detroit; Hint of Racketeer," *New York Times*, 24 July 1930, 1.

56 "Lays Buckley Killing to Bowles Campaign," *New York Times*, 4 March 1931, 23.

57 "Detroit Plays $50,000 Daily on Digits," *Afro-American*, 10 January 1931, 16.

58 Ibid., 1.

59 Carter, "Numbers Gambling," 53.

60 "Tells on Bandit Trio," *Detroit Free Press*, 27 October 1931, 12.

61 "3 Plead Not Guilty to Robbery Charges," *Detroit Free Press*, 23 December 1931, 8.

62 "Youths Arrested in 'Bookie' Thefts," *Detroit Free Press*, 21 December 1931, 9.

63 "Wife Routs Thugs Buy Firing at Them," *Detroit Free Press*, 31 January 1936, 10.

64 Marian Fields, "Detroit, Michigan," *Pittsburgh Courier*, 6 September 1930, A9.

65 "Fined for Reckless Driving," *Pittsburgh Courier*, 30 July 1932, 1.

Chapter 6

1 Robert Conot, *American Odyssey: A Unique History of America Told through the Life of a Great City* (New York: William Morrow, 1974), 248, 259.

2 Ibid.

3 "Numbers War on in Detroit," *Pittsburgh Courier*, 23 July 1932, 4.

4 Gustav Carlson, "A Study of a Culture Complex" (PhD diss., University of Michigan, 1940), 140.

5 "Weisberg Held in Policy Raid," *Detroit Free Press*, 13 September 1938, 4.

6 Swanson Carter, "Numbers Gambling: The Negro's Illegal Response to Status Discrimination in American Society" (Master's thesis, Wayne State University, 1970), 117.

7 Ibid., 119.

8 Ernest Borden, *Detroit's Paradise Valley* (Charleston: Arcadia Publishing, 2003), 15.

9 Carlson, "A Study of a Culture Complex," 156.

10 "Court Cases Reveal Old Practice," *Atlanta Daily World*, 29 July 1935, 6.

11 Conot, *American Odyssey*, 357.

12 Carter, "Numbers Gambling," 119.

13 The People vs. John Roxborough and John Doe alias Wilson Examination before Honorable Henry S. Sweeny, Judge of the Recorder's Court, February 24, 1930, Michigan History Center, Archives of Michigan.

14 "Detroit Plays $50,000 Daily on Digits," *Afro-American*, 10 January 1931, 16.

15 "Idle Protest to the Mayor," *Detroit News*, 25 October 1930, 3.

16 "Welfare Limit Is 7 Million," *Detroit News*, 7 July 1931, 1.

17 "Detroit Stores Displacing Negroes for Whites," *Pittsburgh Courier*, 20 February 1932, 2.

18 A. Philip Randolph, "What the Universal Economic Depression Has Meant to Members of the Race," *Chicago Defender*, 14 January 1933, 8.

19 "Detroit Official Says Race Unemployed Is Big Problem," *Chicago Defender*, 26 March 1932, 4.

20 Conot, *American Odyssey*, 304.

21 Ibid., 306.

22 Ibid., 309.

23 Ibid., 309.

24 Carter, "Numbers Gambling," 107.

25 Margery Miller, *Joe Louis: American* (New York: Current Books, 1945), 26.

26 Joe Louis with Edna and Art Rust Jr., *Joe Louis: My Life* (New York: Harcourt Brace Jovanovich, 1978), 28.

27 Ibid., 30.

28 "Manages Boxer: Latest Sensation!" *Atlanta Daily World*, 14 December 1934, 7.

29 Lewis Erenberg, *The Greatest Fight of Our Generation* (Oxford: Oxford University Press, 2006), 35.

30 Ibid., 33–35.

31 Miller, *Joe Louis*, 33.

32 Joe Louis, "My Toughest Fight," *Salute*, December 1947, 13.

33 Gerald Astor, *And a Credit to His Race* (New York: Saturday Review Press, 1974), 42.

34 Edward Van Every, *Joe Louis: Man and Super-Fighter* (New York: Frederick A. Stokes Company, 1936), 71.

35 Ibid., 72.

36 Louis, *Joe Louis: My Life*, 32.

37 John Roxborough, "How I Discovered Joe Louis," *Ebony*, October 1954, 67.

38 Goldie Walden, "Society Editor Tells Louis' Love for Mother," *Chicago Defender*, 6 July 1935, 7.

39 Erenberg, *The Greatest Fight of Our Generation*, 45.

40 "The Life Story of Joe Louis," *Pittsburgh Courier*, 11 May 1935, A4.

41 Chris Mead, *Joe Louis: Black Champion in White America* (Mineola: Dover Publications, 1985), 55–56.

42 Russ Cowans, "Solid South Decides Joe Louis Must Be Somebody," *Chicago Defender*, 13 April 1935, 17.

43 Miller, *Joe Louis*, 37.

44 "A Forgotten Champion Fights Again," *Life*, 21 June 1937, 19–23.

45 Ibid., 22.

46 "Jobs Scarce for Negroes," *Detroit News*, 27 April 1935, 15.

47 Joseph Ator, "We Bet 5 Billion: How Lotteries Claim an Army of Suckers; Numbers Racket Preys on the Small Fry," *Chicago Daily Tribune*, 25 October 1936, E10.

48 Mark Mellen, "Numbers Racket," *Easy Money* (September/October 1936): 19, 94.

Chapter 7

1 "Seize Mr., Mrs. E. I. Watson in Chicago, Ill.," *Michigan Chronicle*, 17 February 1940, 1.

2 Russ Cowans, "Round N Bout the Highspots of Detroit," *Chicago Defender*, 8 June 1935, 7.

3 Ibid., 8.

4 "Policy Racket Czar Eludes Police Raid," *Detroit Times*, 13 July 1935, 3.

5 Nathan Thompson, *Kings: The True Story of Chicago's Policy Kings and Numbers Racketeers* (Chicago: Bronzeville Press, 2006), 114–15.

6 "Policy Barons Shift Place of Meeting to Hot Springs," *Chicago Defender*, 25 April 1936, 1.

7 Mark Mellen, "Numbers Racket," *Easy Money* (September/October 1936): 18.

8 "Heart Attack Fatal to Duncan McCrea," *Detroit Free Press*, 26 May 1951, 15.

9 "Vice-Conspiracy Convictions Cap Stormy Careers for Principal Defendants," *Detroit Free Press*, 29 April 1941, 16.

10 "Several Names Found on Lists," *Detroit News*, 28 May 1936, 1.

11 John Carlisle, "Night Riders' Chief Tells of Founding," *Detroit News*, 27 May 1936, 1, 2.

12 "McCrea in Black Legion? He Was Just a Joiner Then," *Detroit News*, 26 May 1936, 1.

13 "Ryan Gives Up to Grand Jury Ending Search," *Detroit Free Press*, 10 May 1940, 18.

14 "Ex-Officer Is Granted Immunity," *Detroit News*, 4 May 1940, 1.

15 "Court Studying Watson Appeal," *Detroit Free Press*, 6 April 1940, 3.

16 "McCrea and Aide Got $80,000 Graft, Ferguson Charges," *Detroit Free Press*, 17 April 1940, 1, 7.

17 "Everett Watson Promotes Financial Corporation," *Detroit Tribune*, 20 February 1937, 1.

18 "Watson Enterprises Made Steady Progress Last Year," *Detroit Tribune*, 28 January 1939, 3.

19 "History of Paradise Valley Distributing Company," *Detroit Tribune*, 6 September 1941, 8.

20 Sunnie Wilson and John Cohassey, *Toast of the Town: The Life and Times of Sunnie Wilson* (Detroit: Wayne State University Press, 1998), 46.

21 Roxborough v. Roxborough Docket No. 25, Supreme Court of Michigan, 269 Mich. 569; 257 N.W. 747; 1934 Mich. Lexis 955.

22 Russ Cowans, "Wife of Louis' Manager Gets Divorce, Cash," *Chicago Defender*, 6 November 1936, 12.

23 Roxborough v. Roxborough Docket No. 25, Supreme Court of Michigan, 269 Mich. 569; 257 N.W. 747; 1934 Mich. Lexis 955.

24 "Mrs. Roxborough Is Given Divorce," *Chicago Defender*, 7 November 1936, 23.

25 Cowans, "Wife of Louis' Manager Gets Divorce, Cash."

26 Jay Gould, "Race Track Gossip," *Chicago Defender*, 9 March 1935, 17.

27 Gustav Carlson, "A Study of a Culture Complex" (PhD diss., University of Michigan, 1940), 46.

28 "Roxborough Team Wins Championship," *Detroit Tribune Independent*, 24 August 1935, 8.

29 Bill Gibson, "John Roxborough, Louis's Manager, Is Detroit's Santa," *Afro-American*, 22 June 1935, 20.

30 Earl Morris, "Grand Town Day and Night," *Pittsburgh Courier*, 12 December 1936, A6.

31 Gladys Johnson, "Chesterfields Score Again in Gay Party," *Michigan Chronicle*, 22 July 1939, 6.

32 "Joe Louis Wins Ribbons in America's First All-Negro Horse Show at Detroit," *Life*, 11 July 1938, 45.

33 Lewis Erenberg, *The Greatest Fight of Our Generation* (Oxford: Oxford University Press, 2006), 45.

34 Floyd Calvin, "Give Julian and Johnny a Hand," *Chicago Defender*, 17 July 1937, 20.

35 Fred Cousins, "Policy Racket-Busters Kick Over Valley's Pot of Gold," *Detroit News*, 16 September 1938, 16.

36 "Roxborough to Face Charges of Inventor," *Michigan Chronicle*, 15 January 1949, 3.

37 "Living Costs Are Higher in Detroit than in Any Other City," *Pittsburgh Courier*, 21 May 1938, 6.

38 "Roxborough Robbed," *Detroit Tribune*, 10 December 1938, 1.

Chapter 8

1 "The Rise and Fall of Richard Reading," *Detroit Free Press Editorial Magazine*, 4 January 1942, 1.

2 "Skrzycki Tells of Reading Graft Talk," *Detroit News*, 7 November 1941, 1.

3 "The Rise and Fall of Richard Reading."

4 "Reading, 22 Others Guilty," *Detroit News*, 16 December 1941, 2.

5 "Paradise Valley's Mayor," *Chicago Defender*, 31 October 1936, 27.

6 "Reading Gave Vague Pledge," *Detroit News*, 6 November 1941, 4.

7 "Ryan Gives Up to Grand Jury Ending Search," *Detroit Free Press*, 10 May 1940, 1.

8 Ibid., 10.

9 "The Rise and Fall of Richard Reading."

10 "Cordial Hosts Fete Party in the East," *Chicago Defender*, 6 July 1938, 7.

11 Ibid.

12 "Witnesses Get Guards to Halt Alleged Spying," *Detroit Free Press*, 8 May 1940, 12.

13 "Reading Gave Aid to Racket Ferguson Told," *Detroit Free Press*, 7 May 1940, 1.

14 "Witnesses Get Guards to Halt Alleged Spying."

15 "Reading Gave Aid to Racket Ferguson Told."

16 Ibid., 4.

17 Ibid., 1, 4.

18 "Witness Gone: Quiz Cut Short," *Detroit Free Press*, 16 June 1940, 4.

19 "Suspended Police Inspector Says Reading Took $18,000 in Nine Months as Share of Graft from Policy Houses," *Detroit Free Press*, 5 May 1940, 1.

20 "Policy Racket 'Pay-off' Man Faces Trial," *Chicago Defender*, 15 November 1941, 9.

21 "Detroit's 'Rackets' Smashed," *Atlanta Daily World*, 27 September 1938, 6.

22 "Open Gaming Found in City," *Detroit Free Press*, 3 September 1938, 2.

23 Russ Cowans, "Cops Raid Roxy's Safe," *Afro-American*, 17 September 1938, 2.

24 "Police Seize 86 in Policy Raids upon 11 Houses," *Detroit Free Press*, 9 September 1938, 1.

25 "Will White Mobsters Dominate 'Numbers'?" *Detroit Tribune*, 24 September 1938, 1.

26 "Federal Agents Enter Detroit's War on Racket," *Detroit Free Press*, 11 September 1938, 3.

27 Ibid., 1.

28 Ibid.

29 "Grafters Took Policy Winnings," *Chicago Defender*, 25 October 1941, 1.

30 "'Numbers' Rise Told by Gambler," *Detroit News*, 12 September 1938, 4.

31 "Policy Evil Is Assailed by Pickert," *Detroit News*, 11 September 1938, 1.

32 Ibid., 15.

33 "$2,000 Is Seized in Policy Raid," *Detroit Free Press*, 21 September 1938, 5.
34 "Policy a Game for Poor Man," *Detroit News*, 24 April 1940, 14.
35 "Paid Reading $18,000, Frahm $7,200, Boettcher Asserts at Graft Hearing," *Detroit News*, 5 May 1940, 2.
36 "Policy Racket 'Pay-off' Man Faces Trial."
37 Forrester Washington, "Slants on Sports: There Would Be No Joe Louis without John Roxborough," *Atlantic Daily World*, 23 July 1939, 7.

Chapter 9

1 "Reading's Son Named in Graft Quiz," *Detroit News*, 18 November 1939, 1.
2 "She Kills Self, Child after Bribe Note," *Detroit Times*, 7 August 1939, 1, 2.
3 "I'm Just a Small-Time Guy McBride Insists to Police," *Detroit News*, 9 August 1939, 1, 2.
4 "She Kills Self, Child after Bribe Note," 2.
5 "Death Notes Charge Police Bribery," *Detroit News*, 7 August 1939, 1.
6 "She Kills Self, Child after Bribe Note," 1.
7 "Note Makes Charges to Federal Men," *Detroit News*, 7 August 1939, 2.
8 "Operators Motivated by Inquiry," *Detroit News*, 8 August 1939, 1.
9 "I'm Just a Small-Time Guy McBride Insists to Police," 2.
10 "U.S. Wary of Jury Quiz on Police Graft Charges," *Detroit Free Press*, 21 August 1939, 1.
11 "Death Cheats Graft Inquiry," *Detroit News*, 11 November 1939, 1.
12 "Graft Storm Unabated on Anniversary of McDonald Suicide," *Detroit News*, 4 August 1940, 5.
13 "FBI Calls Robinson in McBride Quiz," *Detroit News*, 9 August 1939, 2.
14 "U.S. Wary of Jury Quiz on Police Graft Charges," 2.
15 "Graft Quiz Called Off by McCrea," *Detroit News*, 10 August 1939, 1.
16 "Policy a Game for Poor Man," *Detroit News*, 24 April 1940, 14.
17 "Graft Storm Unabated on Anniversary of McDonald Suicide," 5.
18 "Policy a Game for Poor Man," 14.
19 "Witnesses Get Guards to Halt Alleged Spying," *Detroit Free Press*, 8 May 1940, 12.
20 "Pastor Echoes Probe Demand," *Detroit Free Press*, 21 August 1939, 2.
21 "Police Graft Inquiry Put in Their Hands," *Detroit News*, 21 August 1939, 2.
22 "Six Are Jailed in Policy Raid," *Detroit Free Press*, 23 August 1939, 3.
23 "Gamblers Flee before Grand Jury," *Michigan Chronicle*, 26 August 1939, 1.

24 "Number Houses Close Doors," *Detroit Tribune*, 26 August 1939, 1.

25 "Idle Gamblers Paid State Aid," *Detroit Free Press*, 28 January 1940, 4.

26 People of the State of Michigan vs. Walter Norwood et al., Testimony of George Washington–Walter Norwood RG 2011–37, Box 915, Folder A24008, July 12, 1940, 165.

27 "Policy Game Is Termed Unmolested," *Detroit Free Press*, 10 October 1941, 1.

28 "Walter Norwood Names Police Graft Takers," *Detroit Tribune*, 8 November 1941, 2.

29 John Roxborough and Julian Black, *Official Souvenir Scrap Book: World's Heavyweight Champion Joe Louis* (Detroit: Self-published, 1939), 1.

30 "Talking About," *Jet*, 17 April 1958, 43. Ruby McCollum became infamous in 1952 when she killed Clifford Leroy Adams Jr., a white physician and newly elected Florida state senator. Although married to Sam, Ruby had an affair and a child by the married Adams, who was considered the most prominent man in Live Oak. It was speculated that Sam paid off Adams and the town's law enforcement to operate his numbers business. Sam also looked the other way while his wife carried on an affair with Adams. On August 3, 1952, Ruby shot and killed Adams in his office over an alleged unpaid medical bill. The trial received national and international attention because Ruby, a black woman, had killed a white man in Jim Crow Florida. Ruby testified that Adams had forced her to have sex with him and made her bear his child. She was tried, found guilty, and sentenced to be executed; however, her sentence was eventually adjudicated, and she was found to be criminally insane. She was committed to a mental institution for several years before being released in 1974.

31 "Negroes Outdid Selves at Gate," *New York Amsterdam News*, 7 October 1939, 15.

32 "Paradise Valley Kicks the Stars: Joe Wins Again," *Detroit Free Press*, 21 September 1939, 1, 15.

33 Henry McLemore, "Joe Louis Is Called Most Mild-Mannered Champion," *Detroit News*, 21 September 1939, 47.

34 "Hotel Gaming Rouses Police," *Detroit Free Press*, 2 September 1939, 1.

35 "Death Cheats Graft Inquiry," 1.

36 "The Rise and Fall of Richard Reading," *Detroit Free Press Editorial Magazine*, 4 January 1942, 1.

37 "Robinson Case to Be Delayed," *Detroit Free Press*, 26 January 1940, 15.

38 Ibid.

39 "FBI Calls Robinson in McBride Quiz," *Detroit News*, 9 August 1939, 1.

40 "Dual Slaying Recalls Case of Robinson," *Detroit News*, 7 August 1939, 1.

41 "State Investigation of Paroles Is Sought in Robinson Expose," *Detroit Free Press*, 24 January 1940, 1, 7.

42 "Supt. Fred Frahm Resigns after Suspension by Eaman," *Detroit Free Press*, 14 January 1940, 1, 2.

43 "Quitting Job Today, Farris Blurts Out in Tantrum at Jail," *Detroit Free Press*, 30 January 1940, 4.

44 "Report Accuses Prosecutor of Collecting Vice Payoffs," *Detroit Free Press*, 24 February 1940, 1.

45 Ibid., 4.

46 Riley Murray, "Their Letters Shook up a City," *Detroit Free Press, Sunday Magazine*, 14 February 1960, B1.

47 "McCrea's Raiders Try to Invade Jury Room; Driven Off as O'Hara Calls Riot Squads," *Detroit Free Press*, 5 March 1940, 1, 10.

48 "Ouster of Wilcox Will Be Sought on Grand Jury Charges of Graft," *Detroit Free Press*, 6 March 1940, 1.

49 Morgan Oates, "Law Mixed with Fun? Tom-Tom Was the Man," *Parade, Detroit Free Press*, 22 January 1961, 2.

50 "Wilcox and Aides Split up $121,000 Graft, Court Told," *Detroit Free Press*, 7 April 1940, 11.

51 Oates, "Law Mixed with Fun? Tom-Tom Was the Man."

52 "Raids Died Out after '35, McCrea's Aide Declares," *Detroit Free Press*, 5 April 1940, 19.

53 "Wilcox and Aides Split up $121,000 Graft, Court Told," 1.

Chapter 10

1 "Reading Indicted in Policy Graft Quiz," *Detroit News*, 24 April 1940, 1.

2 Ibid., 2.

3 "Roxborough the Brains of Joe Louis Management," *Detroit Free Press*, 25 April 1940, 19, 20.

4 Ralph Matthews, "Watching the Big Parade: In Defense of Numbers Baron," *Afro-American*, 11 May 1940, 4.

5 Edgar Rouzeau, "Roxborough Keeps Joe's Linen Clean," *New Journal and Guide*, 11 May 1940, 18.

6 "Eight Policemen Named in Warrant Wednesday," *Detroit Tribune*, 27 April 1940, 1.

7 "80 Police Arraigned as Grafters; Among 134 Named with Reading; Wholesale Arrests Cripple Force," *Detroit Free Press*, 25 April 1940, 1.

8 "O'Hara Booed by Defendants," *Detroit News*, 19 June 1940, 3.

9 "Graft Case Point Won for Reading," *Detroit News*, 7 May 1940, 1.

10 "Stench Bomb Hurled into Hotel Lobby," *Chicago Defender*, 18 May 1940, 2.

11 "Detroit Digit Witness Held on $500 Bond," *Chicago Defender*, 15 June 1940, 5.

12 Swanson Carter, "Numbers Gambling: The Negro's Illegal Response to Status Discrimination in American Society" (Master's thesis, Wayne State University, 1970), 52.

13 "McCrea, Wilcox, Garska and Staebler Guilty with 20 Others on Vice-Graft Plot Charges," *Detroit Free Press*, 29 April 1941, 1.

14 Lucius Jones, "Joe Louis Subject of Eight-Page Feature in Current LIFE," *Atlanta Daily World*, 15 June 1940, 5.

15 "Letters to Editor," *Life*, 8 July 1940, 4.

16 "Joe Louis Flies Home for 123rd Willkie Speech," *Detroit Free Press*, 4 November 1940, 3.

17 "Three Watson Enterprises Show Rapid Growth in Business during the Past Several Years," *Detroit Tribune*, 15 June 1940, 1.

18 "Jury Picked, Trial Starts for Reading," *Detroit Free Press*, 9 October 1941, 1.

19 John W. Roxborough, Petitioner, v. the People of the State of Michigan, 1944, 98/323 U.S. 749/65 S Ct. 80/89 L. Ed. 600/5-24-1944.

20 "Officer Arrests Northend Resident on Policy Charge Because He's Negro," *Detroit Tribune*, 18 August 1942, 1.

21 "Don't Gamble!" *Detroit News*, 29 August 1941, 7.

22 "An Objectable New Trend in White Advertising," *Detroit Tribune*, 6 September 1941, 1.

23 "Mail and Phones Censored in Jury's Private Hotel Wing," *Detroit News*, 15 October 1941, 9.

24 "Cheating in Policy Revealed at Trial," *Detroit Tribune*, 18 October 1941, 2.

25 "State Probes Tampering Hint in Reading Trial," *Detroit Evening Times*, 30 October 1941, 3.

26 "Policy Fraud Told in Court," *Detroit News*, 11 October 1941, 9.

27 "Judge Prods Slow Memory," *Detroit News*, 28 October 1941, 5.

28 "Graft Witness Quiz Ordered," *Detroit News*, 30 October 1941, 24.

29 "Grafters Took Policy Winnings," *Chicago Defender*, 25 October 1941, 1.

30 "Reading, 22 Others Guilty in Graft Conspiracy Case," *Detroit Free Press*, 16 December 1941, 1.

31 Ibid.

32 "Reading, Watson, Roxborough Guilty: Court Frees Eleven," *Detroit Tribune*, 20 December 1941, 1, 2.

33 "Reading, 22 Others Guilty," 2.

34 "Ex-Detroit Mayor Gets Prison Term," *New York Times*, 8 January 1942, 22.

35 Kenneth McCormick, "Reading Gets 4 to 5 Years; Will Appeal," *Detroit Free Press*, 8 January 1942, 1.

36 Ibid., 2.

37 "Roxy and Watson Appeal Sentence," *Detroit Tribune*, 10 January 1942, 1.

38 "Roxborough—The Paradox in the Joe Louis Saga," *New Journal and Guide*, 24 January 1942, A11.

39 "On the Line with Considine," *Washington Post*, 20 December 1941, 19.

40 John W. Roxborough, Petitioner, v. the People of the State of Michigan, 1944, 98/323 U.S. 749/65 S Ct. 80/89 L. Ed. 600/5-24-1944, 15.

41 Ibid., 15–16.

42 "Watson Insurance Agency Becomes Second Negro Company to Sell Bonds," *Detroit Tribune*, 10 October 1942, 1.

43 Art Carter, "Joe's Charity Fight for Navy Will Help Us All—Roxborough," *Afro-American*, 27 December 1941, 1.

44 John B. Williams, "Details of Bout Told to Courier," *Pittsburgh Courier*, 22 November 1941, 1, 5.

45 Dan Burley, "Louis Meets Baer for Navy Friday Night; All Seem to Be Getting a 'Taste' but Joe," *New York Amsterdam Star-News*, 10 January 1942, 14.

46 Margery Miller, *Joe Louis: American* (New York: Current Books, 1945), 160.

47 Ibid., 161.

48 Ibid., 165.

49 Meyer Berger and Barney Nagler, "Part Two of Joe Louis' Story," *Life*, 15 November 1948, 139.

50 Ibid.

51 "New Bowling Alleys for Detroit Keglers," *Chicago Defender*, 11 April 1942, 20.

52 "Negro Leaders Acclaim Attorney Edward Simmons for Councilman," *Detroit Tribune*, 18 September 1943, 2.

53 Ibid.

54 Thomas Sugrue, *The Origins of the Urban Crisis: Race and Inequality in Postwar Detroit* (Princeton: Princeton University Press, 1996), 42–43.

55 "Mystery Fire Destroys House in Watson's New $2,000,000 Project," *Detroit Tribune*, 7 October 1944, 1.

56 "Cop Hires Youths to Burn Negro Homes," *Chicago Defender*, 14 October 1944, 1.

57 Ulysses Boykin, *A Hand Book on the Detroit Negro* (Detroit: Minority Study Associates, 1943), 111.

58 "17 Face Trial in Gambling," *Detroit Free Press*, 25 August 1944, 13.

59 Kathleen Hauke, interview from the papers of Peter Cassey Jr., Roxborough Family Papers, Burton Historical Collection, Detroit Public Library.

Chapter 11

1 Fuller Hit, interview by the author, 12 December 2012, Detroit.

2 "Charges of Vice Dropped against Dr. Haley Bell," *Detroit Tribune*, 22 January 1944, 1.

3 Alfred Lee and Norman Humphrey, *Race Riot* (New York: Dryden Press, 1943), 84–86.

4 "Colored Business Booms as Result of Detroit Riot," *Afro-American*, 17 July 1943, 13.

5 "They Got Their Chance," *Atlanta Daily World*, 19 July 1943, 6.

Chapter 12

1 Kenneth McCormick, "Fred W. Frahm Dies in Work He Loved," *Detroit Free Press*, 25 August 1948, 17.

2 Morgan Oates, "Law Mixed with Fun? Tom-Tom Was the Man," *Parade*, *Detroit Free Press*, 22 January 1961, 2.

3 "Heart Attack Fatal to Duncan McCrea," *Detroit Free Press*, 26 May 1951, 15.

4 Neal Shine, "The Cat in the Hat Ended Up behind Bars," *Detroit Free Press*, 25 May 1986, 8.

5 "Reading Dies," *Detroit News*, 9 December 1952, 1, 4.

6 Earl Wegmann, "Ex-Mayor Reading Dies at 70," *Detroit Free Press*, 10 December 1952, 1.

7 "Ex-Mayor Reading of Detroit Is Dead," *New York Times*, 10 December 1952, 10.

8 "Ex-Mayor Reading Near Death," *Detroit Free Press*, 9 December 1952, 1.

9 Gloster Current, "Paradise Valley," *Detroit Magazine*, June 1946, 32.

10 Russ Cowans, "I Cover the Town," *Michigan Chronicle*, 7 October 1944, 20.

11 "Wives of Negro Millionaires," *Jet*, 17 January 1952, 58.

12 "What Happened to . . . ?" *Michigan Chronicle*, 27 March 1954, 7.

13 Russ Cowans, "Valley Pioneer Succumbs," *Michigan Chronicle*, 23 January 1960, 5.

14 Ibid.

15 "Roxborough, Bomber's Manager, Leaves Prison," *Chicago Defender*, 19 October 1946, 1.

16 "Roxborough and Louis Hold Reunion," *Detroit Free Press*, 5 October 1946, 11.

17 Ulysses Boykin, *A Hand Book on the Detroit Negro* (Detroit: Minority Study Associates, 1943), 111.

18 "$83,000 Paid in Roxy Divorce," *Chicago Defender*, 30 April 1956, 8.

19 Russ Cowans, "Years Rest Lightly on 'Roxie,'" *Pittsburgh Courier*, 15 April 1961, 23.

20 Bill Sudomier, "Out on the Boulevard, John Roxborough Remembers a Boy Named Joe," *Detroit Free Press*, 14 August 1966, 12.

21 "Joe Louis' Mentor, John Roxborough, Dies," *Jet*, 8 January 1976, 8.

22 John Roxborough, "How I Discovered Joe Louis," *Ebony*, October 1954, 65.

23 Gerald Astor, *And a Credit to His Race* (New York: Saturday Review Press, 1974), 35.

24 Lewis Erenberg, *The Greatest Fight of Our Generation* (Oxford: Oxford University Press, 2006), 29.

25 Sudomier, "Out on the Boulevard, John Roxborough Remembers a Boy Named Joe," 8.

26 "He Loved Life," *Detroit News*, 19 December 1975, 11A.

Chapter 13

1 Swanson Carter, "Numbers Gambling: The Negro's Illegal Response to Status Discrimination in American Society" (Master's thesis, Wayne State University, 1970), 53–55.

2 "Ex-Policy King Edward Jones Is Dead at 65," *Chicago Tribune*, 28 November 1964, 7 section 1A.

3 William Leonard and Sandy Smith, "How the Gang Operates," *Chicago Tribune*, 25 October 1959, 14.

4 "Police Stumble over Own Plans to Nab Kidnaper," *Chicago Tribune*, 20 May 1946, 4.

5 "Guns Topple Old Policy Kings," *Chicago Tribune*, 19 January 1955, 2.

6 "Roe Bosses Huge Policy Empire; Defies Syndicate," *Chicago Tribune*, 20 June 1951, 2.

7 "Chicago 'Policy Baron' Kills 1, Routs 3, in Kidnap Try," *Jackson Advocate*, 30 June 1951, 1, 6.

8 "Ted Roe Bares Inside Story of Jones Kidnaping," *Chicago Tribune*, 23 June 1951, 4.

9 "Slay Wealthy Boss of Chicago Gambling," *Capital Times*, 5 August 1952, 1.

10 Ernest Borden, *Detroit's Paradise Valley* (Charleston: Arcadia Publishing, 2003), 25.

11 "Globe News and Gossip," *Chicago Defender*, 16 April 1938, 10.

12 The People vs. Thomas Hammonds, et al. Examination before Honorable Arthur E. Gordon, Judge of the Recorder's Court, November 12, 1940, 84–92.

13 "Globe News and Gossip," *Chicago Defender*, 8 October 1938, 10.

14 "Globe News and Gossip," *Chicago Defender*, 28 December 1940, 10.

15 "Negro Syndicate Buys $250,000 Gotham Hotel," *Detroit Tribune*, 23 October 1943, 1.

16 Ziggy Johnson, "Zagging with Ziggy," *Michigan Chronicle*, 18 July 1964, B5.

17 Robert Conot, *American Odyssey: A Unique History of America Told through the Life of a Great City* (New York: William Morrow, 1974), 413.

18 Ibid., 414.

19 Edward Littlejohn and Donald Hobson, *Black Lawyers, Law Practice, and Bar Associations 1884 to 1970: A Michigan History* (Detroit: Wolverine Bar Association, 1987), 23.

20 The People vs. Thomas Hammonds, et al. Examination before Honorable Arthur E. Gordon, Judge of the Recorder's Court, November 12, 1940, 75, 116.

21 "NAACP Protests Race-Labeling of Crime News by Newspapers," *Pittsburgh Courier*, 2 February 1946, 3.

22 "A Monument to Our Race," *Detroit Tribune*, 20 November 1943, 5.

23 Borden, *Detroit's Paradise Valley*, 32.

24 Frank Bolden, "Gotham Hotel in Detroit Gains Nationwide Fame," *Pittsburgh Courier*, 8 March 1947, 11.

25 Borden, *Detroit's Paradise Valley*, 10.

26 Ibid., 38–39.

27 Ibid., 26.

28 Ibid., 37.

29 Langston Hughes, "A Minor Miracle," *Chicago Defender*, 26 May 1945, 12.

30 Bolden, "Gotham Hotel in Detroit Gains Nationwide Fame."

31 "Mile-Long Resort for Negroes Picked on Lake St. Clair," *Escanaba Daily Press*, 12 April 1949, 12.

32 Elaine Latzman Moon, *Untold Tales, Unsung Heroes: An Oral History of Detroit's African American Community, 1918–1967* (Detroit: Wayne State University Press, 1994), 188.

33 Betty DeRamus, "The Gotham Was the Cream of Black Hotels," *Detroit Free Press*, 17 February 1984, 10.

34 Peter Hammer and Trevor Coleman, *Crusader for Justice: Federal Judge Damon J. Keith* (Detroit: Wayne State Press University, 2014), 60.

35 John Dancy, *Sand against the Wind* (Detroit: Wayne State University Press, 1966), 115–16.

36 Ibid., 114.

37 Ibid., 116.

38 E. Franklin Frazier, *Black Bourgeoisie: The Rise of a New Middle Class* (New York: The Free Press, 1957), 211.

39 Ulysses Boykin, "Phenomenal Rise of Prophet Jones Recounted after 6 Years in Detroit," *Detroit Tribune*, 22 April 1944, 1.

40 Ibid., 2.

41 Justine Wylie, *Detroit's Near Eastsiders: A Journey of Excellence against the Odds, 1920s–1960s* (Detroit: Detroit Black Writers Guild for the Near Eastsiders, 2008), 76.

42 Gladys Johnson, "Is Prophet Jones at the End of the Road?" *Pittsburgh Courier*, 3 March 1956, A6.

43 People v. Brynski, Docket No. 75, Calendar No. 46, 326. Supreme Court of Michigan, 347 Mich. 599, 1957.

44 James Oliver Slade, "Numbers and Negroes," *Michigan Chronicle*, 10 September 1949, 8.

45 Bill Gold, "Study Finds Numbers Racket Economy, Not Race Problem," *Washington Post and Times Herald*, 10 January 1958, A3.

46 "The Battle That's Brewing: The Blacks vs. The Mafia," *Detroit Scope Magazine*, 15 February 1969, 11.

47 Investigation of Organized Crime in Interstate Commerce, *Hearings before the Special Committee to Investigate Organized Crime in Interstate Commerce*, United States Senate, 82nd Cong., Part 9, Michigan, February 8, 9, 19, 1951 (Washington, DC: Government Printing Office), 61.

48 David Bird, "Peter Joseph Licavoli Sr. 81; Ex-Crime Leader in Detroit," *New York Times*, 12 January 1981, 1.

49 Earl Wegmann, "Licavoli Knows His Rights—and Nothing Else," *Detroit Free Press*, 9 February 1951, 12.

50 U.S. Senate Special Committee to Investigate Organized Crime in Interstate Commerce, *Kefauver Committee Final Report Aug. 31, 1951*, 82nd Cong., 1st Sess., No. 725 (Washington, DC: Government Printing Office), 1.

51 Ralph Nelson, "Police Schedule Drive against Numbers Game," *Detroit Free Press*, 27 April 1953, 3.

52 Investigation of Organized Crime in Interstate Commerce, *Hearings*, 65–66.

53 Nelson, "Police Schedule Drive against Numbers Game."

54 Ralph Nelson, "How Gamblers Fleece the Poor, Pay Off Cops," *Detroit Free Press*, 21 March 1954, 1.

55 "Crime Movies," *Detroit Free Press Graphic Sunday*, 2 September 1951, 4.

56 "No More Numbers Playing?" *Detroit Tribune*, 3 November 1951, 1.

57 "U.S. Fails to Halt Michigan Gambling," *Chicago Defender*, 14 February 1953, 5.

58 "J. White Gets 90 Days, Fine," *Detroit Tribune*, 5 June 1954, 1.

59 "'Low' Pressure Grand Jury," *Detroit Free Press*, 16 August 1959, 24.

60 Jack Schermerhorn, "Hotelman Faces Quiz on Cash," *Detroit Free Press*, 27 January 1955, 5.

61 Federal Bureau Investigations, Record Number: 124-10342-10372, Eddie Wingate, 9 December 1963, 3–4.

Chapter 14

1   Robert Conot, *American Odyssey: A Unique History of America Told through the Life of a Great City* (New York: William Morrow, 1974), 401.

2   Thomas Sugrue, *The Origins of the Urban Crisis: Race and Inequality in Postwar Detroit* (Princeton: Princeton University Press, 1996), 49.

3   Conot, *American Odyssey*, 402.

4   "Detroit Tops Nation in Negro-Owned Businesses," *Detroit Free Press*, 3 March 1953, 20.

5   City of Detroit, *Detroit: The New City, Summary Report Detroit Community Renewal Program* (1966), 8, copy in author's possession.

6   City of Detroit, *Urban Renewal and Tax Revenue: Detroit's Success Story* (1958), 1, copy in author's possession.

7   "The Battle That's Brewing: The Blacks vs The Mafia," *Detroit Scope Magazine*, 15 February 1969, 1.

8   Conot, *American Odyssey*, 413.

9   Jeff Leen, "From Segregation to Authority," *Detroit Free Press*, 26 July 1985, 1A, 10A.

10 Sugrue, *The Origins of the Urban Crisis*, 261–62.

11 Mary Stolberg, *Bridging the River of Hatred* (Detroit: Wayne State University Press, 1998), 146.

12 Ibid., 164.

13 Ibid., 125.

14 Ibid., 204.

15 Elaine Latzman Moon, *Untold Tales, Unsung Heroes: An Oral History of Detroit's African American Community, 1918–1967* (Detroit: Wayne State University Press, 1994), 188.

16 Russ Cowans, "Hundreds Attend Wake for Gotham," *Michigan Chronicle*, 15 September 1962, 1.

17 Robert Kennedy, *Statement by Attorney Robert F. Kennedy to the Permanent Subcommittee on Investigations of the Senate Government Operations Committee*, 25 September 1963, 12.

18 George Edwards, "Detroit: A Lesson in Law Enforcement," *Annals of the American Academy of Political and Social Science* 347 (May 1963): 69.

19 Ibid., 68–69.

20 Ibid., 71.

21 Federal Bureau Investigations, File 162–899, Eddie Wingate, 31 January 1963.

22 Ibid., 68.

23 Ibid., 71–72.

24 Ibid., 72.

25 "T-Men Hit Gotham Hotel Like Raging Football Team," *Michigan Chronicle*, 17 November 1962, 1.

26 Ibid., 4.

27 Ibid. It is of some interest to note that numbers gambling had an unintentional benefit for blacks in law enforcement. To build cases against black numbers operators, black officers and agents were needed to go undercover and secure evidence. Because of this, agencies like the IRS, which for years had been closed to blacks, were forced to hire them. For black agents, this was bittersweet. As one of the first black agents in the IRS noted, the attitude was if you were black, you had to know everything about numbers gambling, and for many this was not the case. The black agents, like the white agents, were highly educated and had worked hard for the opportunity and expected assignments similar to those of their white counterparts. Instead, black agents were often placed on assignment alone without any support. One such agent became bitter with his assignment and noted he had worked hard in college to become a well-respected professional, only to be forced to work and live in dangerous ghettos as an undercover agent. Hilton Owens, *Three of the First* (Pittsburgh: Dorrance Publishing, 2011), 150.

28 "T-Men Hit Gotham Hotel Like Raging Football Team."

29 "Those Aren't My Cards, Owner John White Claims," *Michigan Chronicle*, 15 December 1962, 1.

30 "Keep Writing, Folks," *Detroit Free Press*, 9 January 1963, 3.

31 "Those Aren't My Cards, Owner John White Claims," 4.

32 "Here's What Edwards Told Senators," *Detroit Free Press*, 11 October 1963, 8B.

33 Federal Bureau Investigations, File 162–899, Eddie Wingate, 31 January 1963.

34 John Griffith, "Yule Spirit Moves Judge to Leniency," *Detroit Free Press*, 16 December 1954, 17.

35 "Here's What Edwards Told Senators."

36 John Muller, "Racketeers' 'Summit' Here Bared," *Detroit Free Press*, 31 October 1963, 1.

37 "No Even Break for Suckers in Numbers Game," *Detroit Free Press*, 21 June 1963, 3.

38 Federal Bureau Investigations, File 162–899, Eddie Wingate, 31 January 1963.

39 Ibid., 11.

40 David Bird, "Peter Joseph Licavoli Sr. 81; Ex-Crime Leader in Detroit," *New York Times*, 12 January 1981, 1.

41 "Detroit Racket Blackout Is Blamed on Feared Cosa Nostra," *Atlanta Daily World*, 17 November 1963, 2A.

42 Pete Waldmeir, "Rip Koury Played by the Numbers," *Detroit News*, 18 March 1990, 1C.

43 Sunnie Wilson and John Cohassey, *Toast of the Town: The Life and Times of Sunnie Wilson* (Detroit: Wayne State University Press, 1998), 163.

44 Harry Golden Jr., "Echoes of Music and Dice as the Gotham Passes," *Detroit Free Press*, 18 July 1963, 3.

45 Berl Falbaum, "Harmony, Discord, Echo No More at Gotham Hotel," *Detroit News*, 31 July 1963, 2A.

46 Moon, *Untold Tales, Unsung Heroes*, 78.

47 Betty DeRamus, "The Gotham Was the Cream of Black Hotels," *Detroit Free Press*, 17 February 1984, 10.

48 Frank Saunders, "Frankly Speaking," *Michigan Chronicle*, 18 July 1964, B1.

49 Ziggy Johnson, "Zagging with Ziggy," *Michigan Chronicle*, 18 July 1964, B5.

Chapter 15

1 "Remembering the Life and Legacy of Mr. Eddie Wingate," obituary, 5 May 2006, 2, copy in author's possession.

2 "If You Can Sing Dig This!" *Pittsburgh Courier*, 11 November 1957, 7.

3 Federal Bureau Investigations, File 162–899, Eddie Wingate, 19 October 1962.

4 "Talking About," *Jet*, 17 April 1958, 43.

5 Federal Bureau Investigations, File 166–899, Eddie Wingate, 14 May 1964.

6   Federal Bureau Investigations, File 162–899, Eddie Wingate, 7 December 1961.

7   Al Kent, *Custodians of the Hummingbird* (Pittsburgh: Rosedog Press, 2017), 342.

8   Arthur Kempton, *Boogaloo: The Quintessence of American Popular Music* (Ann Arbor: University of Michigan Press, 2005), 232.

9   Federal Bureau Investigations, File 162–899, Eddie Wingate, 31 January 1963.

10   Federal Bureau Investigations, File 166–899, Eddie Wingate, 14 May 1964.

11   "Motel Used for Vice, Suit Says," *Detroit Free Press*, 4 October 1967, 6B.

12   "Detroit's Newest Motel," *Detroit Free Press*, 30 July 1966, 2B.

13   Tom Ricke, "Numbers Today: A Tough Job," *Detroit Free Press*, 7 March 1972, 2A.

14   Ibid., 1A.

15   Ibid., 2A.

16   Tom Ricke, "Numbers Runners Sell Dreams," *Detroit Free Press*, 5 March 1972, 8A.

17   Ibid.

18   Ricke, "Numbers Today: A Tough Job," 2A.

19   "The Battle That's Brewing: The Blacks vs. The Mafia," *Detroit Scope Magazine*, 15 February 1969, 10.

20   John Carlisle, "FBI Seize 58 in Record Betting Roundup," *Detroit News*, 12 May 1970, 1A.

21   Ibid., 12A.

22   John Carlisle, "Chancy Games People Play," *Detroit News*, 12 May 1970, 6C.

23   "Talking About," *Jet*, 4 June 1970, 43.

24   "Numbers Survive Hugh Raid," *Afro-American*, 30 May 1970, 18.

25   "Bankers, Not Runners Real Culprits, Says Detroit Judge Crockett," *Jet*, 4 May 1972, 55.

26   Ibid.

27   Tom Ricke, "Numbers Golden Era Fades," *Detroit Free Press*, 6 March 1972, 1A.

28   "Mutuel Numbers Combine Broken in Detroit Raids," *Holland Evening Sentinel*, 26 October 1972, 17.

Chapter 16

1 Elizabeth Schroeder Schlabach, *Dream Books & Gamblers: Black Women's Work in Chicago's Policy Game* (Urbana: University of Illinois Press, 2022), 45, 53.

2 In this instance, with permission from Bridgett M. Davis, real names were used.

3 The Westsiders, *Remembering Detroit's Old Westside, 1920–1950: A Pictorial History of the Westside* (Detroit: Bookcrafters Book, 1997), 85.

4 "Home Ownership Brings Satisfaction, Security," *Detroit Free Press*, 11 November 1951, 9B.

5 E. Franklin Frazier, *Black Bourgeoisie: The Rise of a New Middle Class* (New York: The Free Press, 1957), 211.

6 LaShawn Harris, *Sex Workers, Psychics, and Numbers Runners: Black Women in New York City's Underground Economy* (Urbana: University of Illinois Press, 2016), 39.

Chapter 17

1 John Hamilton, "Hamilton Favors Law to Legalize Gambling," *Detroit Free Press*, 15 December 1940, 6.

2 Peter Fisher, "Should the Numbers Racket Be Legalized?" *Michigan Chronicle*, 22 July 1939, 5.

3 J. R. Humphreys, "57 Per Cent of Detroiters Give Approval to Legislation of Gambling by State Law," *Detroit Free Press*, 15 December 1940, 6.

4 "Here's What the People Say About: Should the Numbers Game Be Legalized?" *Michigan Chronicle*, 26 February 1949, 4.

5 William Ackles, "What They're Saying," *Detroit Tribune*, 26 January 1952, 7.

6 Edward Turner, "Should Gambling Be Legalized in Michigan?" *Detroit Tribune*, 2 February 1952, 2.

7 Jefferson Jordan, "Legalize Gambling Here?" *Detroit Tribune*, 16 February 1952, 3.

8 James Dewey, "Voters Ok State Lottery," *Detroit Free Press*, 17 May 1972, 5A.

9 Ibid., 1A.

10 Ibid., 5A.

11 Al Sander, "Voters Ok Lottery by 3–1 Margin," *Detroit News*, 17 May 1972, 3A, 18A.

12 Dewey, "Voters Ok State Lottery."

13 John Oppedahl and Roger Lane, "Gribbs Eyeing Lottery for Detroit," *Detroit Free Press*, 18 May 1972, 3A.

14 State of Michigan Legislative Council, *1972 Michigan Compiled Laws through PA 200*, McCauley-Traxler-Law-Bowman-McNeely Lottery Act 239, 1972, 1–2.

15 Ibid., 3.

16 "Lottery May Cost 50 Cents," *Detroit Free Press*, 2 August 1972, 1A.

17 Tom Ricke, "Numbers Racket Doesn't Fear Lottery," *Detroit Free Press*, 23 October 1972, 10A.

18 Ibid.

19 Ibid.

20 "Police Bear Down on Numbers Ring," *Detroit News*, 28 October 1972, 2B.

21 State of Michigan Bureau of State Lottery, *Annual State Lottery Report*, 1973, 1.

22 Gary Schuster, "State's 1st Lottery Drawing Set for Nov. 24 at Cobo Arena," *Detroit News*, 27 October 1972, 5A.

23 State of Michigan Bureau of State Lottery, *Annual State Lottery Report*, 1973, 2.

24 Ibid., 4.

25 Jim Neubacher, "The Losers Win, Too, in Lottery," *Detroit Free Press*, 24 November 1972, 1A, 2A.

26 Schuster, "State's 1st Lottery Drawing Set for Nov. 24 at Cobo Arena," 5A.

27 Roger Lane, "Lottery Drum Rolls Nov. 24," *Detroit Free Press*, 28 October 1972, 1A.

28 Ibid., 1A, 2A.

29 Ibid., 2A.

30 Schuster, "State's 1st Lottery Drawing Set for Nov. 24 at Cobo Arena," 1A, 6A.

31 Ibid., 1A, 8A.

32 State of Michigan Bureau of State Lottery, *Annual State Lottery Report*, 1973, 6.

33 Ibid., 6–9.

34 Ibid., 8–9.

35 Ibid., 7–9.

36 Ibid., 14–15.

37 Ibid., 9.

38 "State to Start Numbers Game," *Detroit Free Press*, 4 December 1976, 2.

39 Peter Gavrilovich, "Gambler Tells All about the Numbers," *Detroit Free Press*, 25 June 1975, 1B.

40 Commission on the Review of the National Policy Toward Gambling, *Gambling in America: Final Report—Appendix 3, Summaries of Commission Hearings* (Washington, DC: GPO, 1976), 262.

41 State of Michigan Bureau of State Lottery, *Annual State Lottery Report*, 1977, 4.

42 "Pick Your Own Number and Play," *Detroit Free Press*, 9 June 1977, 20A.

43 Tom Hennessy, "His 137 Winner a Loser for Lottery," *Detroit Free Press*, 9 June 1977, 3A.

44 "State to Start Numbers Game," 2.

45 State of Michigan Bureau of State Lottery, *Annual State Lottery Report*, 1977, 4.

46 State of Michigan Bureau of State Lottery, *Annual State Lottery Report*, 1978, 4.

47 Nathan Rubenstein, "The Daily Dream Machine," *Detroit News Magazine*, 27 May 1979, 13.

48 Ibid., 32.

49 Ibid., 15.

50 Diane Katz, "Lottery Addict Hopes to Win Freedom," *Detroit News*, 23 May 1985, 1E.

51 Ibid., 4E.

52 Eric Freedman, "Long Prison Term Upheld for Gambling Mother," *Detroit News*, 16 July 1986, 4B.

53 Commission on the Review of the National Policy Toward Gambling, *Gambling in America*, 289.

54 "7 Arrested, 8th Sought in Bet Ring," *Detroit Free Press*, 7 September 1977, 6C.

55 Helen Fogel, "Police Fear Inside Leak to Mafia," *Detroit Free Press*, 7 October 1977, 1A, 18A.

56 Brian Flanigan, "21 Locations Hit by Cops in Numbers Raid," *Detroit Free Press*, 10 November 1982, 3A.

57 Chauncey Bailey and Robert Ankeny, "Illegal Numbers Games Thrive Despite State Lottery," *Detroit News*, 7 August 1989, 1B.

58　Ibid., 2B.
59　Ibid.

Chapter 18

1　"9 on Trial for Ford Numbers Ring," *Detroit Free Press*, 13 November 1944, 1.
2　"15 Arrested in Gambling," *Detroit Free Press*, 28 January 1945, 1.
3　"More Ford Firings Loom in Gambling," *Los Angeles Times*, 24 September 1947, 1.
4　"Aid Pledged Plants to Halt Gambling," *Detroit Free Press*, 24 September 1947, 1.
5　"How Much Do Gamblers Take from Your Plant?" *Business Week*, 21 August 1948, 94.
6　Ibid., 95.
7　Ibid., 94.
8　Ibid., 94–95.
9　Ibid., 96.
10　Ibid., 95.
11　"Ford Fires Aids in Gaming Probe; Jury Quiz Asked," *Chicago Tribune*, 4 July 1948, 10.
12　"Ford Mutuels Ring Broken," *Detroit Free Press*, 3 July 1948, 1.
13　Investigation of Organized Crime in Interstate Commerce, *Hearings before the Special Committee to Investigate Organized Crime in Interstate Commerce*, United States Senate, 82nd Cong., Part 9, Michigan, February 8, 9, 19, 1951 (Washington, DC: Government Printing Office), 203–4.
14　Ibid., 211.
15　Ibid., 212.
16　"Crackdown on Numbers at Ford's Places Hester on $3,000 Bond," *Detroit Tribune*, 10 July 1948, 1.
17　Investigation of Organized Crime in Interstate Commerce, *Hearings*, 202–21.
18　"Response to NCAA Official Inquiry," *University of Michigan*, 25 October 2002, 1–2.
19　Ibid., 1–5.
20　Ibid., 1–6.

21 Ibid.

22 Anonymous, letter to author, 6 August 2012.

23 State of Michigan Bureau of State Lottery, *Annual State Lottery Report*, 2010, 3.

24 "The Battle That's Brewing: The Blacks vs. The Mafia," *Detroit Scope Magazine*, 15 February 1969, 11.

25 Commission on the Review of the National Policy Toward Gambling, *Gambling in America: Final Report—Appendix 3, Summaries of Commission Hearings* (Washington, DC: GPO, 1976), 260.

Chapter 19

1 Swanson Carter, "Numbers Gambling: The Negro's Illegal Response to Status Discrimination in American Society" (Master's thesis, Wayne State University, 1970), 53.

2 Ines Marie Bridges, "Paradise Valley: Detroit's Black Bottom" (Unpublished paper, Folklore Archive, Wayne State University, 1975), 6.

3 Gustav Carlson, "A Study of a Culture Complex" (PhD diss., University of Michigan, 1940), 149.

4 Ibid., 146.

5 Sunnie Wilson and John Cohassey, *Toast of the Town: The Life and Times of Sunnie Wilson* (Detroit: Wayne State University Press, 1998), 66–67.

6 Keith Davis, "The Case for and against Business Assumption of Social Responsibilities," *Academy of Management Journal* 16, no. 2 (1973): 312.

7 Tom Ricke, "Numbers Runners Sell Dreams," *Detroit Free Press*, 5 March 1972, 8A.

8 George Gmelch, and Petra Kuppinger, eds., *Urban Life: Readings in the Anthropology of the City* (Long Grove, IL: Waveland Press, 2018), 207.

9 Bhikhu Parekh, *Ethnocentric Political Theory: The Pursuit of Flawed Universals* (Cham: Palgrave Macmillan, 2019), 4–6.

Index

blaming for their poverty, 205; as lottery players, 12–13, 174; middle-class blacks unable to identify with lives of poor blacks, 46; as numbers players, 32, 46, 113, 205; as policy players, 20–22. *See also* community building and solidarity

population of Detroit: black migration from South, 6, 21–22, 25–27, 145, 155, 164, 194; black population (nineteenth century), 20; black population (early 1900s), 21–22; black population (1920–30), 6, 21–22, 25–27; black population (1951), 144; melting pot of ethnic population (1950s), 144–45; racial composition (1880), 15

pride, black: from Joe Louis's success, 63, 70, 89. *See also* community leaders

private policemen and investigators, 39–40, 46, 66

Prohibition and bootleggers, 24–25, 43–44, 46, 51, 75, 83, 112

Purple Gang, 75, 90

race: Detroit's mix (1880), 15; of numbers players, 43–44, 59, 64–66, 113, 136–37, 195–96, 202; of policy players, 8, 16, 18–22, 64; racial solidarity and numbers gambling, 6–8, 9, 131, 146, 185, 202

race relations: disturbances (1925), 50; Edwards as police commissioner on, 147–48; efforts to improve black conduct for, 25–27; formerly white-only hotels integrating, 148; Joe Louis's responsibility to, 61–63; in 1940s, 6, 9, 130; numbers operations and, 202. *See also* racism

racetracks, winning numbers from. *See* horse races

racism: arrests of black number operators (1972), 162; of Black Legion, 67; Detroit newspapers and, 2, 16–18, 130–31; Detroit police and, 129–30, 147; firing blacks to hire white replacements, 60; housing practices, 109; increasing in late nineteenth-century Detroit, 20; Jim Crow practices of U.S. military and navy, 106–8; jury selection in graft trial (1941), 99, 106; Joe Louis facing, 63–64, 108; in New Orleans, 23; in 1940s Detroit, 129–30; numbers as way to meet financial and social needs in face of, 6–7, 28; self-made black entrepreneurs and, 5; uncouth behavior of blacks blamed for, 25–26; YMCA ban on blacks, 24. *See also* Ku Klux Klan

raids by law enforcement: for failure to pay sufficient protection money, 73; FBI's largest gambling raid (1970), 160–61; Ferguson's office (on order of indicted McCrea), 91–92; Ford's Rouge plant, 187; forewarning of gambling and vice establishments, 92; General Motors plant for drug dealing, 198; Gotham Hotel, 148–52; Great Lakes Mutuels Company, 77, *78*; mafia-owned operations (1982), 184; mob hits precipitating (1929), 54; Norwood's numbers house, 97; war on gambling, 58, 75, 77, *78*, 87–88; on Watson, 48, 66, 75; Wilcox ordering, 53; Wingate's Twenty Grand Motel, 162, 175. *See also* crackdown on numbers operators

Ray, Reuben, 68

Ray Music Company, 121

Reading, Clarence (son), 103, *104*, 105, 121